WOMEN OF INTELLIGENCE

WOMEN OF INTELLIGENCE

WINNING THE SECOND WORLD WAR WITH AIR PHOTOS

CHRISTINE HALSALL

To all those men and women who, in the air, at sea or on the ground, contrib-uted to the Allied victory in the Second World War by obtaining and exploiting air photography.

First published 2012 by Spellmount
This edition first published 2017

The History Press
The Mill, Brimscombe Port
Stroud, Gloucestershire, GL5 2QG
www.thehistorypress.co.uk

British Library Cataloguing in Publication Data.
A catalogue record for this book is available from the British Library.

ISBN 978 0 7509 8245 0

Typesetting and origination by The History Press
Printed and bound by CPI Group (UK) Ltd

CONTENTS

FOREWORD

The Allied Central Interpretation Unit at RAF Medmenham was a remarkable wartime establishment. When I first arrived there, I was at once aware that I was in a very unusual environment, more akin to that of an academic institution than a services unit.

Although the administration was run on orthodox lines, the work of photographic interpretation, which was the purpose of the place, was carried out by an extraordinarily interesting collection of individuals from surprisingly varied peacetime occupations, notably academia, the arts, business and industry. Together with a proportion of army, navy and Allied personnel, many of the interpreters were RAF officers who had been commissioned into the services almost overnight from their civilian occupations, primarily because of their existing skills of acute observation, meticulous attention to minor details, the capacity to make perceptive inferences from small clues, and sometimes to make inspired leaps of imagination. So among them there were archaeologists, geologists and people from the oil industry, many of whom were already experienced in using air photographs, but there were also actors and creative artists.

The outstanding feature of Medmenham, however, that distinguished it from almost all other service establishments, was that a substantial proportion of the highly skilled specialists were women who ranked absolutely equally with their male colleagues, and in some cases were their superiors. These women played a major part in the important contribution that ACIU made to the ultimate victory and this book is a well-deserved tribute to their achievements, little appreciated until now.

Geoffrey Stone

Geoffrey Stone was a wartime photographic interpreter in the Army and Communications Sections at RAF Medmenham; subsequently at the Army Photographic Interpretation Section, HQ 11 Armoured Division in the European campaign and HQ 1st Airborne Corps in the Far East; finally Officer Commanding, Field Security Wing at the School of Military Intelligence; Major, G2, Intelligence Corps.

PREFACE

The first British aeroplane to cross the German coast following the declaration of war on 3 September 1939 was a Blenheim reconnaissance aircraft from which air photographs were taken to confirm the position and number of enemy warships in the port of Wilhelmshaven.

One of the last flights of the war, made while victory in Europe was being celebrated in May 1945, was by a reconnaissance Spitfire that flew over the port of Kiel to determine by photography if German ships and troops were preparing to leave for a last stand in Norway.

In the years between those flights, Allied reconnaissance aircraft flew over the whole of Europe, the Middle and Far East, taking millions of photographs. Day after day the lens of the camera captured on film what was happening in enemy and occupied territory below. Once the film had been processed, photographs were plotted to mark the location where they were taken. They were then passed to photographic interpreters who analysed them to extract every scrap of information that could be seen, or deduced, from the image. Photographic reconnaissance and interpretation provided one of the largest sources of intelligence on enemy actions and intentions, and was used in the planning for virtually every Allied operation.

Women played an important role in photographic intelligence. Female and male photographic interpreters from all three services worked alongside each other and the Women's Auxiliary Air Force (WAAF) formed the majority of the workforce in the processing and plotting sections. Their eyes were the first to see the Ruhr dams breached, the *Tirpitz* battleship contained in its Norwegian fjord, the D-Day beaches and the sites of German vengeance weapons aimed at England.

This book is an account of the women who worked with air photographs at RAF Medmenham, at associated units and overseas. They describe their work, their off-duty hours and the humour they found in adverse situations. The wartime thoughts and memories of these remarkable women were written or spoken by them and provide a record of their significant role in gaining the Allied victory.

Christine Halsall

Glossary of Terms

ACIU	Allied Central Interpretation Unit
ACW1	Aircraftwoman 1
ACW2	Aircraftwoman 2
ATS	Auxiliary Territorial Service
AOC	Aircraft Operating Company
A/S/O	Assistant section officer, the most junior WAAF commissioned rank, equivalent to RAF pilot officer
Capt.	Captain
CIU	Central Interpretation Unit, renamed ACIU in 1944
Cpl	Corporal
ENSA	Entertainments National Service Association – provided entertainment for British armed forces personnel during the Second World War
F/O	Flight officer, a commissioned WAAF officer rank above SO, equivalent to RAF flight lieutenant
Fw	Focke-Wulf, a German aircraft manufacturer
HQ	Headquarters
Int. Corps	Intelligence Corps
LACW	Leading aircraftwoman
Me	Messerschmitt, a German aircraft manufacturer
Mess	The building where personnel ate, socialised and sometimes lived. There were separate messes for officers, NCOs, airwomen and airmen.
NAAFI	Navy, Army & Air Force Institute, which ran canteens and recreational establishments for the British armed forces, and particularly those of junior rank, during the Second World War
NCO	Non-commissioned officer
OR	Other rank
PI	Photographic interpretation or photographic interpreter

PIU   Photographic interpretation unit from January 1940 to April 1941
PR   Photographic reconnaissance
PRU   Photographic reconnaissance unit, e.g. 1 PRU
RAF   Royal Air Force
RE   Royal Engineers
RFC   Royal Flying Corps
RN   Royal Navy
RNVR   Royal Naval Volunteer Reserve
2nd Officer WRNS commissioned rank, the equivalent of RN lieutenant
SD   Special duties
S/O   Section officer, a commissioned WAAF rank above A/S/O and the
            equivalent of RAF flying officer
Sgt   Sergeant
Sub   Subaltern, ATS commissioned rank, the equivalent of an army lieu-
            tenant
USSR   United Soviet Socialist Republic
VE Day   8 May 1945, when victory in Europe was celebrated
VJ Day   15 August 1945, when victory over Japan was celebrated
WAAF   Women's Auxiliary Air Force
WAC   Women's Army Corps (from 30 September 1943), USA
WRNS   Women's Royal Naval Service
USAAF   United States Army Air Force
YWCA   Young Women's Christian Association, provided servicewomen with
            companionship, support and recreational activities during the Second
            World War

To avoid confusion, throughout the book women are referred to by the surname
(which was usually their maiden name) that they had on joining the WAAF, ATS
or WRNS, even though they may have subsequently married while still in the
service. The end notes and index give, where appropriate, their married surnames
alongside their maiden name.

Please note that RAF Medmenham was referred to by several different names
during the war. RAF Station Medmenham was its official designation, often
shortened to Medmenham; the sole unit at RAF Medmenham was the Central
Interpretation Unit (CIU), later renamed the Allied Central Interpretation Unit
(ACIU); many personnel referred to it also by its pre-war name of Danesfield
House. They were all one and the same place.

1

THE ROAD TO MEDMENHAM

The Duke of Wellington is quoted as saying: 'All the business of war, and indeed all the business of life, is to endeavour to find out what you don't know by what you do; that's what I call "guessing what was on the other side of the hill".'[1]

Throughout the history of warfare, commanders on land and at sea have sought ways of seeing over 'the other side of the hill' to gain knowledge of their enemy's force dispositions and resources before engaging in battle. The introduction of aircraft to gain a bird's-eye view of the enemy, and of photography to provide an objective and permanent record of his capabilities, made this possible and changed the nature of warfare. Not only was military information 'captured' for use on the battlefield; it also provided longer-term intelligence in the planning of future operations.

Aviation and photography, developing along parallel paths, became an entirely new profession in the world of military intelligence and was first used to considerable effect in the First World War. In the Second World War, in terms of quantity, aerial photography produced more information on enemy activity than any other source. Moreover, the information was factual, could be provided very rapidly in comparison with most other sources, and could also be directed to provide intelligence on almost any territory required and on a wide variety of subjects.

It was during the period 1939–45 that women played a significant part in photographic intelligence, a role that continues to the present day. With their male counterparts, a large number of them were based for most of that time in an ornate mansion overlooking the River Thames in the small village of Medmenham, in Buckinghamshire. Today, the house is a luxury hotel providing comfortable and peaceful surroundings for its guests. In wartime, with rather fewer creature comforts, the men and women who worked there analysed air photographs and saw over 'the other side of the hill' into enemy and occupied territories. The intelligence gained from their observations and reports was used in the planning of virtually every Allied wartime operation.

Just after the war, Cyril Ticquet, an RAF officer at Medmenham wrote:

Let me introduce you to a spy. Not the kind you read about in novels, but the real, live 1939–45 version. The kind that saw to it that the Germans could pull no surprises, and then did the same for Japan. He is middle-aged with lined cheeks and thinning hair. You would guess that he used to have a school or university job, and you would be right. He, and hundreds of other men and women like him, spent their days staring at the innermost secrets of the enemy, discovering in advance his most hidden schemes.[2]

While the many young men and women at RAF Medmenham during the Second World War would have raised their eyebrows at the 'lined cheeks and thinning hair' description, they would have recognised Ticquet's description of their wartime work.

The history and development of aviation and photography have been well documented. Women's achievements in these spheres are less well known, despite being involved from their inception, and this short account will seek to redress the balance.

Although it was work by an English physicist on the density of hydrogen in the latter half of the eighteenth century that provided the means whereby humans could take to the air, it was the French who dominated early ballooning. On 15 October 1783 Jean-François de Rozier was the first person to ascend into the air in a balloon tethered to the ground by an 80ft rope. Just six weeks later, the first free (non-tethered) flight, with passengers, took place over Paris.

It could be assumed that involvement in early ballooning was an exclusively male preoccupation, with ladies' feet staying firmly on the ground; however, in May 1784, just seven months after Rozier, three French ladies ascended in a tethered balloon. It was a French opera singer, one Elizabeth Thible, who was credited with being the first woman ever to leave the ground in free flight. On 4 June 1784 she ascended in a hot air balloon and floated for over a mile above Lyon as part of a group entertainment for the King of Sweden.

One of the most colourful early balloonists was Sophie Blanchard, whose husband Jean-Pierre, together with a colleague, had been the first balloonist to cross the English Channel from France in 1795. Sophie's first ascent came in 1804 when Jean-Pierre's entertainment business was losing money and she was sent aloft as a 'novelty' to help solve their financial problems. She enjoyed it so much that she became the first woman to turn professional and pilot her own balloon. When her husband died in 1809, after suffering a heart attack and falling out of his balloon, Sophie set about paying off their debts by performing stunts to attract the crowds. Staying aloft all night, crossing the Alps, parachuting dogs (and herself on several occasions) and launching fireworks were just a few of the exhibitions that drew huge crowds from all over Europe. Napoleon appointed her 'Aeronaut of the Official Festivals' and she reportedly planned a balloon invasion of England. Alas, in 1819, while setting off a firework display from her hydrogen-filled balloon in a display over the Tivoli Gardens in Paris, the gas ignited and

Sophie gained the dubious distinction of becoming the first woman to be killed in an aviation accident.[3]

The potential advantages of using balloons for military reconnaissance purposes was soon recognised on both sides of the Channel. In England, the first balloon ascent and the first military flight of 20 miles by an army officer took place in 1784. The British military establishment remained unimpressed, however, and while recognising that making observations by balloon had advantages over climbing the highest vantage point available, they decided not to pursue the possibilities. The French were initially more enthusiastic, using a balloon for aerial observation in two engagements in the 1790s, but then discontinued the venture. Although military ballooning then fell into abeyance, or abandoned altogether by the European powers until the mid-nineteenth century, ballooning for entertainment purposes, many of which included women, continued to attract appreciative crowds.

As progress in aviation, other than for 'amusements', was put on hold, photography became the new popular pastime and this time the English led the field. In January 1839, Henry Fox Talbot reported to the Royal Society in London on his 'art of photogenic drawing', a process called 'Calotype' that based the prints on light-sensitive paper: his first image was of a lattice window in his home at Lacock Abbey. Three weeks earlier Louis Daguerre had displayed his 'Daguerreotypes', which were pictures on silver plates, to the French Academy of Sciences. Fox Talbot made further improvements to his process that reduced the exposure time necessary for the image to develop and, by introducing the use of a fixing solution, enabled the picture to be viewed in bright light. Most importantly, the negative image of the Calotype process could be used repeatedly to produce more positive prints. It was this unique quality that led to its universal adoption and the demise of Daguerreotypes. The reproduction of any number of positive prints was a tremendous boon for private and commercial photographers and raised possibilities for military use.

One of the great Victorian inventions had arrived. By the mid-nineteenth century photography had been taken up with enthusiasm by the leisured classes, interested in both the arts and sciences, and with sufficient money and time to pursue the new hobby. From the very beginning, women on both sides of the Atlantic were active in the field of photography. Fox Talbot's wife, Constance, while assisting him in his work, also took her own pictures and processed them. Anna Atkins (1799–1871) used photography at an early stage to record her botanical specimens. In 1843 she became the first person to print and publish a photographically illustrated book, with 424 photographs of British algae.[4]

The marketing of the first camera for amateur use by Kodak in 1888 put photography within the reach of many more people and increased its popularity. Another popular optical form actually pre-dated photography; this was the stereoscope, which gave the viewer a three-dimensional image of the subject when used with two offset pictures. Although originally only used for entertainment purposes, stereoscopy and the 3D image were to be of paramount importance to military intelligence in the years to come.

In the spring of 1858, the skills of aviation and photography were brought together by Felix Tournachon, a French photographer and journalist, bearing the pseudonym 'Nadar'. Tournachon took the first aerial photographs over Paris, using a camera fixed to the basket of his tethered balloon. He was soon producing excellent aerial views despite the tendency of the balloon to spin and the problem of having to sensitise, expose and develop the wet photographic plates while still aloft. The possibilities of combining balloons and photography revitalised the interest of the military establishment in several countries. The production of more accurate battlefield maps was made possible by using the overall perspective gained from a balloon combined with photographs. Tethered balloons were used in the American Civil War for reconnaissance purposes and to direct artillery fire by a system of predetermined flag signals or telegraph.

In England, photographs were taken successfully from free balloons, at a higher altitude than Nadar, in 1863, and dry gelatine plates that could be developed after descending were introduced. Once again the military establishment considered ballooning too expensive to pursue, but a change of mind soon came about, for in 1878 a training establishment was set up by the Royal Engineers at Woolwich with the advancement of military ballooning, including photography, as its raison d'être. In 1883 cameras were fitted to free balloons and timed by clockwork to take exposures in a regular pattern. As the nineteenth century drew to a close, extensive use had been made of balloons by the French and British for reconnaissance and communication purposes in several military campaigns.

The invention and development of the internal combustion engine caused the science of flight to change forever on 17 December 1903. On that day the first manned flight was accomplished by Orville Wright in a powered, fixed-wing aeroplane called *Flyer* at Kitty Hawk, North Carolina. The first flight lasted only 12 seconds, and the aircraft travelled just 120ft over the sand dunes, but by the end of the day Orville and his brother, Wilbur, had achieved a 59-second flight of 852ft. Flight was no longer totally subject to the vagaries of wind and weather, as the 12hp engine and a movable, vertical rudder put the pilot in charge of the aircraft's speed and direction.

Flying fixed-wing aircraft was taken up with tremendous enthusiasm in countries all around the world, by men and women. Each year saw new milestones reached, and then exceeded, in pilot achievement and aircraft construction. Photographs were first taken from aeroplanes in 1909, with America and France leading the way. John Moore-Brabazon was the first Englishman to make an officially recognised aeroplane flight in England in May 1909. He also transported the first live cargo in an aeroplane that November, when he put a piglet into a wastepaper basket strapped to a wing strut, thereby proving that pigs could fly.

The years 1910 and 1911 were ones of firsts in aviation. On 8 March, Moore-Brabazon was awarded the Aviator's Certificate No. 1 and became the first person to be granted a pilot's licence in Britain. In France, on the very same day, Raymonde de Laroche, an actress and experienced balloonist, received her pilot's licence from the Aéro-Club de France, the first to be awarded to a woman. She also carried the distinction of being the first woman in the world to fly solo. Edith Cook was reportedly the first British woman to pilot a plane, in the early months of 1910, but she died a few months later while parachuting out of a balloon. That summer Hilda Hewlett opened Britain's first flying school at Brooklands, a motor-racing circuit in Surrey, and it was there that she became the first woman in Britain to receive a pilot's licence on 29 August 1911. She received Certificate No. 122 from the Royal Aero Club after completing the test in her own biplane. Also in 1911, Harriet Quimby was awarded a pilot's certificate by the Aero Club of America and became the first woman to fly the English Channel, but died in an aircraft crash the following year.

Following the Wright brothers' initial flight in 1903, the French military showed renewed enthusiasm for further involvement in powered aircraft. The War Office was not so encouraged, preferring to continue with experiments on airships, and even after a successful military flight in England in 1908, banned further aircraft work due to the cost. However, on 25 July 1909 Louis Blériot flew a monoplane across the English Channel in 37 minutes, causing widespread consternation at the ease with which Britain could apparently be 'invaded' from the air. This was just one factor that nudged the War Office into setting up the Army Aircraft Factory in 1911 at Farnborough, Hampshire. Amid concerns about the growing air power of France and Germany, the Royal Flying Corps (RFC) was formed on 13 April 1912, and much pioneering work was done at Farnborough in the years leading up to the outbreak of war in August 1914.

The First World War saw Photographic Reconnaissance (PR), the acquisition of film, and Photographic Interpretation (PI), the analysis of that film, firmly established as a prime source of intelligence. For the first time in warfare, a controlled aircraft with a camera could travel 'over the hill' and return with an objective record from which information could be extracted. At first the aircraft were primitive, with a box camera containing glass plates fixed to the side and operated by the pilot leaning out of the cockpit. The quality of the imagery, though, taken from a relatively low altitude, could be remarkably good and enabled commanders to see their own and the enemy's trench patterns, barbed-wire entanglements, weapons pits and much else. Aircraft design, range and capability gradually improved as manufacturers strove to provide the RFC with machines that could fly high and fast enough to escape German aircraft, while also providing a stable platform from which photographs could be taken.

When the first RFC Photographic Section was set up in France in January 1915, Lieutenant Moore-Brabazon was appointed to command it, with Flight Sergeant Victor Laws, a young photographer who took every available opportunity to ascend in airship, balloon, kite or aircraft to take photographs, as a member of the new unit. These two men, with the active support of more senior officers, largely established the principles and practice of aerial reconnaissance and photographic interpretation. Alongside the progress made in aircraft, Laws worked with camera

A First World War BE2c biplane with a C-type plate camera fitted to the fuselage.

manufacturers to improve design and establish the introduction of film, which replaced glass plates over time.

In Palestine, Lieutenant Hugh Hamshaw Thomas pioneered the use of air photographs and stereoscopy to produce the first maps of desert areas. He also set down many of the procedures that formed the principles of photographic interpretation in two world wars. Both he and Laws returned to serve with distinction in the RAF during the Second World War and Victor Laws' daughter, Millicent, joined the WAAF in 1939 to serve in photographic intelligence.

By 1917 the massive casualty losses on the Western Front had resulted in acute shortages of manpower. The authorities, albeit reluctantly, decided to set up women's forces to replace men with female recruits – but only in carrying out clerical or domestic duties. The Women's Army Auxiliary Corps (WAAC) and the Women's Royal Naval Service (WRNS) were formed in 1917 and the Women's Royal Air Force (WRAF) was established in 1918. All three services were disbanded shortly after the Armistice, by which time more than 100,000 women had served in uniform. Although none had worked in photographic intelligence, two women who served in different capacities during the Great War were to join up again in the Second World War and serve as photographic interpreters at RAF Medmenham.

One was Dorothy Garrod, who was born in 1892, the only daughter of a distinguished medical family. She entered Newnham College, Cambridge, in 1913 where she read history and graduated three years later, although without a degree

Flight Officer Constance
Babington Smith headed
the Aircraft Section at RAF
Medmenham.

as the University of Cambridge did not award degrees to women at that time. By 1916 two of her three brothers had died of wounds on the Western Front and the third was to die in the 1919 Spanish flu pandemic. From 1916–19 Dorothy was a worker in the Catholic Women's League huts in northern France and the Rhineland, nursing wounded troops and refugees. The death of all her brothers convinced her to pursue an academic career herself. In the years between the wars, she studied archaeology, led several pioneering expeditions to Iraq and then went to Palestine, where in the Mount Carmel cave deposits she found the first evidence of Neanderthal people outside Europe. In 1933 she took up the post of director of studies in archaeology and anthropology at Cambridge.[5]

Charlotte Ogilvy, later to be Lady Charlotte Bonham Carter, was born a year after Dorothy Garrod and her initial service in the First World War was in the Voluntary Aid Detachment when she worked as a nurse. She was then employed in the Foreign Office where at one stage she was seconded to the infant MI5 and involved in tracking Lenin as he crossed Germany before the Russian Revolution. She was also on the secretariat of the Peace Conference at Versailles in 1919.[6]

Although photographic intelligence was recognised as indispensable by the end of the First World War, it had been employed principally for battlefield use rather than strategic planning. This was largely due to the technical limitations of cameras and the restrictions on the range of aircraft. Through the interwar years little thought was given to PI by the RAF other than as a means of estimating bomb damage, and the aircraft assigned for reconnaissance were slow, low flying and of relatively short range. The army was sufficiently interested, as a result of their experiences in the Great War, to run advanced photo-reading courses. While not giving full PI training, these at least provided a nucleus of people who could be quickly trained up when the British Expeditionary Force (BEF) moved into France in 1939.

Meanwhile, the interwar years saw the civilian world go 'aviation mad' and many of the men and women flyers who had the money to pursue the new craze became celebrities. Amy Johnson and Amelia Earhart became two of the best-known pilots of the era, the former for being the first woman to fly solo in 1930 from England to Australia, and the latter for making the fastest crossing of the Atlantic on record in 1932. In Germany, Hanna Reitsch was the first woman to qualify as a civil and military aviation pilot, the first to fly a helicopter and, at the outbreak of war, the rocket-propelled fighter, the Me 163 Komet. A woman who was not an aviator herself during the 1930s, but acquired a great deal of technical knowledge on aircraft and aviation was Constance Babington Smith. Writing as 'Babs', she attended air shows and aviation meetings in Europe as a staff journalist and photographer for the British journal, *The Aeroplane*. Constance was the PI who identified the Me 163, a great threat to Allied aircraft, in 1943 on an air photograph at RAF Medmenham.

Photography also took great strides forward between the wars, with many women able to earn their living in various forms of the art. Dorothy Wilding, who concentrated on portraits, attracted film stars and celebrities to her studios in Bond Street, London, and in New York. In 1937 she was awarded a Royal Warrant to be the official photographer at the coronation of King George VI and Queen Elizabeth, the first such award presented to a woman. Ursula Powys-Lybbe was a professional photographer who set up a studio in Cairo in the 1930s, moving to London later on to establish a business called the 'Touring Camera'. Instead of photographing her subjects in a studio, she photographed 'Society at Home' on visits to country estates and town mansions, where her sitters positioned themselves in their everyday clothes among favourite objects. In 1937 Ursula walked into the offices of the society magazine *Tatler* with a composite portrait of Lady Mary Lygon, surrounded by images of beloved pets and the family home of Madresfield Court in Worcestershire. Mary was the third daughter of the 7th Earl Beauchamp and was considered to be one of the great beauties of the age. It was claimed that her beauty was such that it once caused the band to stop playing when she entered a ballroom. The *Tatler* promptly commissioned Ursula to produce a series of similar portraits that ran until the outbreak of war in 1939, when she joined the WAAF and became a PI.[7] By coincidence, Lady Mary's younger sister and devoted companion, Lady Dorothy, also became a WAAF PI and served with Ursula at Medmenham.

In 1938, with war on the horizon, a brash unconventional Australian named Sidney Cotton was recruited by the Secret Intelligence Service (MI6) to pioneer new methods of reconnaissance to investigate the build-up of German armaments. Cotton had First World War flying experience and had spent the interwar years in various entrepreneurial activities such as seal spotting in Newfoundland, setting up aerial survey companies in Canada and buying up a controlling interest in a colour film company. In the course of promoting the latter business, Cotton frequently flew to Germany and was on good terms with influential Nazi officials. Having agreed to the spying plan, he bought a fast aircraft and fitted hidden cameras in the fuselage that could be activated at the press of a button to take clandestine photographs. Throughout the months leading up to the outbreak of war Cotton flew to and from Germany on so-called business trips, taking secret photographs of military installations, airfields and naval bases. He flew the last civilian aircraft out of Berlin only a few days before war was declared, and despite being warned not to divert from his route, managed to get photographs of the German fleet on his flight home. In a few short months he, and the experienced pilots who had joined his daring enterprise, had provided invaluable information on German military forces.

'Cotton's Club', as he liked to call it, was based in a hangar tucked into one corner of Heston Airfield, a civilian airport for British Airways Ltd, west of London. Shortly after the declaration of war, the RAF took over Cotton's Heston flight and he was commissioned as an acting wing commander to be its commanding officer. He had proved conclusively that if reconnaissance pilots were to be effective in taking the required photographs and out-fly enemy planes, their aircraft had to fly fast, fly high, be highly manoeuvrable and merge into

Flight Officer Ursula
Powys-Lybbe was head
of the Airfields Section at
RAF Medmenham.

Heston Aerodrome, West London, in 1939, where Sidney Cotton's planes were based.

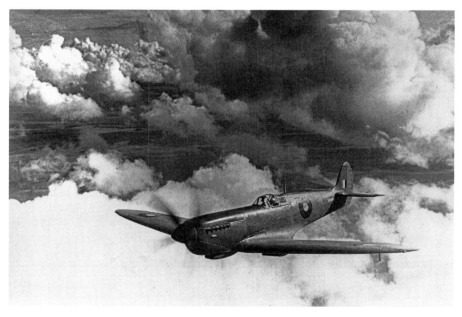

A reconnaissance Spitfire of 16 Squadron, 1944.

a blue-grey background. Cotton managed to acquire Spitfire aircraft that were just coming into service; they were ideal for reconnaissance purposes after certain modifications had been made. All the unnecessary items of armour, ammunition and radios were stripped out and cameras were fitted into the space created. Extra fuel tanks were fitted in the wings to increase the aircraft's range and the overall reduction in the weight of the aircraft made it more manoeuvrable. An application of blue-green 'Camotint' paint helped the aircraft merge into the colour of the sky. Reconnaissance pilots flew alone in the extreme cold for long distances; they were unarmed and navigated by dead reckoning and in radio silence. To escape from enemy fighter planes and anti-aircraft fire the pilots relied on the supreme manoeuvrability of the Spitfire and its operating height of up to 33,000ft, plus their own flying experience and skill.

There was another urgent problem to solve. Having photographed the enemy targets successfully, the PR pilots returned to base, the photographs were processed and then … what? The almost complete absence of PI training in the interwar years had resulted in just one experienced RAF interpreter and a handful of photo-readers being in post at the Air Ministry in the summer of 1939. Photographs waited at least several days to be analysed, which was useless when enemy movements were changing by the hour. Cotton tackled this problem in his usual maverick way. Bypassing the official service route, he contacted an old friend from his days in Canada, Major Hemming, who owned a civilian aerial survey company called the Aircraft Operating Company (AOC) in Wembley, north-west London. The AOC produced detailed reports for geological and survey companies using aerial photographs and the most up-to-date measuring machines available, manufactured in Switzerland. One machine, the Wild A-5, was capable of maximising information on the small-scale photography that Spitfires had taken at high altitudes. The Wild operators readily adapted to interpreting military targets instead of commercial subjects and, most importantly, their reports were delivered to the relevant HQs within hours of a photographic flying sortie rather than days.

The Aircraft Operating Company in Wembley, North London, with sandbag protection in 1939.

A three-phase system of interpretation was set up at Wembley to ensure the timely analysis of photographs and delivery of reports. First-Phase interpretation was a selective analysis of top-priority photographs carried out by the PIs who worked at the airfield from which the aircraft had flown. The process was normally completed in less than 2 hours and could trigger an immediate tactical response; on occasion the decision whether or not to launch an attack rested solely on the PI report.

Second-Phase interpretation examined all the photographic sorties flown in northern Europe in a day and then issued twice daily up-to-date reports on every aspect of enemy activity. Any photograph that raised a query was passed on to the Third-Phase specialist sections, which were concerned with longer-term strategic analysis. The three-phase system was simple in concept but extremely effective in practice, ensuring that reports on enemy activity were issued to the relevant HQs according to their level of priority, in the most efficient and timely way. The system transferred successfully to RAF Medmenham, was replicated in all the overseas reconnaissance and interpretation units, and was adopted by the Americans when they entered the war.

In a matter of months Sidney Cotton had revolutionised the principles of photographic reconnaissance and engineered the changes in the organisation of photographic interpretation. He was also instrumental in pioneering the employment of women as interpreters; a highly skilled, responsible job, very different from the clerical and domestic roles women had been confined to in the First World War. The attributes of patience, attention to detail and persistence, which Cotton considered women to possess naturally, made them highly suitable for PI work. In the months leading up to war, his girlfriend, Pat Martin, accompanied him on his secret flying exploits over Germany to get photographs of military installations; she was taken because she was a good photographer, not because she was a woman. Cotton records his spying flight on 27 August 1939, just five days before Hitler invaded Poland, over German-held islands with a co-pilot and Pat operating a Leica camera with instructions to look out for fighter patrols: 'I had hardly spoken when she tapped my arm and pointed out of her window. There, not 300 yards ahead and to starboard, flying on an opposite course, was a German fighter.' Cotton put their escape down to the 'Camotint' paint.[8]

By the middle of 1940 WAAF officers were being posted in to work as PIs at Wembley – the earliest date that WAAF regulations at that time would allow. Mollie Thompson was one of these officers. In 2009 she wrote:

> I do not remember any tinge of 'the old boy network' or 'the glass ceiling' at Wembley or Medmenham. As far as the interpreters were concerned you did your job, you were capable and whether you were a man or a woman did not matter.[9]

This opinion was echoed by many of the women concerned: the most competent person to do a particular job got it on merit – regardless of gender.

An air photo of RAF Medmenham taken in 1945, showing Danesfield House, the gardens and the huts used as working and living space.

The RAF took over the Heston Flight and the AOC at Wembley in January 1940. For the first fifteen months or so of the war, reconnaissance flights were flown from Heston and the air photographs obtained were interpreted at Wembley. Heston Airfield was bombed with high explosives and incendiaries on an almost nightly basis throughout the summer of 1940 and, although Wembley suffered less, its work was regularly disrupted by bombing and the consequent damage to buildings. The increasing numbers of male and female personnel put space at a premium on both sites and larger premises were urgently sought.

At the end of 1940, the Heston unit moved to RAF Benson in Oxfordshire and was renamed No. 1 Photographic Reconnaissance Unit (1 PRU), remaining there for the rest of the war. Several senior PIs from Wembley set about finding a new, suitable home for photographic interpretation. The requirement was a property large enough to house the growing numbers of PIs and their equipment, conveniently close to RAF Benson and to High Wycombe, where HQ Bomber

Command was sited. They found what they were looking for in a Thameside village in the Chiltern Hills.

Medmenham – we have the Anglo Saxons to thank for the tongue-twisting name of the village, meaning followers of the Saxon leader Meda. Even today it is a small village standing on a wooded road 3 miles equidistant from Henley-on-Thames and Marlow. A string of houses and some old timber-framed cottages line the lane that leads down to a slipway on to the River Thames, where once there was a chain ferry. The population totalled less than 1,000 in the 2001 census; it was probably larger in 1086 when the value of its lands and livestock were sufficient to be recorded in Domesday Book. Seven centuries after that, the ruins of its Norman abbey achieved national notoriety as the location for Sir Francis Dashwood's infamous Hell Fire Club. The other Norman building, St Peter's church, still stands beside the Henley road with the sixteenth-century Dog and Badger Inn opposite.

On the site of an Iron Age hill fort adjacent to the village, the present-day Danesfield House, destined later to become RAF Medmenham, was built. Robert William Hudson, son and heir to the 'Sunlight' Soap fortunes, bought the estate in 1897 and set about having a new house built for himself on the plateau overlooking a curve of the River Thames below. When it was completed in 1901, however, Hudson chose to sell it and a series of owners followed. Over 100 years later it is still a striking sight, built in the locally quarried white rock chalk. The flamboyant Italianate style of architecture provided the mansion with a gatehouse, courtyards, towers, large latticed windows, a sprinkling of crenellations and tall, decorated chimneys.[10] Captain Derek van den Bogaerde (better known as the post-war actor Dirk Bogarde), who worked there during the war, referred to it somewhat disparagingly as 'The Wedding Cake'. It was Winston Churchill, the wartime Prime Minister, who reputedly coined its more familiar name, referring to it as 'The Chalk House with the Tudor Chimneys'. He visited the house more frequently than is officially recorded to examine particularly interesting air photographs and to visit his daughter, Sarah, who worked there.

In 1938 the house was sold to a Mr Stanley Garton who renovated it just in time to see it occupied by eighty boys, evacuated from a London school at the outbreak of war. In 1941, the boys having departed, Danesfield House was occupied once more, this time by the RAF, who requisitioned it to rehouse the unit from Wembley. It was renamed the Central Interpretation Unit (CIU) and of the fifty-three PIs who had moved to their new home by April 1941 one-third were commissioned WAAF officers.[11] The RAF was administratively responsible for the CIU and designated it as RAF Medmenham, part of Coastal Command. It was one of the first truly joint-service organisations to be established, with army, navy and air force personnel working alongside each other. It was international too, with representation from the Dominions, European occupied countries and America. In recognition of this, the CIU became the ACIU (Allied Central Interpretation Unit) in 1944.

The women's uniformed services were re-established before the outbreak of war. The new Auxiliary Territorial Service (ATS) was authorised by Royal Warrant in September 1938, its role being to provide female volunteers who would undertake certain non-combatant duties in connection with the military and air forces. After a hard fight by Director ATS, a Defence (Women's Forces) Regulation dated 25 April 1941 was published and among its provisions was the commissioning of female officers and a declaration that women enrolled for service with the Women's Auxiliary Air Force (WAAF) and the ATS were deemed to be members of the armed forces of the Crown with military rank, with female officers enjoying equal status to male officers. Despite the fact that women replaced men on a one-for-one basis, they received only two-thirds of male pay rates – a disadvantage universal throughout the Allied women's services and one that still rankled many years later.

The Women's Royal Naval Service (WRNS) was speedily re-established in 1939 and had its own code of regulations. Members of the WRNS were not given equivalent naval ranks to men, could not wear the distinguishing marks of naval officers and their officers were not entitled to a salute. In this respect they were unique among the British women's services, and there was a long-running dispute over the fact that they were denied the full status granted to both the ATS and the WAAF.

The recruiting drive that followed the setting up of the ATS in 1938 also produced the personnel to form forty-eight RAF companies within its framework. At first all recruits wore the ATS-issue khaki uniform, with the forty-eight companies wearing RAF distinguishing insignia. The Director ATS argued that a blue uniform for these companies 'would encourage loyalty, enthusiasm and good discipline', and in March 1939 the new uniform of RAF blue was authorised, although stocks of material were not immediately available. These forty-eight companies were transferred as the nucleus of the WAAF when it was formed in June 1939, although the volunteers had to improvise by wearing a mixture of issued uniform items and civilian clothing for several months.

With manpower shortages becoming critical by mid-1941, the War Cabinet announced the conscription of women on 2 December 1941; a step not systematically adopted by any other combatant power. All unmarried women and childless widows were made liable for compulsory service. At first only those between the ages of 20 and 25 were called up; the limit was later dropped to 19 and could be extended to 30 if required.[12]

A number of the earliest volunteers in the WAAF became clerks (special duties) and were sent to train as plotters in operations rooms where they were soon to be engaged in helping to direct the action throughout the Battle of Britain and subsequent bombing raids. Mary James, who was a plotter in the 'ops' room at Fighter Command's HQ at RAF Bentley Priory in north London, wrote:

At first the authorities had been reluctant to use women in this role, claiming that they did not have enough mental dexterity. They were also thought unsuitable because of the need for high security – some would surely chatter about their work.

How little they knew about women:

> It soon became obvious that the Waafs were far more dextrous and speedy than
> the men. Their job was to mark the positions of enemy and RAF formations in
> ever changing situations, from information fed to them by radio: new raids would
> be given to them while they were still working on earlier ones. It was gruelling,
> demanding, technically challenging work with great responsibility for accuracy –
> knowing that pilots and civilians could die if they made a mistake. At times when the
> 'Ops' rooms rocked with the bombing, the girls (their average age was 20) stood to
> their work with quiet coolness.[13]

Several of these WAAFs were later selected to train as PIs and were posted to
RAF Medmenham, where they joined many others involved in the same work,
some recently out of school, others older. Their analysis of air photographs and the
accuracy of their reports could affect the success, or otherwise, of a planned raid or
operation and the lives of those taking part in it. They were continually examining the facts, hints and snippets of information to be gleaned from photography,
trying to determine what the enemy was doing, why they were doing it and, most
importantly, what their intentions were. They worked for months on producing
precise information for the landings in North Africa, Italy and Normandy. If any
hint of a leak or gossip of what they saw and knew had reached enemy ears, it
could have had disastrous consequences for the Allies and, more particularly, for
the troops concerned. There were no leaks, there was no gossip. Friends working
in adjacent rooms did not talk to each other about what they were engaged in, and
decades later some have still been reluctant to discuss their work.

More words from Flight Lieutenant Cyril Tiquet:

> Who are they, these men and women who saw so much? In the RAF they call them
> photographic interpreters. They would smile if you called them spies. They get their
> information, not by adventurous journeys into enemy territory, but by sitting at a
> desk poring over pictures. They peep, not through keyholes and forbidden places, but
> through the twin lenses of a stereoscope. They are armed, not with gun and dagger,
> but with a slide-rule and a mathematical table.[14]

Now is the time to meet some of these women.

2

THE FIRST RECRUITS

As soon as Britain declared war on 3 September 1939, women started volunteering to join the services. Some had enrolled during the preceding months as the inevitability of war increased, while others joined up as soon as possible once war was declared, ready to serve in any job to which they were directed. Many were selected for specialist training later on, including those in photographic interpretation.

The first women PIs of the Second World War were different, however, as they were recruited to learn and fulfil a specific role and were employed as civilians. In the early weeks of the war four women joined four RAF officers to train as PIs at Heston Airfield where Wing Commander Sidney Cotton, newly commissioned by the RAF, was in command. Their employment was possibly at the behest of Cotton, who considered that women naturally possessed the necessary attributes for PI work. WAAF regulations at that time required all recruits to serve six months in the ranks before being commissioned, so in order to train them immediately as PIs, these women had to be employed as civilians.

One of the four was Angus Wilson, who owed her unusual forename to her father; having decided on the name, he was not to be deterred by the gender of the new baby. Angus, with her colleagues Cynthia Wood, Mary Chance and Mary MacLean, learned the art of PI largely by trial and error, constant practice and gained experience. In early 1940 they moved to the temporary HQ Bomber Command, which had its own PI section, where they carried out exactly the same work as the RAF officers, but being civilians, were not entitled to eat in the officers' mess. One day they were having their picnic lunch at their desks as usual, when Cynthia decided that her bottle of milk was a bit off so tipped it out of the upstairs window. Her timing was perfect, unfortunately, for down below was a senior officer in pristine uniform, and the milk landed on top of him – his reaction can be imagined.[1] Within a few months the women were transferred to the new underground HQ Bomber Command near High Wycombe, with the PI section office adjacent to the operations room, where they assessed the accuracy of RAF bombing operations and the extent of the damage caused. Shortly after

Millicent Laws was initially a WAAF plotter at RAF Bentley Priory, the headquarters of Fighter Command, during the Battle of Britain.

the move they were commissioned into the WAAF and joined by another recruit, Honor Clements, who replaced Mary Chance.

In 1938 Millicent Laws had tried to join the Auxiliary Territorial Service (ATS) at the Duke of York's Territorial Army HQ in Chelsea:

> I wanted to learn to drive lorries but there were no vacancies, so I continued work-ing in a solicitor's office until 7 September 1939, when I joined the WAAF. Once again I was turned down as a driver and, wanting a change from secretarial duties, became a Clerk (Special Duties) and was sent initially to RAF Hendon where we just did lots of drilling.[2]

When her father, Group Captain Victor Laws, found that his daughter had only been issued with a raincoat, beret and kitbag, he sent her off to Moss Bros, the tailors, for a made-to-measure uniform. So as a very junior aircraftwoman second class (ACW2), Millicent wore a smart bespoke uniform. Within a few weeks she was posted to the operations room of HQ Fighter Command at RAF Bentley Priory in Stanmore, north London, where she plotted the course and numbers of incoming enemy aircraft on a large map:

> The duty rosters were run on the hours of naval watches and the worst part of the job was having to crawl out of bed for the one that started at 4am, especially as the winter of 1939/40 was one of the coldest on record and there was often deep snow.

In May 1940 Millicent was commissioned and posted to train as a plotter of air photographs at Heston. Like the first civilian PIs, who had by then departed for Bomber Command, her 'training' meant 'learning on the job'. Wing Commander Cotton was no longer to be seen at Heston, as in June 1940 he had been relieved of his command. Although he had revolutionised PR and PI practices in the early months of the war he was too much of a maverick to work for anyone but himself. His deputy, Squadron Leader Geoffrey Tuttle, a regular RAF officer and supporter of women in PI, replaced him.

When Heston was taken over by the RAF in 1940, the commercial side of the airport ceased and all the aircraft were used for PR purposes. Nightly enemy bombing raids all through the summer threatened to stop flying, and the Photographic Section, which was working round the clock on processing and plotting the films, was particularly badly affected. The work continued day and night, however, although the plotters had to shuttle back and forth many times from the plotting hut to air-raid shelters while the bombs fell outside:

> The bombs on the airfield did not bother me as much as the two mile cycle-ride back to my billet after working a shift. I was only nineteen, but often had to escort another girl, ten years older than me, an extra mile to her billet because she was scared of the bombing, then I quickly pedalled back home alone.

The plotter's job was to mark the exact position at which each photograph was taken on to a map before the prints were sent for interpretation. Their only guide was the trace the pilot made over his map showing the route he had taken, but even this was often inaccurate. The task was made harder in the early days by battling with out-of-date lists, inaccurate information from reference books and the ancient machinery used for copying the plots. The frequency of bombing raids at Heston progressively disrupted operations and relocation became essential. On 26 December 1940 Millicent and her fellow plotters moved with 1 PRU to RAF Benson, Oxfordshire.

Meanwhile, at the AOC in Wembley, taken over by the RAF in January 1940, more PIs were needed to handle the increasing volume of photographs coming from 1 PRU. The civilian PIs contacted former university colleagues experienced in working with aerial photographs, and very soon a number of archaeologists and geographers were employed at Wembley and they rapidly adapted their knowledge to military requirements. Newly trained WAAF officers and the handful of PIs at the Air Ministry moved to the AOC in 1940.

Mollie Thompson had completed her BSc (Economics) degree at University College, London, in 1937 and was in her first job in the research department of the Portland Cement Company in Westminster when war broke out. The company decided to evacuate to the country with a smaller staff and encouraged its younger members to join one of the services by offering to subsidise their service pay until it matched the level of their civilian salary. In September 1939 Mollie joined the WAAF as an ACW2 in Coastal Command and was later posted to the Air Ministry for training in PI. Mollie wrote:

I knew nothing about photography before the war and always assumed that the reason I was picked for PI was because of the nature of my university degree. A BSc (Econ) then comprised compulsory courses in economics and banking, one major subject, one minor subject plus two languages. My major subject was economic geography which included maps and map making, some geology, some meteorology, trade and industrial products. Economic history included world trade, industrial development and transportation. My languages were French and German. As you can see, much of this fitted neatly into PI work.[3]

Mollie was commissioned and posted to Wembley where she was very soon analysing air photographs of the coastlines of France and the Low Countries.

After the Dunkirk evacuation in June 1940, the expectation of an attempted enemy invasion of Britain became a near certainty. The only reliable means of securing information on where the German invasion force was gathering, and the strength and readiness of its troops and transport, was by air reconnaissance. This intelligence was of paramount importance in planning the British defensive response and photographic cover was flown whenever possible, often several times a day, to determine aircraft movements, troop concentrations and the positions of naval vessels. Throughout that summer, the Wembley PIs monitored the build-up of the German invasion force along the Channel coast, examining each photographic sortie for increased enemy activity and a first sighting of the barges necessary for transporting an invasion force. Day after day reconnaissance aircraft returned to base with photography, and in July five barges were spotted under construction in a Rotterdam shipyard, quickly followed by more seen in Antwerp and Amsterdam. Successive air photographs showed a concentration of barges at the French and Belgian Channel ports with a supporting force of E-boats and merchant vessels moving into position. The daily count and recount of the assembled lines of moored barges preparing to load continued as PIs reported on their numbers and readiness. By 17 September the number of barges was over 1,700 and the invasion was thought to be imminent. Winston Churchill, the Prime Minister, warned Parliament in secret session that a major assault might be launched on Britain at any moment.

The aircraft used to obtain this photography were the modified Spitfires introduced by Cotton. The pilots relied on the aircraft's superior speed, height and manoeuvrability to evade enemy fighters, photograph the invasion preparations and return to base. However, the small-scale photography produced at such high altitudes could only be exploited by one machine in the whole country. The Wild A-5 stereo-comparator at the AOC, manufactured for civilian survey purposes, could, with a few adaptations, be utilised to analyse the Spitfire photography. Michael Spender, a civilian geographer and arctic explorer, was the expert on using the Wild A-5 and headed the team of PIs scrutinising the highest priority photographs in order to determine the invasion situation.

Two women who worked with Michael Spender were Ann McKnight-Kauffer, who was determined to be a PI before she had even joined the WAAF, and Eve

Holiday, who arrived at Wembley by a more circuitous route. Early in 1939 she had enrolled in the WAAF:

> I attended evening classes in a barracks in Leeds during which I and other volunteers took rifles to pieces and cleaned them, did physical training, country dancing and cooking![4]

Eve was called up at the outbreak of war, spent ten days as an ambulance driver, a few days in one kitchen, a few weeks in another and several months as a map clerk. When interviewed for PI training she impressed the questioner with her knowledge of coke oven battery designs learnt from her engineer father.

Throughout 1940 increasing numbers of WAAF personnel arrived at Wembley for PI training and were immediately put to work. When the Germans failed to gain air supremacy in the Battle of Britain, their invasion force remained in readiness and the repeated checking of barges continued. At last, in October, while the London Blitz continued, the PIs reported signs of lessened activity on the quaysides and shortly afterwards the dispersal of the fleet indicated that the threat of invasion was over. In that same month, the AOC building received a direct hit and during the winter PIs often had to wear raincoats and put umbrellas up over their desks to protect the photographs. The search for new premises resulted in Danesfield House being requisitioned and renamed RAF Medmenham. When the Wembley interpreters relocated in April 1941 one-third of the total PI personnel were WAAF commissioned officers.

While the PIs at Wembley were monitoring the enemy preparations for invasion, other WAAFs were working as plotters throughout the Battle of Britain in the operations rooms of Fighter Command.

Stella Ogle, a future PI, was on holiday in Devon and, like many other people on 3 September, heard on the wireless that Britain had declared war on Germany:

> While the news had been expected, the reality of it brought an extraordinary feeling that life as I knew it had simply come to an end. While viewing the unknown future with mixed feelings of fear and exhilaration, I was most anxious to return home to Winchester, where I was an art teacher, certain that if I did not get back within the next day or two I would be too late to join my chosen service.
>
> I had had a chance of joining the ATS earlier in the year; two Winchester bright, young things were very keen on my joining, as they explained that if I started drilling now I should be able to have a direct commission before the war actually started. Well, neither drilling in the Drill Hall nor the direct commission appealed to me very much. I was more interested in the fact that the ATS uniform was the most unbecoming colour imaginable for my rather sallow complexion and if I had to choose between khaki, navy blue or air force blue, the last was obviously the best for me. So the Air Force it was to be.[5]

After volunteering Stella read a brief notice in *The Times* newspaper inviting applications for a job of 'the greatest secrecy and importance' that the RAF was

Stella Ogle, another early recruit to plotting, who worked in the operations room at RAF Bentley Priory.

about to undertake. Off she went to the recruiting office again and was sent to Southampton where a harassed woman told her that:

> She did not actually know what the job was, except that it was very, very secret and needed all sorts of qualifications, but she didn't know what they were, but she thought I would be very suitable for them!

Stella found herself at RAF Leighton Buzzard with eight other girls on a similar quest, one of whom lorded it over the others as she had been drilling all summer and had become an acting lance corporal:

> As we sat in a crowded assembly hall chatting and wondering when we would get a cup of tea, an immaculate figure came to the front of the stage – auburn hair in a strict Eton crop and a beautifully cut officers' uniform. She spoke, in a very icy tone, 'Has anyone here had any previous experience in the WAAF?' Up shot the arm of the eager beaver acting Lance Corporal. 'Indeed', continued the chilling voice, 'and how is it that you are remaining seated in the presence of an officer?'

As they all hastily scrambled to their feet for the remainder of their short, sharp harangue, Stella realised that life had indeed changed. After a very serious talk on security and signing the Official Secrets Act, Stella was sent to be a plotter at HQ Fighter Command at RAF Bentley Priory, where the ballroom had been hastily adapted as an operations room:

> We plotted the course of the enemy raids as they came over the coast into England and passed that information on. On our accuracy and alertness depended not only the success of the interception of the incoming bombers by our own fighter aircraft, but frequently the lives of the pilots themselves.

The hours were 4 hours on, 8 hours off, interspersed with 24-hour rest days; and like Millicent, she hated turning out of bed for the 4 a.m. shift. The work was concentrated yet, especially during the Phoney War, the anxious hours could also be frustrating. They waited in a high state of alertness and in perfect silence, around a map of England, listening for one of the outstations to contact them. On the balcony above they could hear the murmur of officers' voices, a telephone bell ringing, the arrival of a messenger; and all the time the duty officer would be leaning over the banister, watching intensely, like them, for something to happen. When a message came, it was in the form of a plot, and the WAAF linked to the outstation marked the exact position of the incoming aircraft on the map, adding more coloured buttons as the numbers were assessed, before repeating the plot aloud to attract the attention of the duty officer. Some time later Stella trained as a PI and was posted to Medmenham.

Many girls volunteered for service on their eighteenth birthday; and some before, having 'boosted' their age to meet the entry requirement. Suzie Morrison had spent the last few months of her school life evacuated to Chatsworth House in Derbyshire. She joined the WAAF in September 1940 and was sent for two weeks' basic training at Harrogate, in what had been the Grand Hotel:

> The hotel was stripped of all creature comforts and we slept four to a room on three square mattresses called 'biscuits'. These had to be neatly stacked at the end of our beds every morning for room inspection. The food was AWFUL – corned beef in every disguise for breakfast, lunch and tea. I have never eaten corned beef since then. A strict RAF sergeant drilled us each day, swearing and shouting at us, and using words I had never heard before! Having just left boarding school, I accepted the drill and discipline and liked wearing the new uniform. Others found it very hard. I spent my first week's pay – 5 shillings I think – by going to Fuller's Café and having afternoon tea and a slice of iced walnut cake, which has always been my favourite. My mother came up to Harrogate, uninvited, thinking that she would take me home but by then I was fully signed up for the duration of the war, and no way was I going to desert![6]

Suzie was posted as a plotter to 11 Group's operations room at RAF Kenley, in Surrey, one of the three Group HQs responsible for the wartime air defence of London. RAF Kenley was extensively bombed on 18 August 1940 and the operations room was moved to a standby location. When Suzie started her plotting career a few weeks after the raid:

> It was in a large room behind a butcher's shop in nearby Caterham hastily converted to an Ops Room which we entered through a large archway; meanwhile the butcher carried on business as usual in his shop at the front! I was there when there were a lot of night raids on London. When the sirens went we had to sit with our tin hats on and we were kept busy plotting with large numbers of 'bandits' coming in.

Later on, Suzie became a map clerk at RAF Bircham Newton, in Norfolk, handing out target maps and charts to air crews of Coastal Command:

> I was promoted to Corporal and still aged 17, put in charge of airwomen old enough
> to be my mother. When they questioned my authority, in no uncertain terms, to stop
> them leaving the camp in the evenings, I called upon my recent experience of being
> a school prefect to instil discipline!

Suzie's commanding officer recommended her for a commission, which was rather awkward, as having joined underage, she was only just 18 years old instead of the required 19 or 20:

> Nevertheless, I went ahead and went up to the Air Ministry and they said that I was
> a little bit young at the moment, but they would call for me in 3 months time. Three
> months later to the day I was called back and told I had a commission. Then I trained
> as a PI.

After graduating from Oxford University with a degree in philosophy, politics and economics, Lavender Bruce had spent several months of the summer of 1939 travelling around Argentina with her father who was involved with the expansion of the railway system. On 3 September she boarded a cargo ship at Buenos Aires to return home:

> and heard the news that war had been declared. The ship could not take its scheduled
> route to Britain, so we sailed south, through the Magellan Straits, spent some time
> in Chile and then northwards to pass through the Panama Canal. We then sailed to
> Jamaica where bananas were loaded, but instead of setting off across the Atlantic, the
> ship turned north to Halifax, Nova Scotia where we became part of a large convoy.[7]

Having gone some way to circumnavigating the American continent, Lavender eventually arrived in Liverpool and joined the WAAF. She was another plotter at RAF Bentley Priory who was later commissioned and trained as a PI.

Hazel Furney had enrolled before war was declared and she had reported to RAF Farnborough in autumn 1939. She and her colleagues were issued with raincoats, navy berets with an RAF badge on one side, and black ties, while the rest of their WAAF uniform slowly trickled in. Hazel had the choice of being a typist, a driver or a cook, and chose the latter. She worked in the station cookhouse at Farnborough:

> mixing up huge troughs of plum duff, making yards of sausages and great pots of
> vegetables and stew. I got to be a sergeant butcher having passed a trade test with
> surprisingly high marks, and started a cricket side which we called the 'Hotplates'
> and challenged other teams. We never did very well, not as hot as we hoped.
>   When the 1st Canadian Army arrived in the area they asked us to dances – we
> used to be collected and returned in a lorry with a sergeant in charge. When the

music started, there was a stampede and we were all on the floor 'jitterbugging' like mad. Any idea that the Americans introduced the jitterbug to England is not true! I was selected for a commission and PI training later'.[8]

For many young women in the summer of 1939 life was stiflingly limited and predictable. Although educational opportunities had improved for many girls by this time, attendance at university often depended on personal financial independence or the willingness of a family to pay fees. Even then, passing university exams did not guarantee a woman a degree. When Dorothy Garrod graduated from Newnham College, Cambridge, in 1916, women received certificates instead of full degrees, and were excluded from any part of the governance of the university. Despite becoming a professor and renowned archaeologist, Dorothy did not receive her degree until 1948, when Cambridge University at last awarded them to women.

While job opportunities had also increased in the professions, many girls left school at the age of 14 to take an unskilled job, while others completed a training course for a skill that would enable them to seek a steady, secure post. The expectation for many young, middle-class women was to live at home with parents until meeting and marrying a suitable young man with good financial prospects. Her job would then be given up to care for the house and the children that followed. Nineteen-year-old Joan Bawden lived in a pleasant Surrey village with her parents and worked as a shorthand typist in London, but her ambitions were to write, travel and become famous. Seemingly impossible aspirations, until the declaration of war presented the opportunity to change her comfortable lifestyle. On 20 September 1939 Joan joined the WAAF and was sent to RAF Hendon in northwest London as a clerk typist and told, as she had hoped, that she could be posted abroad. Later on Joan trained as a PI, but initially:

> I'll explain my reasons for joining. Firstly, doing one's bit. I suppose that's there, though it doesn't seem particularly in evidence at the moment. Secondly, this life will get me away from home, make me adult and independent. Thirdly, it's a change and an adventure. Fourthly, and at present most strongly, I want to swank around in a uniform.[9]

Dorothy Colles, aged 22 at the outbreak of war, was an assistant teacher in a private school and attended art college. Her headmistress was not only surprised but totally baffled at Dorothy's decision to throw up her safe job and join the WAAF. She became a clerk SD and was sent to RAF Leighton Buzzard, where the new recruits were housed in what had been the local workhouse. Uniform was in short supply so they dressed in navy overalls for several weeks, until: 'At last I have a uniform and I'm glad to be a proper WAAF! We are transported to and fro in a van, like sardines in a tin. It creates a sensation in the town and all the RAF men put their thumbs up to us.'[10]

The uniform was a major factor in Susan Bendon's decision to join the Mechanised Transport Corps in 1940:

I was not at all interested in mechanics or transport but an officer-type uniform was available and it was very stylish. It comprised a khaki jacket with lots of brass, a leather belt similar to a 'Sam Browne' and a really rakish forage cap. Having so far in my life been involved in haute couture and films, all this appealed to me. A rude awakening awaited.

My job was as an ambulance driver, working 12 hour shifts during the London Blitz. It was a frantic time – we drove our ambulances with sirens screaming, bombs and incendiaries dropping all around, and took the wounded to St Mary's Hospital, Paddington where there were the most terrible sights.[11]

Her 'rude awakening' does not refer to the hospital sights, but to the living conditions at their base where they waited to be called out: a large room, furnished with a few wooden chairs and two-tier metal beds strewn with dishevelled grey army blankets shared with the other drivers. After her initial horror: 'I vowed to myself that I would muck in with whatever was in store from then on.' Susan joined the WAAF in early 1941.

After the emergency measures necessary in 1939–40, conditions of entry and training became regularised in the women's services.

Myra Murden, a shorthand typist in Reigate, was offered a 'safe' job by a family friend, so she could continue to live at home throughout the war. Determined to do something more adventurous, Myra promptly enrolled at the WAAF centre in Croydon on her eighteenth birthday, having turned down the WRNS because they only wanted cooks. Two months later she reported to RAF Bridgnorth in Shropshire for 'kitting out':

First came another medical examination, followed by vaccinations for typhoid and paratyphoid and a check to see that I was FFI – Free From Infection, which meant no head lice.[12]

The uniform items issued were a jacket, skirts, an overcoat, shirts with separate collars for starching plus collar studs and a black knitted tie, black lace-up shoes, grey lisle stockings and a service hat, which completed the outerwear. Less glamorous were three pairs of interlock bloomer-style knickers and two pairs of 'passion killers' – striped flannelette pyjamas. Other essentials were the three square 'biscuits' to make into a mattress, which caused endless troubles and disturbed nights to recruits. A groundsheet, gas mask in a box, brass button-polishing equipment and a kitbag completed the issue.

Many recruits then proceeded to the WAAF Depot at Morecombe. This holiday resort on the north-west coast of England had its ample number of boarding house rooms taken over for the duration of the war to house WAAFs for ten days' basic training. Without exception their opinion of the experience was 'dreadful'. Peggy Hyne remembers: 'It was bitterly cold with bracing winds and doing PT on the pier in January was a real challenge!'[13]

The recruits learned to march on the sea front and Myra also recalls a lecture that included instructions on how to use a wash flannel: 'FFF – Face, Fanny, Feet!' Her pay was 15s a week. On leaving Morecombe she was posted as a clerk to 'an office in London' and forbidden to give any details to anyone, not even her parents. The 'office' was underground and was, in fact, the Cabinet War Rooms, where she worked for a year before being posted to RAF Medmenham.

Susan Bendon commented:

We were billeted at a boarding house on the sea front with very basic accommodation and a landlady who hated us all. The place was not very clean, the food terrible and she was so frugal that she counted the number of tinned peas on each plate as she served them. Drilling included performing exercises in our knickers (dark blue, extending to the knee) on the pier above the frozen sea – it was so cold that sheets of ice floating on the waves beneath. After two weeks everyone received their posting notices – except me. Whenever I went to the various WAAF offices, I was brushed aside and told to try elsewhere. Eventually it became clear that my papers had been lost and no-one knew what to do with me – I simply didn't exist in the Air Force. Before it was resolved, I spent seven weeks in that ghastly boarding house where, in spite of my pleas, my sheets were never changed and the landlady's dislike of her perpetual lodger became almost a joke as new batches of recruits came and went.[14]

To pass time, Susan bought a notebook and went each morning to the large reception area for new recruits, and looked busy. Before long she became an accepted member of staff until eventually her posting to RAF Biggin Hill came through. Later on she was sent to learn PI at Medmenham: 'Why was I given such a wonderful opportunity? I never discovered the reasons – but it was a prize beyond prizes.'

Learning to live in close proximity with women of all backgrounds, ages and attitudes came as a great shock to many. Jane Cameron, who described herself as extremely shy, without close friends and reticent, joined up in 1939:

I found my freedom as a six-digit number, an aircraftwoman in the WAAF, inside a high wire-mesh fence, behind the guarded gates of a Coastal Command station. My shyness, my reticence dissolved like mist in a barrack room shared with twenty-nine other women. I wore a uniform, but at five feet nine inches tall and with shoulders broader than my twenty-two inch waist I wore the uniform better than the other twenty-nine. When I elected to lie on my cot and read a book instead of going to the NAAFI with them they told me with cheerful frankness that I was a 'queer one' but implied that they accepted me as I was.

When, within a few weeks I became corporal in charge of them, I watched them, listened to them, helped them write their letters home, bullied them to bed when they came in drunk, forced them to wash and mend their underwear, man-handled them apart when they indulged in hair-tearing, clawing quarrels and discovered some nine months later, when I was posted to be commissioned as an officer, that I

Joan 'Panda' Carter sketched some of her fellow ATS recruits on parade.

loved them. They were sad, one or two shed tears and the oldest of them, a woman of nearly forty, summed up their thoughts when she sighed and said: 'Well, we're not surprised.' I had never known so much raw, rumbustious, uninhibited life.[15]

Although WAAF personnel were in the majority at Medmenham, a few WRNS officers and a number of ATS officers and NCOs also served there. In 1939 Joan 'Panda' Carter had a job in the Admiralty Drawing Office, and, after being called up into the ATS, was sent to Talavera Camp in Northampton for basic training. Of the twenty-four recruits in her hut:

Two had their heads shaved because of lice, one wet the bed nightly and another had regular nightmares and walked in her sleep. Our four weeks training was like a complete new world. Each day, come rain, shine or snow, when the camp was ship-shape, we spent many hours learning how to march and obey commands. I enjoyed it after a while, and even knew my left from my right. Our uniforms fitted smartly and we were medically A1, having had all the appropriate injections.

The last part of our training consisted of a variety of tests to decide for what kind of work we were most suited. It was like being back at school. We had to sit several written papers, and then take a practical test of assembling wooden puzzles, fitting pegs into holes. There were also odd bits of machinery to find out if we were mechanically minded. I had just one aim, to become a draughtswoman. When it was my turn to be interviewed by the Commanding Officer, she asked me what I would like to do. When I told her she handed me a huge book about architecture. She asked me if I understood it, and I told a deliberate lie. I said I understood it all. She obviously didn't believe me, and said I was just the right type for a clerk. I tried to protest by telling her I could not spell. Her answer was, 'None of us can'. So that was that. My case was lost. My heart sank – how boring.[16]

Barbara Rugg applied to join the ATS in 1938 and was put on a waiting list. In September 1939 she volunteered and although she was nearly 19 years old her mother opposed the idea, claiming that Barbara was 'not strong enough'. However, the doctor declared her medically fit and her father signed the form. Barbara was in a group of twenty-four women sent for basic training to an army camp at Larkhill on Salisbury Plain. Their arrival was not welcomed and they were billeted, with bags of straw for bedding, in a redundant church; in fact, it was a tin shack that had just been painted, and the paint was still wet. While some of the younger soldiers, who had only recently been called up themselves, were helpful, the older regulars resented the women and booed them when they first went to the mess for meals:

> It was awful to start with but we couldn't write home and say so because our mothers would have been saying 'I told you so!' So we all kept quiet. I was there for two years and worked in the Drawing Office of the School of Artillery. There was a different atmosphere by then.[17]

Jeanne Adams describes her experiences at the WAAF Depot in Morecombe in November 1941 as:

> Very grim. It was terribly cold and we were all very young, very green and very, very, home sick. Our TAB injections made all of us rather ill for a couple of days and we lay under our miserably thin blankets wishing we could go home. It was interesting to observe, even at this early stage, that officer qualities came to light and revealed those who were going to lead us; they comforted us, urged us to get out of bed, eat some food and cheer up!
>
> I was posted to Medmenham, but first I had to get there. There was only one train and that departed at 6am from Morecombe. I was billeted one and a half miles away and the only way to get there was to walk. So at 5.30am I set off in pouring rain, carrying a kit bag and gas mask, a tin hat and a suitcase and clad in something called a ground sheet, a substitute for a mackintosh. They were standard issue and because I was small I kept tripping over mine, so I struggled along the front, feeling very sorry for myself, and caught the train.[18]

On her first day at Morecombe, Jeanne had met a vivacious redhead, Sarah Churchill, the second daughter of the Prime Minister, who had become a stage dancer and actress in 1935. She married a well-known stage entertainer in 1936 against her parents' wishes, but by 1941 her marriage was breaking down and she asked a rare favour from her father: 'I had decided to join the Services and asked him to arrange it as soon as possible. I was in the WAAF within forty-eight hours.'[19]

Felicity Hill (later Dame Felicity Hill, director WRAF 1966–69) was in the wartime Inspectorate of WAAF Recruiting:

> One day we received a message telling us that the Prime Minister's daughter, Sarah, would be coming to Victory House to join the WAAF. Sarah Churchill was then recently married to the comedian Vic Oliver. Mrs Oliver arrived in a very lively mood after lunch at the Savoy, and I interviewed her in the inner office. I smiled to myself as I went through the motions of asking her the usual questions for completion of the application form (though I skipped over Father's Name and Address, and the question of references seemed inappropriate to Winston Churchill's daughter). I enrolled her as a Plotter, told her something of recruit training, and looking at her beautiful and abundant red hair suggested she should have it restyled, for I shuddered at the thought of what the camp barber would do to it. Sarah was later commissioned as a Photographic Interpretation Officer, a branch in which she and many other WAAF officers did valuable work in detecting and deducing intelligence material from aerial photographs.[20]

Sarah continues:

> In October 1941 I became an Aircraftwoman Second Class. My choice of the WAAF was influenced by the colour of the uniform. I was enrolled and despatched on a long

Jeanne Adams plotted where each photograph was taken on photographic reconnaissance sorties.

Sarah Churchill, the Prime Minister's second daughter, was a plotter before training as a photographic interpreter.

train journey to Morecombe for the inevitable 'square bashing' and wrote plaintively to my mother about the first few days, largely concerned, as always, with my appearance. The shoes were a particular horror – not a pair fitted, all were hideous and you simply could not do anything but 'clump' in them. We left for Morecombe at four o'clock in the morning to catch an eight o'clock train. We had to carry full equipment, including gas cape and gas mask strapped on one's back – full-sized kitbag on one's shoulder, smothered in an enormous topcoat and clutching a suitcase with civilian clothes in the other hand. I never imagined an eight hour journey could be a rest cure! It was a wonderful system though, watching a straggly bunch of nervous civilians change in about forty-eight hours into fairly passable looking WAAFs. Another forty-eight hours saw a change in deportment and manner, and one would march away with a look of pity towards the next bunch of sad-looking individuals being herded in the entrance gate.[21]

Although commissioned later, Sarah started in the ranks as an ACW2 clerk (special duties) and worked as a plotter at RAF Medmenham before training as a PI. She was respected as a hard-working, generous person who never used her illustrious parentage to 'pull rank'.

Elspeth Macalister had read archaeology at Cambridge University, including the use of air photography, and her tutor, Dorothy Garrod, suggested that she apply to the Air Ministry to be a PI. Elspeth was duly interviewed, soon heard that she was accepted and in July 1942 met up with three other Cambridge graduates, Sophie, Ena and Lou, to travel to RAF Bridgnorth for 'kitting out'. After getting their uniform they were herded into a large hall to complete an IQ test with rows of numbers and odd shapes to match, which Elspeth found extraordinary:

Pat Donald was just 18 years old when she joined the WAAF.

Next day were the interviews to help us find our niche in the war machine. I was interviewed by Theresa Spens – we had been in the same form at school and never liked each other. She showed no sign of recognition. She asked me if I could cook. 'No'. Then she said, 'We don't know quite where to place you. Your IQ is very low – educationally subnormal'. I had just achieved a good Cambridge degree and muttered something about PI. I was ignored, obviously I was useless.

On the last day the postings went up. I was to go to RAF Duxford; having joined the WAAF to see the world I would be six miles from home! My work as an unskilled clerk in Sickquarters was to write out, in longhand, a list of the kit of aircrew lost on bombing missions – a sad job.[22]

Women came to PI from widely diverse backgrounds and experience. Some were not long out of school, such as Pat Donald who volunteered for the WAAF in London with a friend, just before their eighteenth birthdays. They were sent initially to RAF Gloucester where they were so homesick that they would have left after four weeks (as they were entitled to do) but stuck it out as the inevitable 'I told you so' comments at home would have been even more unbearable.[23]

Many younger women were looking for adventure, while others had put their chosen careers on hold for the duration of the war, and several, including Dorothy Garrod and Charlotte Bonham Carter, were of an age that would have exempted them from conscription. By various routes all these entrants to the women's services came to serve at RAF Medmenham, where a new era in photographic interpretation had begun.

3

LEARNING THE ART

When the RAF took over the Aircraft Operating Company at Wembley in January 1940 to become the centre for photographic interpretation, it also assumed the responsibility for training the increasing numbers of new interpreters that were urgently required. Instruction was undertaken by a number of the PIs already working at the newly named Photographic Interpretation Unit (PIU), most of whom had acquired their specialised knowledge of military targets by applying and adapting their previous civilian knowledge of air survey. Squadron Leader Alfred 'Steve' Stephenson was put in charge of organising all PI training courses for the RAF from the early days at Wembley until the end of the war. He was well qualified for the post, being one of the first geographers to use aerial survey on Arctic and Antarctic expeditions in the 1930s, with a wide knowledge and experience of the photogrammetric and optical machines associated with survey and PI. In Antarctica, a colleague had said that Stephenson was the ideal companion in difficult conditions: equable, efficient and with great organising ability. He had infinite patience with students, a quality he shared with Douglas Kendall, another pre-war air surveyor and mathematician, who would later be responsible for all PI carried out at Medmenham. Soon, RAF selection boards were identifying suitable candidates who showed the attributes required for interpretation training. From the middle of 1940, these included WAAFs who had by then served their regulation first six months in the ranks; Mollie Thompson was one of the earliest candidates to join a PI course at Wembley.

Finding enough space for courses to be run became a problem after bombing raids had damaged the PIU main building and damaged or destroyed many houses in the Wembley neighbourhood. Ann McKnight-Kauffer and Constance Babington Smith met on their PI course in December 1940, held in the upstairs room of a small terraced house opposite the PIU. It was bitterly cold and as the gas fire only operated intermittently, they wore their thick woollen WAAF greatcoats all day. Fortunately there was a canteen on the premises where they could warm up with tea and stodgy buns, or sausages known as 'bread in battledress'. Their group of RAF and WAAF students learnt the skills of interpretation using recent photography taken over Germany and France, identifying ships in Kiel Harbour and analysing a dump of tangled French aircraft on an airfield at Bordeaux. In her final oral exam Ann was asked a catch question: were there more armoured divisions or horse-drawn ones in the German army? She fell into the trap and guessed 'armoured', which was wrong, but it taught her the basic principle of never making an assumption or a guess.

PIs were instructed that, if less than totally convinced of the identification of an object, they were to use the terms 'possible' and 'probable'. For instance, they might be positive that what they were looking at was a tank and almost sure, but not quite, that it was a German Tiger. So they would describe it in their report as a 'probable Tiger tank'. On the other hand, with the tank wreathed in smoke and impossible to clearly distinguish, they would describe it as 'a possible tank'.

Ann was impressed, above all, by Kendall's kindness and even temper to all the students on the course, and this was a feature of teachers found by prospective PIs on subsequent courses. The support, encouragement and patience of instructors were essential for students to gain self-confidence in their own knowledge and decision making. They would soon be writing reports on photography that they had interpreted, which could result in an immediate tactical response or affect future planning; in either case, loss of life was possible if action was undertaken based on an inaccurate report. Much could be gained by students from senior colleagues' experience and specialist knowledge, with each individual adding their own particular skills to the team. PI was an art that could not be learnt by rote or by following a set of instructions; that would be merely recognition of what is present and visible. Interpretation was about defining the unknown, and asking not only what and where objects could be seen but, all importantly, why they were there and the meaning that could be deduced from that knowledge.

With the move of the PIU to RAF Medmenham in April 1941, the School of Photographic Interpretation was established in the main building of Danesfield House. Joan Bawden arrived at Marlow, the nearest railway station, in May to attend the first course to be held there. Transported to Medmenham with her luggage in the unit's motorcycle and sidecar, her first impression of Danesfield House, in common with most other newcomers, was one of amazement at the size of the place and its resemblance to a castle or an abbey. Initially Joan, Helga O'Brien and two other WAAFs shared a small, bleak room above the stables, but within a week they were moved into more salubrious accommodation in the main building, a room with lattice windows, window seats and a view over one of the courtyards.

By the following year, Medmenham had grown to such an extent that, despite the rows of Nissen huts erected in the gardens, the space taken up by the PI school was needed for working sections. The school made two temporary moves before settling into its final wartime home at RAF Nuneham Park, just south of Oxford and a few miles from Benson and Medmenham. Nuneham Park was a handsome Palladian-style villa built for the 1st Earl Harcourt in 1756, surrounded by a park landscaped by 'Capability' Brown. After being requisitioned and designated RAF Nuneham Park, it housed the model-making school, part of the Photogrammetry

Section and the School of Photographic Interpretation. As with Danesfield House, accommodation huts and temporary buildings, including a theatre, sprouted in the grounds and the Thameside mansion became another Allied Joint Service establishment. PIs drawn from all three services of the Allied forces were trained here, although as the need for PIs increased, army and ATS personnel attended similar courses at the School of Military Intelligence in Matlock, Derbyshire.

Diana Byron had grown up in Newlyn, Cornwall where she enjoyed living near the sea and watching the movements of ships. After training as a teacher at the Froebel Institute, she took a post teaching art at a boy's preparatory school, where she was the first woman to be appointed to the teaching staff. With the declaration of war Diana joined the WAAF and trained for radar work at RAF Cranwell. Postings to two Chain Home radar stations in Kent followed; her work was to pass the details of incoming German aircraft ('bandits') to the appropriate group operations room, where WAAFs plotted them on to a central display table. The Chain Home ring of coastal stations formed the first area radar intercept system for the protection of Britain throughout 1940, when the country was threatened with invasion, and beyond. Later on, Diana was selected for PI training and attended the first course to be held at RAF Nuneham Park in 1942, where she and her fellow WAAFs were joined by WRNS, RAF officers and USAAF personnel. Diana said: 'The course covered everything you could imagine, from silhouettes of shipping

American personnel in the PI School at RAF Nuneham Park.

and aircraft and information about Europe. It was not only about aerodromes but also everything to do with harbours, seas, the whole lot – it was fascinating. What makes a good interpreter? Curiosity in the unusual.'[1]

In the selection process for PI training, the candidate's personal qualities were considered more important than paper qualifications. Visual memory, an ability to sketch and an attention to detail headed the list of necessary qualities, together with an enquiring mind and a sense of the significance of events and objects. Women were noted for their dogged pursuit of a particular subject over a period of time, while men often had scientific knowledge about a specialised subject. Under Stephenson's guidance, his staff taught the principles and practice of photographic reconnaissance and interpretation and inspired the students to become 'curious in the unusual'.

The first lecture of each course was an explanation of the three phases of interpretation, which was at the core of the efficient organisation of the examination of air photographs. From the early days at Wembley, where the system was devised, to the end of the war and beyond, it provided an effective means of prioritising the examination of an ever-increasing volume of photographs. Urgent prints were dealt with immediately, while those used for monitoring purposes were available within 12 hours, leaving others to be dealt with on a longer timescale. This deceptively simple system ensured that photography was analysed and reported on in a time frame dependent on its priority, and was used in Allied interpretation units all around the world.

First-Phase interpretation took place on the reconnaissance base that the photographic sortie was flown from, with the PIs living close to the airfield to ensure 24-hour cover. Photographs of high-priority targets were selected and analysed as swiftly as possible, or within a maximum of 2 hours of the aircraft landing. An immediate report was then signalled to the relevant command, which could trigger an instant tactical response if, for example, the PIs had sighted a concentration of enemy tanks or the departure of an enemy battleship from its anchorage.

RAF Medmenham was the home of Second-Phase interpretation, keeping an up-to-date record of all enemy movements, activities and new constructions relating to land, sea and air forces. This formed a most detailed, comprehensive record of what the enemy was engaged in from day to day. With this knowledge, it was possible not just to predict, but to know for certain what the next enemy move would be, giving an opportunity for an Allied countermeasure to be put into operation. The Third-Phase sections, around thirty in total and specialist in nature, were also housed at RAF Medmenham. Each was designated by a letter of the alphabet and concerned with one specific aspect of enemy activity.

Comparing photographs of an area or activity with others taken on previous cover was the only way of establishing if any changes had taken place. Comparative cover was one of the most useful tools the PI could use, for without comparison over time there was no way of knowing what was, or was not, normal. An air photograph of an enemy airfield might show a single track leading to a runway for light passenger aircraft. One month later the track could have become a well-surfaced road with several heavy transport planes visible among different types of aircraft, indicating that something was happening: comparative cover would show the change in use and purpose. It was then the responsibility of the PI to find the answers to the questions and report on them. Captain Dirk Bogarde summed up the fascination that PIs had for their work:

> You needed observation, an eye for detail and memory. I loved the detail, the intense concentration, the working out of problems, the searching for clues, and above all, the memorising.[2]

Intervals between flying photographic sorties could range from a matter of hours in a rapidly changing situation, to a regular 'watching brief' of days or weeks. When an operation was being planned, one of the first orders would be for a significant increase in photographic cover of the area concerned, which would form a major part of the intelligence gathering and influence the planning and decision-making process. Even when intelligence came from other sources, for instance by electronic or human means, it invariably had to be verified with photographic cover. The plans for virtually every wartime operation included the words: 'The photographs show …'

Maps and charts are fundamental to every armed force activity on land, sea or air, and constitute one of the earliest forms of intelligence. This part of the course put the mathematical skills of the students to the test. Dorothy Colles passed her PI course in 1941 despite a few doubts:

> On the last course all the WAAFs and half the RAFs failed. I have looked at all the manuals and am overwhelmed – not that one does it in a few weeks, but that one does it at all! I can see some most involved mathematical calculations ahead of me![3]

By the afternoon of Diana Byron's first day, the students were immersed in learning the standard procedures of basic scaling, recognition, identification and measurement that all PIs follow when looking at an air photograph. On each desk was set out the 'tools of the trade': a simple, pocket-sized stereoscope, which looked like a pair of spectacles mounted on a fold-up stand, a magnifier with graticules for measuring, photogrammetric tables and sets of trigonometry tables, a slide rule and an anglepoise lamp to provide a strong and adjustable source of light.

The scale of an air photograph had to be determined in order to identify objects correctly by size and recognition. The process involved the accurate measurement of the size of an object relative to its size on the ground; sometimes the object was little more than a speck seen on a photograph taken at a height of 30,000ft. Before the invention of the pocket calculator, the slide rule was the most commonly used calculation tool in science and engineering. Looking like an overlarge folded-up ruler, it was used to multiply and divide and calculate functions such as roots, logarithms and trigonometry. Hazel Furney and Sarah Churchill were together on their course at Nuneham:

Five of us shared a room. I liked Sarah very much – she had an awful inferiority complex and was terrified of letting the family down. One day we all did a test report on an aerial photograph of which she had got the scale wrong, and then she asked me why she had got so much of her interpreting wrong. When I realised and told her what she had done, she disappeared. Later I found her sobbing her heart out on her bed, convinced she had failed. Needless to say, she wasn't sent away.[4]

Sarah's abilities with a slide rule improved and she passed the course, although she still lacked confidence in her mathematical capabilities. So she devised an ingenious solution to her problem:

When faced with the complexities of setting a slide-rule, I would tiptoe downstairs and ask a friend, one of the model makers, to do it for me. In fact, I got two slide rules, so that I would not have to change the setting if the photographic sorties used cameras with different focal lengths. David would set them both, once I knew the areas I was working on, and I would then carry them gingerly back upstairs.[5]

Ursula Powys-Lybbe, who had been a professional photographer before the war, enjoyed mastering scaling and the slide rule:

Generally all that had to be done was to pull out the map sheet of the area covered by the photographs, make a note of its scale (1:25,000 for example), multiply that by the distance between two points measured on the map, and divide that total by the distance between the same two points seen on the photograph, and the answer is the scale of the photographs. It was then possible to arrive at the measurement, say, of the wingspan of an aeroplane in feet ... I can say with pride that it took nearly a week for me to be able to multiply and divide with the help of the slide rule, and I was so gratified that I wrote a 'Child's Guide in the Use of the Slide Rule (Simplified Version) with Illustrations', to make it easier for limited persons like myself.[6]

Like repeating a mantra, students muttered 'size, shape, shadow, tone and associated features' to remind themselves of the five elements of interpreting an air photograph. Colour film was rarely used in air photography as black-and-white prints revealed varying tones far better, making identification easier even when an object was camouflaged. As familiar objects become unfamiliar and unrecognisable when seen from above due to the loss of normal perspective, many hours were spent learning to recognise the shape of every feature of a landscape shown on an air photograph. The silhouettes of military and naval equipment were committed to memory from recognition charts and manuals.

In binocular vision, each eye records an image and the brain fuses those two separate images, resulting in vision with depth, which we accept as normal. An ordinary photograph merely provides a flat two-dimensional representation, but the Victorian novelty of stereoscopy could change that into a three-dimensional picture. Stereoscopy had proved its value to military intelligence in the First World

War and now, in the second, stereoscopy teamed with superior measuring devices allowed minute objects on very small-scale photography to be measured and identified. When a reconnaissance pilot flew over a target area, the cameras were automatically set to expose the film at calculated intervals, causing each frame to overlap its successor by 60 per cent. When the PI adjusted the two overlapping prints, termed a 'stereo-pair', under a stereoscope, the two separate images 'fused' and the three-dimensional effect of normal vision was reproduced. Using two images, rather than one, greatly increased the knowledge that could be gained from an air photograph. All three dimensions of height, width and depth could be accurately measured, making recognition of an object possible. Stereoscopy also enabled identification of objects hidden on a two-dimensional image: for example, vehicles parked under camouflage were likely to be 'invisible' on a flat photograph, but were revealed under a stereoscope where the 3D effect showed up the depth and the varying tones.

The students spent some time away from their desks discovering the practical side of PI. Jane Cameron recorded a visit:

> We went to Farnborough today by bus to see the shot-down and reconstructed German aircraft and I do so wish aircraft meant a little more to me. Ships are different – ships are like people, gifted with an actual personality and with an infinite capacity to please the eye and mind, but aircraft – no. They are like motor cars, humdrum, soulless machines in which to go from A to B, and no more. Sometimes, in the sky with the sun on them, they are beautiful in a distant sort of way, but in my mind they will never have the awesome beauty of a man-of-war against a thunder sky or the ardent effort of a trawler against a heavy sea.[7]

Time was spent at RAF Medmenham watching experienced interpreters at work and visits made to RAF Benson to learn about air photography from the reconnaissance pilot's viewpoint. Joan Bawden and Helga O'Brien had their first flight on their training course after a young Canadian pilot offered them a trip in a Blenheim bomber. Clambering up the footholds attached to the side of the aircraft, they squeezed into the little space available and were soon looking out on to an aerial view of Medmenham, enjoying the enormous noise of the engine and the wonderful sensation of speed.

Hazel Furney, Molly Upton and Sarah Churchill were invited for a flying trip in Tiger Moths by two pilot instructors at a nearby airfield:

> Our heads were out in the open and the intercom was impossible to hear. At one point my pilot said something I couldn't hear and, on the third attempt, I got the message that I was flying the aircraft, and we were losing height rapidly! After that incident, we caught the train to London and Sarah took us to see a show with Bebe Daniels and Ben Lyon, a well-known show business married couple who appeared in reviews. Afterwards we went to their dressing room and then on to Sarah's flat.[8]

Having passed their final exams and been granted a commission, the new PIs received their first posting, either to RAF Medmenham or to a PRU base. Although they had worked hard and sometimes thought that they would get 'thrown off the course', the students found some time for socialising, as Shirley Eadon described:

> One of the other WAAF officers on my course could swallow a pint of beer without stopping to draw breath. We used to take her around like a performing bear because, thanks to her, we all got free rounds of beer![9]

All PIs at Medmenham held commissioned rank. Why was this considered necessary? A conference of senior PI officers held at the end of the war concluded:

> If interpreters, if the actual men and women who hourly look at photographs, are too rigidly controlled and directed, either by their own organisation or by superior bodies, they will not be able to get out of interpretation all that it can give. The success of British interpretation is probably due first to the decision to use officers as interpreters and secondly to the give and take in the British character that permitted junior officers considerable freedom of initiative, and often responsibility, out of all proportion to their rank. For example, in the early days of the war, when a watch was being maintained on the German Fleet, the disposition of the entire British Fleet would wait upon the word of a single junior photographic interpreter.[10]

On the other hand, in the preface to her book *The Eye of Intelligence*, Ursula Powys-Lybbe refers to the tendency of 'authorities' to question a PI report when few would have the temerity to question the 'intelligence snatched out of the air' by the code and cipher school at Bletchley Park:

> The basis for photographic intelligence, on the other hand, was the ordinary black and white photographic print familiar to the majority of people. It was therefore tempting for the recipients of Medmenham interpretation reports to borrow stereoscopic magnifiers and formulate their own opinions, sometimes overriding the findings of fully trained and experienced PI officers, particularly when the intelligence received was contrary to their expectations. In some cases our interpreters were 'invited' to rewrite their reports, an invitation which not unnaturally they refused.[11]

Most WAAFs who were to be commissioned attended the two-week course at the WAAF Officer Training Unit at Loughborough. Jeanne Adams:

> We learned how and when to salute, to drill a squad, to be an orderly officer and to look after other ranks' welfare. Last, but not least, to learn theoretically how to pass the port at mess dinners, which was a new experience for most of us. I was commissioned as Assistant Section Officer No 5086 and posted back to Medmenham.[12]

Jeanne found that there was another advantage to being an officer:

> When I had my initial medical examination at the Air Ministry on joining up, I was handed a paste pot for a specimen by a dragon who said to me, 'And don't do it all over the floor'. At Loughborough we had a further medical and asked to provide another specimen. However on this occasion the orderly was far more courteous. I was handed a kidney dish covered with a cloth and the request, 'Could you please provide a specimen, ma'am?'

Millicent Laws was one of the few WAAFs who attended an early OTU, temporarily relocated to Bulstrode Park in Buckinghamshire. Unable to recall anything of the content of the course, Millicent's abiding memory is the 'pep' talk given to the cadets on the last afternoon by the then commandant WAAF, Dame Katherine Trefusis-Forbes. Her final words – 'You must have <u>guts!</u>' – rang in their bemused ears as they headed back to their various units.

Elizabeth Johnston-Smith was the only WAAF to take and pass the PI course twice. In June 1940 she was living in Bournemouth and planning to go to art school, when suddenly the town was full of exhausted soldiers who had lost everything in their evacuation from France. It was Dunkirk and the Battle of Britain later on that summer that determined Elizabeth to join the WAAF. She was subsequently commissioned, went into WAAF administration and was posted to 3 Group Bomber Command at RAF Exning, in Suffolk, which she greatly enjoyed:

> Several months later I was called 'out of the blue' to the Air Ministry and interviewed by Douglas Kendall for PI training – I don't know why! It sounded interesting and I duly went to Nuneham Park for the PI course, which I enjoyed and passed. I was then sent to Medmenham to be interviewed by a panel to decide which section I should go in. But when I looked at the 'old bods' on the panel (I was only 20) I thought, 'they look a bit stuffy', and requested a transfer back to Bomber Command. There were no vacancies so I did WAAF Admin in the Midlands until 1943 when I got fed up with that, reapplied to Nuneham Park and passed the PI course again. Steve Stephenson told me that I was the only person to have done the course twice and passed both times![13]

Elizabeth has another unique claim as she is almost certainly the only WAAF ever to have sat on the knee of the Commander-in-Chief, Bomber Command:

> At Exning, I was chosen to play the part of Cinderella in the Christmas pantomime. At the final performance the last song was 'Kiss the Boys Goodbye' and then the cast trooped down to sit on the knees of the top brass sitting on the front row – and I sat on 'Bomber's' much to the delight of the audience! The following morning I encountered Air Marshal Harris at work. I delivered a smashing salute, and received a smile and 'Good Morning Cinders' in reply!

Elizabeth Johnston-Smith passed the PI course twice.

During the latter half of 1941, when the USA was still neutral, the personnel at Medmenham became accustomed to increasing numbers of US navy and marine officers coming to learn about the organisation of British PI. Pamela Dudding recalls a US naval officer being there for two or three months: 'I avoided him at breakfast because he put marmalade on his kippers!'

Helena Ewen tells an interesting anecdote indicating that US preparations for war against Japan were in place before the attack on Pearl Harbor on 7 December 1941:

> In November/December 1941 I attended the first PI course at RAF Benson with six WAAF and six RAF officers plus a WRNS officer. Also attending, but keeping apart from us, were two American civilians. On the morning of Monday 8th December they appeared in American service uniforms and joined in with us fully – now as Allies.[14]

Having passed their PI course and, if not already commissioned, attended an OTU course, the new PIs set off, either to Medmenham or to one of the four PR bases in Britain. RAF Benson was near Wallingford, in Oxfordshire; RAF St Eval on the north coast of Cornwall; RAF Wick in the far north-east of Aberdeenshire; and RAF Leuchars on the coast of Fife, in the east of Scotland.

Mary Grierson, always known as 'Bunny', had joined the WAAF straight from school and worked at Wembley before moving in 1941 to RAF Benson where 1 PRU was based. With four reconnaissance squadrons operating from the base, the PIs were fully occupied. The photographic unit and First-Phase hut were sited just beyond the airfield boundary in the little village of Ewelme, so they could walk or cycle there from Benson through the tranquil countryside, crossing hedges and a stream with watercress beds. A path led to their hut and above them they could see the manor house where Henry VIII had spent his honeymoon with Catherine Howard. Ten PIs, a mixture of RAF, WAAF and USAAF, were on duty at any one time. 'Bunny' wrote:

> First Phase Interpretation was carried out at the aerodrome from which the PRU aircraft operated. It was essentially a report which contained tactical information which affected the day to day course of the war, and consisted of a brief teleprint which was issued as soon as possible after the landing of the aircraft.
>
> Close cooperation between Station Intelligence, the organisations that requested the cover and First Phase Sections was very necessary, especially after the D-Day landings as the programme for flying would be continually changing due to the speed of the Allied advances. It was also important to file data in a manner suitable for quick and easy reference due to the speed at which information had to be issued.
>
> While the process of de-briefing the pilot was in hand with the Station Intelligence Officer, the camera magazine would be removed from the aircraft by the Photographic personnel and rushed to their Section for processing. The time taken to process and print varied according to the number and length of films to be dealt with on the machines available, but one and a half to two hours was an average time taken for the whole procedure of processing, viewing and printing of one sortie.
>
> Once processed the film was taken through to the First Phase Section where it was viewed by rolling it over a desk lit from underneath and checking with the pilot's trace, data relevant to the area and the jobs claimed by the pilot. Speed being one of the essentials, much depended on the memory and experience of the PI viewing the film and if, at moments glance, he or she could determine the unusual from the usual trend of activity on any class of target, the number of prints required could be cut down to an absolute minimum. Specialist PIs were not needed on First Phase, rather a wide knowledge of enemy activities in general, gained through experience.[15]

PR aircraft also flew over target areas shortly after bombing raids had taken place and their photographs were examined by First-Phase PIs:

> The point of our reports of damage assessment on targets was to inform the Bomber department responsible for the raid if it had been successful. If the photography showed that it had not been, and the target justified immediate damage, another attack would follow shortly.

Other targets analysed included ports and anchorages when the positions of all naval ships were reported on, with particular attention being given to U-boats. Convoys, either stationary or in movement, were important too, especially if they were within range of Allied coastal aircraft, when a message would immediately be sent through to the appropriate Coastal Command base and an attack could ensue.

RAF St Eval, near Wadebridge, was used as an operational base for squadrons of Coastal, Fighter and Bomber Commands. It was also well placed for the PR aircraft monitoring the movements of the German fleet off the west coast of France which was a constant threat to the British Atlantic convoys. Ann McKnight-Kauffer was posted to St Eval in February 1941, where she worked initially with one male senior interpreter, keeping a watch over a long list of enemy shipping:

> The whole effort of PI was, of course, focussed on German shipping and there were always two, and sometimes three, PR covers of the ships each day – first the *Hipper*, and then the *Scharnhorst* and *Gneisenau*. There was also a watch kept on the building of submarine pens at l'Orient.[16]

At first the senior PI was rather offhand with Ann, only giving her the boring jobs to do, so she was always counting aircraft; he was also rather fond of his own opinions. One day, after throwing another handful of airfield photographs on to her desk for her to count yet more aircraft, he made a particularly sweeping statement that Ann challenged him to substantiate. It turned out that he was wrong but the confrontation did clear the air and from then on he treated Ann as his equal:

> The pilots were briefed by the Intelligence Officer before a sortie, and some of them then come to the PI section for additional gen. The PR aircraft were all Spitfires at first, but Mosquitos were coming in before I left in 1942. The usual procedure at St Eval was that when the aircraft landed, the pilot went to the Intelligence Officer to give the information he required. Meanwhile, the films were being processed, which took about an hour, and as soon as the negatives were developed the interpreters started working on them with a stereoscope. The PI report was supposed to be written within two hours of the aircraft landing. The pilots, if they were keen, usually looked in to see the negatives.

St Eval was regularly bombed and the Photographic Section was eventually moved off the airfield. Ann remarked:

> You felt closer to it in an unusual way when you had been counting the German bombers at their airfield in the morning, and then that night they attacked your station.

In complete contrast to her work of analysing the movements of the German fleet and being bombed, Ann was flown from St Eval to London for a few days to be photographed in uniform by Cecil Beaton, and featured in a series for *Vogue* magazine. She was later posted back to Medmenham.

Eve Holiday was chosen in January 1941 to go from Wembley with Michael Spender to set up a new PI unit at RAF Wick, an airfield sited on a bleak, treeless plateau on the extreme corner of north-east Scotland. With Norway now under German occupation, the station existed to keep a watch on enemy shipping using the fjords as a base from which they could attack British shipping convoys. Eve recalled:

> When the Germans attacked our airfield, they came in over the sea almost below cliff-top level then swooped upwards to attack the airfield, usually starting with the

Eve Holiday was serving at RAF Wick when the German battleship *Bismarck* was identified.

Officers Mess. There was quite a lot of bombing, and one Heinkel 111 was shot down, the crew landing safely by parachute. For some reason they were brought to the Operations Room, where I happened to be. The Hauptman was brought to our Commanding Officer who was a quiet man. The German did a Heil Hitler to which the CO replied mildly, 'Good Afternoon'. [17]

On 21 May 1941 an urgent phone call was received at RAF Wick from the Admiralty, stating that German ships had been spotted steaming north and must now be off the Norwegian coast. Two PR Spitfires were made ready and took off, one heading for the Oslo area and the other, piloted by 20-year-old Michael Suckling (nicknamed 'Babe' because of his youthful looks), covering the Bergen area. Eve was on duty with the senior PI, David Linton, as they watched them take-off for Sumburgh, on the Shetland Islands, where they refuelled to give them just enough range for their mission. As the aircraft would not return for several hours, Eve and Linton settled down to catch up on some routine tasks. Some time before their expected return, however, Eve heard a Spitfire circling and rushed out to meet Suckling who, as he climbed out of the cockpit shouted: 'I've seen them. Two of them!' When the PIs examined his photographs they identified two German battleships, the *Bismarck* and the *Prinz Eugen*, both at anchor in a Norwegian fjord with destroyers and merchant vessels. The photographs also showed that the protective torpedo booms were open, indicating an imminent move. An immediate warning signal was sent to the Admiralty. The ships did sail and an epic naval and air chase ensued that ended with the *Bismarck* being sunk in the Atlantic Ocean six days later.

Two months later, Suckling failed to return from a PR sortie to La Rochelle. Eve must have remembered the very earnest young pilot. At Wick 'Babe' had evidently regarded her as extremely aged, and when he heard that she was going on a high-altitude flight with one of the pilots, he came to see her rather worriedly, saying: 'Have you cleared it with the medical officer? You know it's not always wise for elderly people to fly at great heights!' Eve was then under 30 years of age!

The fourth PR airbase, RAF Leuchars near St Andrews, was also on the east coast of Scotland but considerably further south than Wick and consequently a whole day was saved when transferring photographs to Medmenham. The return flight from Wick to the Norwegian fjords was at the extreme extent of a Spitfire's range, but the Mosquito, introduced at Leuchars in 1941, had a far greater range. The PI Section was set up with the arrival of the new aircraft and Eve Holiday moved there from Wick for a few months. She described Leuchars as:

> Most cosmopolitan – and fun. There was a Dutch squadron there (who thought mostly about food) and a Norwegian squadron, 'Vikings of the Air', who would take off in any weather and were quite fearless. The WAAFs used to organise games and amusements which the pilots adored, and there was always a crowd – musical evenings when David Linton played his violin, country dancing, fencing, archery and games. There were drinking parties too of course, and sometimes, when I attended morning briefings, I would notice a yellow faced pilot slipping off for a whiff of oxygen in his cockpit. This was recognised as the best antidote for a hangover.

Early in 1942, the newly built 42,900-ton German battleship *Tirpitz* became fully operational and for nearly three years threatened the Allied convoys passing through the Arctic Ocean to and from Murmansk. These convoys carried essential supplies to maintain the Russian ability to fight, and thus it was vital to pinpoint *Tirpitz*, monitor her movements and ultimately destroy her. It was not an easy task as *Tirpitz* hid in the Norwegian fjords, well camouflaged against the steep, wooded slopes. Hundreds of PR sorties were flown, each one bringing back up to 1,000 photographs to interpret which provided the most useful and up-to-date intelligence for the Royal Navy and Bomber Command. *Tirpitz* was prevented from plundering the Arctic convoys but it was late 1944 before she was finally capsized.

Suzie Morrison was posted to RAF Leuchars in July 1942 and for six months followed the movements of *Tirpitz*:

> Knud Hauch, a Danish engineer who had joined the RAF, was in charge of PI at Leuchars and there were two other WAAFs there with me. Cover of the *Tirpitz* was flown every day, at least once. The weather, of course, was always a problem: it could prevent photographs being taken at all or else they were obscured by cloud. Despite this we did often see the *Tirpitz* and reported on the situation.
>
> I managed to get flights in all sorts of aircraft. I once flew to the Shetland Islands where, at that time, no service women were posted. I was walking around and an airman said to me, 'How long are you staying?' and I replied, 'Twenty minutes!'[18]

The German battleship *Tirpitz* was a great threat to Allied shipping. Photographed here vertically from above and at very low level (below) when it was moored and hidden in a Norwegian fjord. Taken on 28 March 1942 by PR pilot Flight Lieutenant Fane.

Several pilots at Leuchars wore the dark-blue uniform of the Royal Norwegian Air Force, having escaped to Britain when their country was invaded. Throughout the war, they piloted flying boats across the North Sea at night to rendezvous with fellow Norwegians in remote fjords and sometimes smuggled them back to Britain. These men would be extensively debriefed to avoid the possibility of bringing an enemy agent into the system who could betray other Norwegians. The PIs briefed pilots on their course for these flights, which were at very low altitudes to avoid being picked up by enemy radar. Information on enemy defences within the narrow confines of a fjord, including the variable height and positions of booms and balloon barrages, was vital to the success of all of these missions.

Some WAAFs enjoyed being in the vanguard of First-Phase PI with the 'buzz' that an operational PR airbase provided. Others preferred the diverse subjects presented to Second Phase, building up a huge amount of day-to-day knowledge about the enemy. Third-Phase sections provided an opportunity to concentrate on a specialist subject. The ACIU was a flexible organisation that responded to current need with sections being opened or closed as prevailing operations demanded, and PIs moved from one section to another as required. The WAAF PI who seemed to have worked in the greatest number of sections was Sarah Churchill, who joined at least six different teams. This arrangement would almost certainly have had mutual benefit for both Wing Commander Kendall, who organised all PI at Medmenham, and her father, the Prime Minister.

Suzie Morrison served at RAF stations Wick and Leuchars in Scotland, monitoring the movements of *Tirpitz*.

4

POSSIBLE, PROBABLE

On a summer's day the sunlight streams through the tall windows of the 'Versailles Room' of Danesfield House Hotel, lighting up the decorated plasterwork on the delicate coloured walls, the high ceiling and the chandeliers. Stepping outside on to the terrace one sees the stone balustrade and steps with the topiary garden below and the specimen trees standing in the parkland. The lawn slopes down to the cliff edge and below is a sweeping curve of the river; it must be one of the most beautiful views of the Thames valley.

In the Second World War, the plasterwork was boarded over, the chandeliers removed and the largest room in the house was known as 'Second-Phase' or 'Z' Section. It was to this section that all air photographs came for inspection after the immediate tactical reports had been made by the First-Phase PIs on reconnaissance bases. Tables were positioned around the room, each with the individual PI's stereoscope, slide rule and anglepoise lamp. Box files and reference books stood on shelves, charts of enemy equipment were pinned to the walls and photographs were everywhere. The room was never empty, for the occupants worked 12-hour shifts every day of each year, and as one group finished their shift, another took its place. The view through the latticed windows was much the same as it is today, if the lines of temporary huts could be ignored and allowance is made for the dug-up garden.

Anyone taking a break from work to admire the view of the river from the terrace would have been in uniform – the air force, navy or army, or the women's services of WAAF, WRNS or ATS. Nationality flashes on the shoulder of some uniforms showed that their wearers came from Canada, Australia and other Dominion or Empire countries – Joan Vyvyan Slade wore a flash with 'NIGERIA' on her tunic.

Later on many wore the uniform of the American services – the United States Army Air Force (USAAF) or the Women's Army Corps (WAC). The occupied countries of Europe were represented too, including officers from Norway, Czechoslovakia, Poland and the Free French. It was in the Second-Phase Section that the international and joint service character of RAF Medmenham was most in evidence.

Among the WAAFs were two Jeans from Australia. Jean Starling had travelled to England from her home in Canberra in early 1939 and was working in London when war was declared. She enlisted in the WAAF soon afterwards and worked in Second-Phase interpretation at Wembley and Medmenham.[1] Jean Youle, from Melbourne, also joined the WAAF early in the war and first served as a telephone operator at RAF Hornchurch in Essex. This was one of the sector airfields of RAF Fighter Command that defended London and south-east England throughout the Battle of Britain. The airfield was located in what was known as 'bomb alley' and the station was frequently attacked throughout the summer of 1940, with particularly heavy raids on 24 and 31 August.

The *London Gazette* records awards made to personnel of all three services. In 1941 the following announcement was published:

Air Ministry, 10th January 1941

ROYAL AIR FORCE

The KING has been graciously pleased to approve the undermentioned awards

in recognition of gallant conduct:-

Awarded the Military Medal

881906 Acting Sergeant Jean Mary YOULE – Women's Auxiliary Air Force.

In August 1940, Sergeant Youle was on duty in a Station telephone exchange when the Station was attacked and bombed by five enemy aircraft. Part of the building containing the telephone exchange suffered a direct hit and other bombs fell in very close proximity. The telephone staff were subjected to a heavy rain of debris and splinters and to the noise of the concussion of exploding bombs. It was solely due to the cool bravery of, and superb example set by Sergeant Youle, that the telephone operators carried on with their task with calmness and complete efficiency at a most dangerous time for them. She has at all times set an excellent example of coolness and efficiency to all.[2]

Jean Youle was commissioned on 20 January 1942, trained as a PI and posted to RAF Medmenham where she worked in Second Phase.

The function of the Second-Phase Section was to report fully and immediately on enemy activity, on a day-to-day basis, with the Command that ordered the sortie receiving their report within 24 hours of the flight. The most comprehensive

Joan Vyvyan Slade at work; the run of photographs on the wall is called a mosaic.

and detailed record of all enemy activities from the North Cape of Norway to the Spanish frontier and throughout all the occupied countries of Europe was compiled at Medmenham and constantly updated. The PIs saw every aspect of the German war effort and provided essential intelligence for Allied strategic planning. Diana Byron described a typical day in Second Phase:

> If the day was fine and all the pilots were flying with all cameras whirring, then by 8pm a massive amount of material would be delivered to us. Then it was heads down for 12 hours.
>
> The Duty Intelligence Officer (DIO) gave out the piles of photographs and the first thing was to find out where you were looking at. Next you went to find previous cover of the whole amount of photographs, if possible. Then you compared the new with the old with your mind working overtime, studying photographs, finding out what had been built, what had gone. Were there more or less of anything? We were always comparing.
>
> We all had our pet places that we loved to know about. We followed airfields and also shipping from north Norway, the Baltic, down the European coast, through France and into the Mediterranean as far as Genoa. It was a hefty lot to learn and we got to know the areas intimately and could see from the next cover how much had come and how much had gone. What had happened to the 'Hipper'? Was she

Jean Youle, from Australia, was awarded the Military Medal in 1940.

still under nets? Was the 'Gneisenau' all right or had they actually broken the gates at St Nazaire?

It was the most wonderful thing to be 'in', to be really 'in' the war, but somehow it didn't seem like war, at least not to me as I was doing something that simply fascinated me – finding out about the movements of another nation's Navy, Army and Air Force.

It really was astonishing just how much detail one could get out of photographs. We followed the elite of the German Navy and that was really so difficult. I am no mathematician but we were told to find out not only where they were but also to pinpoint them to an exact location. It sometimes took hours to do this if all you had on the photograph was a rocky speck on one side and a huge German warship on the other. You had to give exactly where it was and if you had no indication from the pilot's trace, it was very time consuming, but we always managed very well, I think. We had a table for working out the speed of the ships.

You came off duty mentally as well as physically exhausted, to life in a world that didn't really exist because, at that time, you were still living amid things that were going on over the other side, and not at home – a very unusual circumstance. All our reports had to be concise, brief, accurate and in good clear English – and they had to be ready to send on within 24 hours. On cloudy days, when photography was impossible, we caught up and finished off any jobs we had left over.[3]

With twenty or more interpreters on duty at any one time, the Section was divided into many smaller sub-sections each assigned to one subject. This flexible organisation allowed additional sub-sections to be opened at very short notice if a new subject of concern arose. Throughout the war, shipping was reported on with as much detail as possible, including a daily watch kept on the whereabouts and movements of the *Tirpitz*. Other capital ships were continuously monitored in port or underway, as they were a perpetual threat to Allied convoys. Records of enemy merchant ships and blockade runners were also kept on a regular, but less frequent, basis as a change in their pattern of movement could be a sign of a future operation. If the normal pattern of activity anywhere changed, the photographic cover flown could be rapidly increased and continued until the reason for the change was established.

Diana Byron married Richard Cussons, a PR pilot from RAF Benson, who in 1942 was detached to RAF Wick, in north-east Scotland, to track and monitor the *Tirpitz*. He flew a Spitfire Mk IV PR, which operated at its extreme range when flying to Norway and back, despite its fuel tanks being filled to overflowing at Wick, then topped up at Sumburgh on the Shetland Islands, so that it was only just possible to get airborne again. The pilot then flew 400 miles or so over nothing but sea, navigating by dead reckoning, until he reached the Norwegian coast when a recognisable point on the map could be picked up. Richard described his PR missions to locate the *Tirpitz* in a book:

> The general idea was to fly fast and high and nip in, take the photos and nip out again before the enemy realised what was happening. Our defence against enemy action depended mainly on 'rubber necking' – that is, keeping a very good look out in all directions!

The author added:

> It took a special courage to fly at great altitude in freezing conditions for hours at a time over the featureless expanse of the North Sea. Spitfire flights to reconnoitre the 'Tirpitz' at this time lasted between four and five and a half hours. Not only had the pilot's navigation to be accurate, but as he either had no radio, or had to maintain radio silence, he had no one with whom to share his lonely flight.[4]

Reconnaissance aircraft carried no weapons or ammunition, these having been stripped out to carry more fuel, and there was a danger of instruments freezing at high altitudes. The pilot's defence, and his life, relied on height, speed, observation and first-class navigation. Having reached the target, which was frequently heavily defended with anti-aircraft guns and intercepting enemy aircraft, the pilot had to fly over it in a certain sequence, north to south photographing one strip, then south to north on a parallel strip. Maintenance of a steady and level course was essential to ensure the whole target was covered and that good quality photographs were taken. If his aircraft was damaged the PR pilot could not communicate with his base and when he failed to return from a sortie it was assumed he was dead – some crashed into the sea to prevent the enemy getting their film. It is small wonder then that all PIs felt a great responsibility for the PR pilots on their lonely, dangerous flights, and ensured that the greatest accuracy of information was provided for their pre-sortie briefings. When it was decided, after interpretation, that the target had not been sufficiently covered and its importance was such that more photographs were essential, the pilot had to re-fly the sortie, knowing that enemy defences would be ready and waiting for him.

The Coverage sub-section worked in watches all round the clock, examining incoming sorties to decide which jobs had been satisfactorily photographed and which must be flown again. A WAAF who worked in Coverage was Ann Sentence-Tapp, known as 'The Polished Tap' for, as Diana remembered, she was always a model of neatness and glamour. In the summer of 1944, members of the American WAC were posted into Medmenham to assist in dealing with the huge increase in photographs to be interpreted due to the Normandy invasions. Two pre-war photographers, Lieutenants Lois Willard and D.T. Cooke joined lieutenants Mabel Menders and P.L. Linder to work alongside their WAAF counterparts in Coverage. Several USAAF personnel were posted in too, one of whom recorded in an amazed tone: 'My immediate boss was a WAAF!' British female emancipation was perhaps some years ahead of America. Both male and female PIs who worked at Medmenham during the war agree that those employed in the unit carried out similar work. It was accepted that the person most capable of doing a job got that job, regardless of gender. As Mollie Thompson wrote, many years later: 'I do not recall any "glass ceiling" at Medmenham.'

Pamela Dudding had been a secretary in the Foreign Office before joining the WAAF, and trained with Joan Bawden. Pamela met her future husband on the PI course and they married in November 1941, claiming to be the 'First Medmenham Alliance':

We lived out in Marlow and bought a Norton motorbike to get to and from Medmenham. Although we both worked on Second Phase, we were often on different shifts, so had to share the bike. It was very large and heavy and I had difficulty in moving it, but the guards on the gate used to get it started for me and see me on my way.

I worked all the time in Second Phase, primarily on ports, which I loved as I come from a naval family. If we were watching a particular port it could be for several weeks with new sorties coming in all the time and we had to pinpoint everything we could see coming and going. Shipping movements were very important so we watched all big ships like hawks to see if there was any hint of them preparing to leave and what was being loaded.

We also had to measure the heights of the balloon barrages, because they were always being changed and that was desperately important for the wretched pilots flying in low. I liked maths at school and was very good at trigonometry. We did not have any of these modern gadgets, like calculators, but I had a slide rule and my knowledge of trigonometry, and one job I liked doing very much was working on balloon heights. I asked for sorties to be flown in sunshine whenever possible as then there was a good shadow of the tethering line on the balloon and it was easier to calculate an exact height.[5]

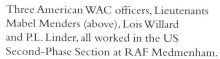

Three American WAC officers, Lieutenants Mabel Menders (above), Lois Willard and P.L. Linder, all worked in the US Second-Phase Section at RAF Medmenham.

Sarah Churchill worked in Second Phase after passing her PI course:

By eight o'clock in the evening, when we started our shift, the photographs and plotted positions would have to be at Medmenham for us. Within twelve hours – we worked until eight in the morning – the photographs had to be interpreted and a full report made, which was then rushed to the Air Ministry. Each area was allocated to a specific interpreter – one of mine was Kiel Harbour and I had to plot the movement of shipping estimating, for instance, when they were shifting smaller craft to make room for a battleship or destroyer. I still have the scraps of paper on which I wrote the measurements of enemy ships, the number of gun turrets and other features – the only means of identifying each ship from the air.[6]

The de Havilland Mosquito, introduced in 1941, had a longer flying range than the Spitfire, and could reach the further reaches of the enemy empire, making it harder to hide secret establishments and industries on more distant border areas. Often photographs provided the only information available of such areas and gave the Allies the opportunity to be one step ahead of future enemy plans. The advances in optics and camera technology enabled photographs to be taken at

Ann Sentence-Tapp worked in the Coverage Section.

Mary Grierson (standing) and Elizabeth Dennis with an RAF PI in Second Phase, with various artwork behind them.

heights previously thought impossible, using cameras with a greater focal length, which made objects on the ground more easily identifiable. By 1943, it could be claimed that anything that moved or was built in enemy or occupied territory was photographed by Allied PR aircraft.

One 'Most Secret' sub-section, set up in 1942, had the title 'Topographical' or GILO (Ground Intelligence Liaison Officer) and among the PIs working there were Ann Sentence-Tapp and Mary Grierson (always called 'Mary' to distinguish her from Mary 'Bunny' Grierson in First Phase). Mary had been a confectioner, decorating wedding cakes, before she joined the WAAF in 1941. After a month at RAF Bridgnorth, Shropshire, being 'knocked into shape', she was posted to 'No. 6 BC' and in her enthusiasm thought: 'Oh good, Bomber Command.' However, it turned out to be No. 6 Balloon Centre at RAF Withall, near Birmingham, where Mary worked as a plotter among the maps in the operations room. Her artistic talents were later recognised and she came to Medmenham to work as a PI in Second Phase.[7]

The work of the GILO PIs was to report on the selection and suitability of the landing and dropping sites in Europe for agents of the Special Operations Executive (SOE). At first the PIs involved were not allowed to know the purpose of their work, although it soon became obvious when they were asked to report in the greatest topographical detail on a specific site, then select and report on further suitable sites within the same area. Their reports were used for the flights of Hudson or Lysander aircraft on a pinpoint bearing to either land or pick up SOE agents, VIPs or refugees in enemy-occupied territory. There were only six PIs in total working in this sub-section, under the leadership of Flight Lieutenant Clive Rouse, an expert on medieval wall paintings and the ideal person for this role, as the same methodical patience and painstaking attention to detail was required in both his civilian and wartime work.

Initially the PIs worked late into the night on the GILO jobs after their usual duty hours, but these were soon separated as a properly rested PI was essential when the lives of agents and infiltrators were at stake, and the interpretation had to be so minutely detailed that every ridge and furrow in the ground, each telephone line and tree, and any minor obstacle had to be highlighted. Flights to France took place almost every night, although the same landing point could never be used twice. An important function of photographic reconnaissance was in the selection of suitable landing sites, in conjunction with the underground groups who would act as reception committees for the landing aircraft. At the beginning of its existence, the GILO sub-section provided an average of five reports a week and this increased until, in one single week in 1945, twenty-one reports were completed; an indication of the extent of clandestine SOE operations in north-west Europe.[8]

The first American service personnel visited Medmenham during spring 1941, eight months before the Japanese attack on the US fleet at Pearl Harbor. The American naval attaché in London had been impressed by the number of enemy secrets revealed at Medmenham and, knowing that there were no trained photographic interpreters in the US navy, had asked for an officer to find out how a similar organisation could be set up in the USA. Section Officer Constance Babington

Smith was responsible for the subsequent three-month visits made by US navy and USAAF officers. After these visits, American personnel started attending RAF PI courses and in 1942, PI schools were established at the US Navy Depot at Anacostia, Virginia, and the USAAF Intelligence School at Harrisburg, Pennsylvania. By June 1942 all PI courses at RAF Nuneham Park included US personnel and, later on, the Americans set up their own PI school in Kensington, London. When the first trained American PIs were posted into Medmenham they were immediately put to work on the preparations for Operation Torch, the planned invasion of North Africa in November 1942 and the first Anglo-American operation of the war.

Although the first male American PIs arrived at Medmenham in 1942, their female counterparts were not posted there until 1944. One of the first American women to arrive was First Lieutenant Lillian Kamphuis, a WAC attached to the USAAF. She came from a farming family in Mobile, Alabama, graduated in 1934 aged 19 from Huntington College in Montgomery and took her first teaching job in a high school in Ozark, Alabama, which she soon left. Two things persuaded her never to teach again: the first was that many of the students were older and larger than she was, and the second was that the state's depressed situation resulted in the faculty being paid with an IOU.[9] Lillian joined the WAC following the Pearl Harbor attack and, after several assignments in the USA, was posted to the 325th Photographic Reconnaissance Wing at the 8th Air Force Headquarters at High Wycombe, England:

> I had two major reasons for having joined up for the war effort. One was, of course, the patriotism, I wanted to help. But I also joined for adventure. It was a chance to leave home, see the world and meet people.
>
> I flew into Scotland in July 1944 and took the train to London where I attended a short two week PI course. I was assigned to High Wycombe where the 325th was located in what had been The Abbey School, codenamed 'Pinetree'. I was immediately detached to RAF Medmenham where I worked as a PI in Second Phase for seven months before being re-assigned to France.[10]

It seems that there were never more than fifteen or so WAC officers at Medmenham and they all worked either in 'Z' Coverage or 'Z' (USA) – a Second-Phase Section that was formed in September 1944 so that the American PIs would be ready to move to the Pacific as a trained group once the war in Europe was finished. The WACs in 'Z' (USA) included Lieutenants Mildred Wilson, M.C. Davidson, Doris Jacobsen and D.E. Forgue.[11]

An individual interpreter may have spent his or her 12-hour shift investigating a specific area or, like Peggy Hyne, analysing photographs of a variety of targets. Before going off duty, every PI added their own reports to the total collection, which would be typed up, assembled and despatched as separate daily reports for individual countries or part of a country. The daily reports contained all the information extracted from the photographs of relevant targets on that one day with comparisons made to earlier cover, if that was available. Also included could be reports on shipping movements, ports and cargoes being loaded, the aircraft on individual airfields, railway movements and marshalling yards, and anything to do with factories and industrial plants. A huge accessible store of knowledge was built up, detailing what the enemy was doing, and where and why he was doing it. This knowledge provided A1 intelligence, meaning it was from a reliable source and almost certainly correct. Future enemy plans could then be predicted with certainty, giving the Allies an important strategic advantage.

There were several artists in Second Phase and a number of PIs who enjoyed putting some aspects of their work into verse. Mary Greirson was one of these, and perhaps she penned the following lines, part of a longer poem, after a particularly frustrating day trying to locate German E-boats on the photographs. E-boats were small, fast, seaworthy motor torpedo boats used to intercept shipping heading to British ports through the North Sea and English Channel. During the Second World War, E-boats sank and damaged many naval and merchant vessels and posed a continuous threat to Allied shipping. Mary wrote:

> The 'E' Boat is so very small
> You cannot make it out at all
> But many sanguine people hope
> To see it through a stereoscope.
> It hides behind enormous docks,
> Conceals itself when on the stocks,
> And in a hundred other ways
> Defies the interpreter's keen gaze ...[12]

While part of Second Phase dealt with the identification and movements of enemy shipping, 'A', the Naval Section, a Third-Phase specialist section, worked on other marine concerns such as port facilities, minesweeping, wrecks, submarine shelters, shipbuilding and ship repairs. Of particular interest was the building of German U-boats or submarines, which were the cause of so many Allied ships being sunk or damaged with consequent terrible loss of life and essential cargoes. A young geographer, Flight Lieutenant David Brachi, had set up the U-boat Building Section at Wembley in early 1940 when, with 'Bunny' Grierson, the process of submarine building in enemy shipyards was monitored. The following year, 'Bunny' moved to RAF Benson and Section Officers Lavender Bruce and Betty Campbell joined Brachi to continue the work at Medmenham.

Day by day, they used air photographs to follow the construction of each individually numbered U-boat, from the first stage of laying down its keel in the shipyard, through each successive procedure until it was completed and fitted out eleven months later, ready to join a U-boat pack. This monitoring was only achieved through the tenacity of the PR pilots who, despite the massive defences around enemy shipyards, repeatedly brought back the photographs. By skilful use of stereoscopy, the PIs saw through the elaborately camouflaged constructions to monitor building progress and accurately calculate when each U-boat would be

Betty Campbell, a WAAF
who worked in the Naval
Section.

operational. Forewarned is forearmed, and as with so much interpretation work at
Medmenham, these reports provided the Admiralty with the authoritative intelligence needed to plan attacks at the optimum time, to cause maximum damage
and disruption to the U-boat construction programme.

In 1944, the numbers of conventionally built U-boats suddenly dropped and
PIs sought to find the reason. They found the answer when they spotted large
sections of submarine hull being prefabricated at different locations and then
transported to shipyards for assembly, thereby cutting the overall building time by
several months. In the same year, midget submarines were found at many seaplane
bases. In both cases, identifying something different or unusual on new photography had triggered a comparison with previous photographic evidence of the area,
which had helped to provide the answer.

Betty Campbell had grown up on Clydeside, near Glasgow, and learnt a lot
about ships and shipping. She trained as a teacher, joined the WAAF and after
PI training, worked in the Naval Section at RAF Medmenham monitoring
enemy U-boat construction. Betty married Willem Skappel, a Norwegian who
had escaped to England in spring 1940, following the Nazi occupation of his
country. He had run an aerial survey and map-making business in Oslo, gaining
an intimate knowledge of the Norwegian coastline. Willem and his brother
were suspected of using their printing facilities to produce an underground
newspaper and his brother was arrested and shipped to Germany. Willem kept
his bicycle outside his office window, and when the expected knock on the
door came, he leapt through the window on to the bike, and headed for the
Swedish border. He was flown to the Shetland Isles and spent two weeks being
debriefed in an internment camp before being cleared for PI work; he and Betty
met on their training course at Nuneham Park. Willem was the only permanent
Norwegian officer at Medmenham and worked in 'Z1', a specialist sub-section

An air photograph used to monitor U-boat construction in Hamburg shipyard. The latticed structures at the bottom are the construction pens designed to conceal building progress – they were unsuccessful.

of Second Phase concerned with Norway and the Baltic, where his knowledge of Norwegian coastal waters was invaluable. He also trained his compatriots in PI before they went to work on operational airfields.[13]

Many special studies and handbooks were produced by the sections at Medmenham, all designed to aid identification and knowledge. Lavender Bruce's future husband, Lieutenant Bryan Westwood RNVR, devised a method of gauging the speed of shipping from the wave patterns shown on air photographs. When a PI reported on a convoy, its location and course would be stated together with the number and types of ships. In addition, the time of arrival at its destination could be calculated from the speed at which the vessels were travelling, providing

'Z1' sub-section, responsible for Norway and the Baltic. Seated from left: Grania Guiness, Mary Howitt, Jean Starling and Elizabeth Dennis. Standing at left is Willem Skappel, who escaped from Norway in 1940. Standing at the back is Vivien Russell.

the navy with important intelligence. Lieutenant Geoffrey Price RNVR, who married an ATS PI at Medmenham, describes his work in 'A', the Naval Section:

> I looked after the contingent at Medmenham which consisted of three RNVR officers and three WRNS officers who were permanent staff; with small contingents of Naval officers coming through on short courses before going to the Pacific to work, mostly, in aircraft carriers. We kept a close eye on the German Navy, the merchant marine and a very sharp watch on the U-boats. This covered both the operation and the building of U-boats. One of the marine movements always under close scrutiny was the passage of cargo ships to and from Norwegian iron ore ports. It was possible from photographic cover to watch each ship, which was individually known to us by its correct name, from its loading in Hamburg or its German or continental port, to its unloading in Narvik or other Norwegian port and then after its cargo of iron ore was loaded and the ship well on its way to Germany we would arrange for it to be sunk. The cargo from Germany was nearly always known as well and, if considered necessary, this would be sunk on the outward voyage. It was rather unsporting to let a vessel load up before being sunk, but of much greater benefit to the war effort.
>
> The economic section followed a similar plan. This section was manned by officers with inside knowledge of the workings of all manner of factories, steel works etc. It would arrange the bombing of them or by other means of destruction or damage.

The rebuilding would then be carefully watched until such time as it looked like coming into production again; when it would be attacked again. Very unsporting![14]

The WRNS officers at Medmenham were few in number and other ranks did not serve there. Second Officers Evelyn Bellhouse and Margaret Binns worked in 'A' Section for some time and other WRNS members included Dorothy Vaughan-Williams and Christine Guthrie, who was later posted to the Allied HQ in Ceylon, in preparation for the planned attacks in the Pacific War.

Mary Winmill was born in Calcutta, returning to England at the age of 7. After leaving school she trained as a secretary before studying in France and Germany and becoming fluent in both languages. A few days into the war Mary and a friend travelled to Edinburgh to join the WRNS and then went to Portsmouth for basic training. She spent the next eighteen months as a cipher officer in Edinburgh, putting secret messages into code to send, and decoding incoming ones. She then transferred to the 'Y' service on radio interception and served at several east coast naval intercept stations, where her linguistic skills were fully utilised:

I listened on Radio Transmission (R/T) to the German E-boat captains as they chattered to each other before leaving ports in occupied Europe to hunt for Allied shipping in the North Sea and English Channel. The information gleaned from these conversations was used on a daily basis to warn Royal Navy and merchant ships of where and when they might be attacked by the enemy, thus enabling them to take evasive action. After several months however, the Germans realised that their social chatter was being intercepted and the practice ceased.[15]

Mary Winmill, a WRNS who worked in the Naval Section.

Mary married an army officer who was a PI and when her service with the interception service came to an end she retrained as a PI. She then joined her husband at RAF Medmenham and worked in the Naval Section, where she was the only WRNS officer at the time.

Other women's services were slightly envious of the Wrens as it was believed that they were issued with black silk stockings, with seams, as part of their uniform – far preferable to the khaki or grey thick lisle stockings which were uniform issue for the ATS and WAAF. At some point during the war, however, a small, extra allowance of clothing coupons was made to all servicewomen, enabling them to buy such things as handkerchiefs, thinner stockings and other non-issue items. Another difference was that WRNS officers wore 'natty little tricorn hats' while the two other services had opted for a cap style more akin to men's headwear for their female recruits. Although, as one WAAF said: 'caps were jammed on to all kinds of coiffeurs – it was the time of the Vera Lynn look.' An unforeseen advantage to the WRNS uniform, as Mary Winmill discovered, was the double-breasted reefer jacket that gradually stretched to became a single-breasted number, allowing her to continue working until just before her first baby was due to be born. WAAFs and ATS could buy themselves a short 'battledress'-style blouson with plastic buttons, which saved the daily metal button polishing. The majority of women took pride in their uniform and accepted the associated pressing and button polishing without complaint, finding satisfaction in being smartly turned out. Practice was required to manipulate the collar studs with which, in common with servicemen, they were issued to anchor their collarless shirts to separate starched collars.

First-Phase army PIs had formed part of the British Expeditionary Force (BEF) to France in 1939, and following the withdrawal from mainland Europe, an Army Photographic Interpretation Section (APIS) was established at Wembley. With the move to Medmenham in 1941 the APIS became known as the Army Section 'B', with the function of providing strategic military intelligence from photographic cover over a large part of Europe. RAF and WAAF personnel worked alongside American, Canadian and British army and ATS in the Section, which followed the practice of forming several sub-sections. Military establishments were watched, including barracks and training areas, where new types of tanks and military vehicles might be spotted. Under continuous scrutiny were the enemy artillery and flak (German anti-aircraft fire) installations that formed the Channel and North Sea coastal defences. Reports and maps showing these were continuously updated and provided essential information for the target data needed for air and seaborne operations. Topographical and detailed defence interpretation was called for in many areas prior to commando raids and paratroop operations, and for this reason army PIs always played an important role in the strategic-planning team for future combined operations.

One of the many incredible accounts of enemy establishments being discovered by PIs at RAF Medmenham was that of the underground factories, for which an army inter-service sub-section – 'B6', under the leadership of Captain McBride – was set up to investigate. The widespread searches made by the Section in connection with enemy secret weapon manufacture in 1943–44 will form part of a later chapter, but during those searches 'B6' had spotted a large number of underground sites all over continental Europe. Although some were just storage depots, many were factories identified by the PIs from the standard building pattern of latrines, which were always the first essential to be built when there were plans to employ large numbers of workers. The construction of a complete aircraft factory, capable of producing fully assembled aircraft, was discovered built deep underground near the Czechoslovakian border near a town called Kahla. The PIs found that the flat top of a long, high ridge had been stripped of trees and a runway constructed; further searches found parked aircraft, later identified as new jet fighters. Geologists determined in which strata of rock the factory would be built and where the entrances were likely to be. The number of workers on the site was estimated by measuring the hutted camp alongside and applying British army standards for the number of bunks permitted in a specific area. Two of the WAAF members of the 'B6' team were Helga O'Brien and Sarah Churchill, who wrote:

> Puzzling and tedious as it often was, there were moments of terrific excitement and discovery. One American interpreter had been watching a particular mountain in his regular checks on an area. Suddenly he noticed a change: it appeared that the top of the mountain had been shaved off. At the mountain's base a railway line disappeared into it. There was no apparent reason for this, but we were never allowed to 'assume' anything. He had been allocated this area so he must survey it constantly. I was in the room one day when, after weeks of unrewarding scrutiny, there was a shout of delight – there was a photograph of a plane being winched up the side of his mountain! The Germans had built an underground factory. Aeroplanes were winched to the top of the mountain then the 'shaved' mountain top was used as a runway.[16]

Subaltern Margaret Hodgson was one of the first ATS officers to be employed as a PI and she joined 'B' Section in 1943, along with Subaltern Bridget Bateman. They had attended army PI courses at the School of Military Intelligence in Matlock, Derbyshire. In common with the WRNS, ATS officers who were PIs at Medmenham were few in number. ATS NCOs who had trained as draughtswomen were posted into Medmenham in the last year of the war. Sergeants Joan 'Panda' Carter, who had reluctantly found herself as a clerk in the Pay Corps, and Barbara Rugg, who had worked in the Drawing Office at Larkhill, achieved their wish and went to be trained as topographical draughtswomen at Wynstay Hall, Ruabon, North Wales. The three-month course, attended by Royal Engineers and ATS, included map drawing, use of a stereoscope, contouring, plotting and learning how to survey with a theodolite.

'Panda' was then posted to the military survey establishment at Esher, in Surrey, to use her cartographical skills:

Margaret Hodgson, ATS, at work in the Army Section with a USAAF officer.

We were put to work on revising maps using aerial photography and photo mosaics to form a comprehensive picture of bombed areas. The Ordnance Survey maps of Europe at the time were about twenty years old and a way had to be found to bring them up-to-date as quickly as possible. It was very exciting to be working on a map and suddenly see a photograph of a town not there twenty years ago or an autobahn cutting across the country.[17]

Barbara became a plotter on army-related photography flown from RAF Benson:

We actually worked at Ewelme in a lovely old house. We had huts in the garden as well and there was a lovely yew tree in the garden. When it was hot weather we would go outside and have our breaks sitting under the tree. We worked long hours and when we came off a night shift we would go to have breakfast in the little café nearby and then cycle straight to the river and row up to Shillingford Bridge, under the bridge and then back.[18]

As more and more men were posted away from Medmenham to mainland Europe, to serve as PIs in support of the advancing Allied forces following the Normandy invasion in 1944, women took over their work. The Royal Engineers Drawing Office at Medmenham was originally composed of men only, but became an entirely ATS section when further demands were made for men to go overseas. It was officially noted that there was nothing to show that the work of the ATS was in any way inferior to the Engineers.

5

OFF DUTY

After the move to Medmenham in 1941, Danesfield House itself was used for a short time as both working and living accommodation, and in common with many other country mansions it was reputed to have a resident ghost. A clerk typist, newly posted into Medmenham, whom we know only as 'Jane', was told the legend of the Grey Lady of Danesfield. The tale, doubtless embellished for each new WAAF's arrival, was of a nursemaid who, in times past, had claimed to hear footsteps ascending the stairs when the moon was shining and the house silent. The story was playing on Jane's mind as she groped her lonely way around the house at dead of night to a room set aside for the official 'hour in bed', halfway through her first 12-hour night shift:

> I ascended the wide staircase to a room four storeys up in pitch darkness. The moon shone through a high circular window on to a mattress bearing rough blankets but no sheets. The calls of owls and sheep came very clearly and I was terrified by the scurry of what could have been a mouse. A bat flapped against the leaded window and a giant moth fluttered helplessly about the moonlit room. When I heard footsteps in the corridor outside I grabbed my skirt and hurried for dear life back to the happy tap of the typewriters in the typing pool.[1]

Accommodation was found for some women in local houses. Pat Donald and three other WAAFs were billeted in Wittington Hall, the house next door to Danesfield, where they lived comfortably in the attics:

> The house belonged to a Canadian named Garfield Weston who owned many food companies, including Fortnum and Mason. He and his wife had a large family so there were always lots of children around. They were very kind and made cocoa for us when we returned at the end of a 12-hour shift.[2]

Susan Bendon commented:

Medmenham is in one of the most beautiful parts of the Chilterns and I was billeted in a dream-like mill house about a mile down a steep hill towards Marlow. The mill was active and was owned by an enchanting elderly couple who seemed to have stepped out of the nineteenth century. In spite of having eleven children, they always addressed each other as Mr or Mrs Broomfield. The PI course was fascinating, with a great atmosphere of camaraderie, there were wonderful pubs all around and it was sheer heaven.[3]

The RAF soon requisitioned another large Thameside building to serve temporarily as the WAAF officers' mess until sufficient huts were built in the grounds of Danesfield House. Phyllis Court was an Italianate-style house built in 1837 close to the centre of Henley, with beautiful gardens overlooking the finish line of Henley Royal Regatta. Some WAAFs lived and ate there, others came from their billets just for meals; buses then transported them to and from RAF Medmenham. Hazel Furney was billeted with a friend in a charming beamed cottage opposite the Angel Inn by the bridge in Henley-on-Thames, where they enjoyed living in a homely atmosphere. They would often punt home from Phyllis Court to Henley after dinner and struggle back with it to have breakfast the following morning.

Section Officer Lady Charlotte Bonham Carter, known at Medmenham simply as 'Charlotte', lived in the mess. She was older than most WAAFs, having served in the First World War with the Foreign Office. Just before war was declared in 1939 she trained for Air Defence and took a flying course, commenting that she missed not having a motor horn when up in the air. She subsequently joined the WAAF at the age of 47 and served initially as an instrument mechanic before being commissioned in 1941 and posted to RAF Medmenham after PI training.[4] She was an efficient officer, remembered with great affection by many former colleagues, for her kindness and her eccentric, unmilitary behaviour. Charlotte always carried an umbrella and a basket or string bag containing food, as she was permanently hungry, even taking a basket of sandwiches on a church parade. She made up marmalade sandwiches at breakfast time in Phyllis Court and tucked them into the envelopes that her post had been delivered in earlier, making it easier to transport them to work on the bus. Thus they were always handy should hunger suddenly strike. She was once detached from Medmenham for a few weeks, and her section gradually developed a smell that increased in pungency. Following a search, a packet of marmalade sandwiches, covered in green mould, was discovered tucked into a filing cabinet.

Rows of huts sprouted up in the gardens surrounding Danesfield House throughout 1941 and these provided living quarters for men and women and all the messes, leaving the house itself to accommodate many working PI sections. 'Jane' wrote:

November 1941 was bitter. Water in the fire buckets froze, the walls in the huts (to which the typists had now moved) ran with moisture and we spent most of our off-duty time huddled in bed drinking steaming cocoa. Sometimes it was so cold that we lay, facing upwards like Russian soldiers left to die in the Baltic wastes, Balaclava helmets over our foreheads and arms straight down by our sides.[5]

Later on, with an increasing need for work and living space, especially with the additional US personnel, more accommodation huts were put up in Wittington Woods opposite the main gates. Diana Byron recalls:

Our hut accommodated nine WAAF officers, ablutions took place in a block outside in the woods and a stove kept us warm – we all took turns in collecting firewood to feed the stove.[6]

Although the huts in the woods were reasonably comfortable, they were damp and the surrounding wildlife took up residence with the humans. Clothes and shoes went mouldy and there was a permanent musty smell. Mice, woodlice and spiders abounded and the hot weather brought out the mosquitoes.

Jeanne Adams:

I did my six months in the ranks at Medmenham living in a Nissen hut with 32 other girls. We all worked on different watches so sleep was a problem for us all. Our only heat was from a huge, black iron stove in the middle of the hut, which had to be stoked frequently, day and night, to keep us warm. The ablutions were primitive with no mains drains and a dreadful cart which came round each day to empty the loos. The baths and showers were shared by four huts full of girls and were pretty grim. I used my tin hat as a very effective shower cap and when inverted it carried my soap and toiletries. One night when the orderly officer came round at about 10pm to ask if we had any complaints, I foolishly told her that we had a blocked drain. I was told to come along with her and unblock it. I learnt not to complain![7]

Corporal Pat Peat was posted into RAF Medmenham in spring 1942 and shared a Quonset hut with fifteen other women:

There was a coal stove in the centre of the hut – some of the women stole coal from the store so we were always warm. Toilets and showers were down at one end of the hut. We had an inspection every morning. There was one bath tub and each week we were each allowed 2 inches of hot water for a bath. A group of five of us decided to pool our hot water ration to make one full tub every week and rotate who went in first. It was heavenly to have a full 10 inches to wallow in. I also went up and down the hut when I first got there to see who did the best cleaning of shoes, the best ironing and so on, then each did the task we were best at for the others. I did the buttons because I was the best at metalwork. We were always the best turned out WAAFs.[8]

Mollie Thompson described the gardens of Danesfield House:

> It was a great pity that the garden was so defaced. The owner had been a well-known
> gardener and his alpine garden (in the valley between the House and the Danes Ditch)
> was full of treasures – clipped yew hedges, a wooded area which in spring was a sheet
> of daffodils (you could pick a hundred and never notice where you had done so), a
> topiary garden at the foot of the steps, a sunken rose garden, a pool garden and acres of
> mown lawns. The cliff edge over-looking the river was clear cut so that standing on the
> cliff path you could look for miles in both directions up and down the Thames valley.
>
> By 1945, the garden was a mass of assorted hutments, and the alpine valley was
> devastated by an enormous sewage pipe with the spoil used to fill up the sunken rose
> garden. The trees in the daffodil plot had been cut down and the trees below the cliff
> edge had been allowed to grow so the house looked 'shut' from the river and the
> view blocked out.[9]

Contemporary photographs indicate that the topiary and part of the garden survived the building works. At least one fishpond with water and fish remained intact, as Myra Murden remembered lying in bed one night listening to splashes and shouts coming from the garden. Their WAAF sergeant, returning to camp on a dark, moonless night in the blackout, had fallen in the pond and the goldfish swam round her legs for some time before she was rescued by her American boyfriend.

The whole wartime population had problems getting around in the darkness due to dimmed lamps on vehicles, blacked-out windows and the mere glimmer of light allowed in public places. Finding the way back to their huts in the middle of the woods on a moonless night after finishing a shift was just one extra challenge for the Medmenham personnel. Dorothy Colles had a brush with the local law in 1941, about a light that was off rather than one that was on:

> On Christmas Eve I went to supper with the Palmers and on the way home got
> caught by a policeman as my back light had gone out. So I had to walk home to

US PIs in the gardens of Danesfield House. WACs Lillian Kamphuis, Lois Willard and Doris Jacobsen stand behind Mabel Menders.

Phyllis Court and arrived cross and tired to find a party in progress with a whole load of pilots from Benson. It was quite spontaneous – they came for a drink and someone started playing and we danced and sang and had a wonderful time. I went to bed at 1am.[10]

Poor lighting was sometimes used to their advantage by the ATS draughtswomen. 'Panda' Carter wrote:

The most dreadful act we committed was to cheat the railway. Buy one return ticket and make it last several journeys. In the Drawing Office we would very carefully paint out the date and put a new one in. We did not think of the crime we were committing. We did it for the thrill of putting the ticket under the collector's nose, watch him turn it over in his fingers and hand it back as he directed us through the barrier.[11]

The personnel who worked at night had the problem of trying to sleep during the day in a hut that housed twenty or more colleagues all working different shifts. An insomniac possibly penned these lines pinned to the door of a hut:

PERADVENTURE HE SLEEPETH
I. KINGS. XVIII. 27

Remember those who sleep by day:
Tread softly when you come this way,
Pray do not whistle, sing, or shout,
It puts the hopeful sleeper out.
And other things that he abhors
Are clattering tools and banging doors.

So QUIET in the daytime PLEASE,
And let the sleeper take his ease.

N.B. This does not give one any right
To make commotions in the night.

Opinions of the food served at Medmenham were universally low, even allowing for rationing and wartime shortages of ingredients. Those working long night shifts who had to eat their main meal in the early hours of the morning were particularly critical, as Diana Byron and Jeanne Adams explained:

We ate in a hut beside Danesfield House. The cooks left the food in huge ovens hours earlier so it was not ideal at midnight with the odd cockroach thrown in – it was quite ghastly.[12]

On night shifts we had breakfast at midnight and another dreadful meal with something like stew at 4 am, with tea made in a coffee urn![13]

Jane Cameron was a PI at Medmenham:

My new unit was a fantastic amalgam of nationalities, Army, Navy, Air Force and
personalities that ranged from Freddie Ashton (later Sir Frederick Ashton, the Master
of the Royal Ballet) to a man who had spent his pre-war working life watching the
movements of herring shoals in the North Sea.
   I remember coming off a twelve-hour night watch and walking to the Nissen hut
mess for breakfast with Pilot Officer Freddie Ashton. The orderly presented each of
us with a plate of dehydrated, re-constituted eggs which had been 'scrambled'. In the
centre of each plate there was a little island of greenish-yellow vomit, washed on all
sides by a little ocean of pale green liquid.[14]

By 1943, a canteen had been established by the Young Women's Christian
Association (YWCA). Clementine Churchill, the Prime Minister's wife, was president of the YWCA and spent much time and energy in raising money to open
more canteens and hostels of a high standard. Hearing from Sarah how bad the
catering was at Medmenham, she intervened to get a YWCA canteen established
there. 'Panda' Carter and her ATS friends certainly appreciated the canteen when
they moved to Medmenham in January 1945:

Near to our Sergeants Mess hut in the woods was a small house run by kind ladies of
the YWCA where we spent our evenings drinking tea and eating buns.[15]

Geoffrey Stone, a young Army PI also recalls the YWCA:

The concert last night was in the YWCA – well furnished, warm and very bright. We
all sat in comfortable armchairs and afterwards had coffee and buns.[16]

The service cooks were clearly capable of producing attractive fare on special
occasions as was shown by the RAF Medmenham menu for Christmas dinner in
1943, which listed roast turkey, chipolata, chestnut stuffing and all the trimmings,
preceded by soup and followed by Christmas pudding and mince pies. Dorothy
Colles recorded in 1941:

There was a very good dinner at Danesfield House on Christmas Day with speeches
and dancing. All the Mess and kitchen staff came in and joined the dance which was
very jolly.[17]

Perhaps the Americans suffered most of all from the unimaginative food, for
when they joined RAF Medmenham they became part of the unit and thus

US PIs enjoy boating on the River Thames. The WACs wear their distinctive uniform 'Hobby' hats.

were subject to British provisioning and rationing restrictions. Leonard Abrams wrote:

> Over a period of two years we Americans never did adjust to the rations. At best, the general level of British cooking was uninteresting, to put it politely. The soggy, dull monotony of the food, the lack of any refrigeration, and the rather casual attitude towards cleanliness in those times, made the Americans bitterly and vocally resentful. We traded cigarettes for food which we cooked illegally in our huts and we challenged other Americans to baseball games so we could eat in their camps.[18]

However awful the food was, the British servicemen and women were also 'bitterly resentful' when they heard the Americans criticising it; after all, they had endured it for far longer. WAAFs taken by their American boyfriends to a US unit at nearby High Wycombe could not believe the variety and quantity of food, drink and other goods available; many were also fiercely critical of these unnecessary commodities taking up precious cargo space in convoys crossing the Atlantic.

A last story about food. One day Charlotte took Hazel Furney's bike, not knowing whose it was, to go out to dinner. Next day the bike was back in its place with a note attached saying who had borrowed it and if the owner went to see her, a bar of chocolate would be given in recompense. Having presented herself for her consolation award, Assistant Section Officer Furney was most aggrieved to be told that as Charlotte had assumed that the bike belonged to an 'other rank', Hazel, as an officer, did not qualify for the chocolate bar![19]

Almost everyone got around locally by bicycle, so it was possible to enjoy a tea nearby, shop in villages or towns or, for the artists of Medmenham, find many attractive places in the surrounding countryside to paint and sketch. 'Jane', the typist, recalled her off-duty time in the summer of 1943:

> I remember boating on the Thames, brambling on Marlow Common, dreaming in Quarry Woods, crossing on the ferry from Medmenham to the opposite bank then walking along the towpath to Hurley to visit a farmhouse for fresh bread and home-made jam.[20]

The chain ferry ran from the slipway at the end of the village lane and cost 2*d* per crossing. It was used by everyone at Medmenham to cross the river, often to enjoy meeting up with colleagues at the Old Bell in Hurley, the village on the opposite bank. The favourite pub for the pilots and PIs from RAF Benson was the White Hart at Nettlebed, where Mrs Clements, the landlady, mothered the PR pilots. The Dutch Café in Marlow was a favourite place and was renowned for the quality of their dried-egg omelettes. A more expensive rendezvous was the Compleat Angler Hotel on the river at Marlow, while the nearest pubs to RAF Medmenham were the Hare and Hounds at the bottom of Marlow hill and the Dog and Badger opposite the village church. Mary Winmill and her new husband, an army PI, had their first married home in the cottage adjoining the Dog and Badger, complete with a convenient, or inconvenient, hatchway from the public bar that opened directly above their bed.

Pat Peat:

> I could not ride a bike until I came to Medmenham and had to learn. The road went through a wood and then down a steep hill almost to the Thames. The hill was scary at first but eventually I took my hands off the handlebars and 'flew' down. I remember there was a gypsy camp nearby with a field of poppies alongside. Sometimes I cycled into Marlow to see a 'Western' at the cinema, but I was a solitary person – not gregarious – and mostly I explored the countryside, sketching and painting in water colours. I never had difficulty in buying paper, paints or pencils; I bought them in 'Boots' in either Marlow or Henley.[21]

Catching the train up to London was a popular off-duty option. Peggy Hyne and her colleagues often went into London to see a matinee performance at a theatre:

> We would take a train from Marlow to Paddington and then go to the Dorchester Hotel which had Turkish Baths in the basement. Then we could lie down and feel more refreshed, very welcome after a night on duty, before seeing a play in the afternoon.[22]

Once Upon a Time was a production staged by the theatre group at RAF Medmenham.

All uniformed personnel were offered, and accepted, lifts in cars and lorries and, although officers were not supposed to 'thumb' a driver down, they too hitched when necessary. Usually all they had to do was walk past the guardroom and out through the main gate of RAF Medmenham for some sort of service or civilian vehicle to stop and offer them a lift. Charlotte had a rather different approach to acquiring transport: arriving at the main gate, she would inform the airman on guard duty where she wished to travel to. Then she waited until a suitable vehicle had been halted and her travel requirements passed on to the driver. Rather similar to a hotel commissionaire hailing a taxi, but it always worked for Charlotte.

Due to the nature and intensity of work at RAF Medmenham, off-duty activities on the station grounds were officially encouraged. After a 12-hour shift concentrating over a stereoscope or working at the other demanding jobs, all physical sports such as football, tennis and running were popular and well supported. Physical training (PT) was compulsory, although Myra Murden managed to avoid a daily session by carefully choosing the right work shift, and Mary Harrison saw it as a way of keeping warm through the chilly winters. There were station sports' days and several rowing 'Blues' took over the boats of the Marlow Rowing Club, temporarily without members due to the war, and held regattas on the Thames in the summers of 1942 and 1943.

The name of this stage production is unknown but clearly required lavish costumes.

With artists and musicians working and living alongside people formerly employed in the theatrical world, it was not long before a variety of entertainments were being staged. The RAF Medmenham Players came into being in 1942 and performed full-length plays, revues and pantomimes. The unit was completely self-sufficient in actors, dancers, scriptwriters, musicians, set builders, costume designers and any other skill necessary to stage a near-professional performance. Men and women from all the services took part in these either on stage or behind the scenes.

The model makers were a group of professional sculptors, artists and architects who readily turned their hand to set designing, building and lighting, while the scriptwriters included a BBC drama writer and producer, Captain Bill Duncalfe, a PI in the Army Section. The Lynx RAF Medmenham Dance Band was on hand to provide the music required and one of the vocalists, Robert Rowell, another army PI, was a professional operatic singer. Props were 'scrounged' from various quarters and the programmes and posters were designed and drawn by renowned cartoonists, such as Julian Phipps and A.E. Beard, who had both worked on newspapers and magazines in pre-war days. The costumes were designed and made by the women at Medmenham who, with inspiration and much improvisation, achieved stunning results.

LACW Myra Murden reported to the unit dental officer one day:

> I had a bottom front tooth needing to come out according to an earlier dentist's decision. I protested as I was going to be in the front line of the chorus in a show being put on that evening and I did not want to appear with a gap in my teeth. So the young dentist agreed to do a root job instead, which incidentally was very painful, on condition that I introduced him to my glamorous friend, Gill Clarkson – she went on to dance at The Windmill after the war. So I got my tooth and the dentist got his date – a good deal all round.
>
> The concerts were great fun – there were one or two a year. In one I was a mermaid, luring an ATS officer (Margaret Hodgson) as a sailor to her death at the bottom of the sea! Photographic silver foil was cut up and made into a scaled fish tail for me – that was Sarah's idea. I was instructed to keep absolutely still to avoid rustling on stage.[23]

First-class productions were ensured by Flight Lieutenant Ken Bandy – who had been the stage director of the Windmill Theatre before he joined the RAF – and Sarah Churchill, a professional dancer as well as a talented stage and film actress. Sarah appeared in four full-length plays at Medmenham, including *Squaring the Triangle* written by Bill Duncalfe, and *Gaslight*, a West End play in which she had taken the role of Mrs Manningham in 1939 and 1941 before joining the WAAF. She also kept colleagues amused on more informal occasions with her memorable performances of the popular 'Egyptian Dance' in the mess, when she used her natural skills of mimicry. A dancer with a more classical background was

Frederick Ashton, although there is no evidence of him being involved with the Medmenham theatrical productions.

Out of the Blue was a revue of singing, dancing and a number of short sketches staged by twelve Medmenham women and had a particularly eye-catching programme, designed and drawn by one of the illustrators. The cast included several singers, Sarah Churchill, model maker Helroise Hawkins and the ATS PI, Margaret Hodgson. The only men performing on stage were 'Kenneth and George' who played duets on two pianos. Revues were also popular in the Central Photographic Interpretation Command set up in Delhi in 1942 where the RAF Players came into being.

Margaret Price was assistant entertainments officer at Medmenham for a while:

> Entertainments were mostly dances at Henley Town Hall, which I think were open to all ranks and members of other units in the vicinity, RAF, Army etc. We had our own dance band at Medmenham consisting of both British and Americans. There was also an RAF man, Alan Potts, who entertained between the dances – he was an excellent 'Carmen Miranda' in full costume, complete with a tall headdress made of fruit. Other events in our Mess such as Halloween were staged by the American officers and the decorations were amazing for war time – they seemed to find the impossible. There were two officers, George Reynolds RAF and Stanley Lashmer-Parsons RNVR, who would play syncopated music together in the Mess and entertain us for hours.[24]

Flight Lieutenant Edward Wood was entertainments officer for eighteen months and in that time he recorded fifty-six dances, forty ENSA (Entertainments National Service Association) film shows, six ENSA concerts, three RAF gang

A Halloween party organised by the Americans.

A poster advertising an exhibition of photographs at RAF Medmenham.

shows and four visits by the RAF Griller String Quartet, one of which was led by Malcolm Sargent in person. Gala and fancy dress dances held in the officers' mess became substantial social occasions when the US personnel came to Medmenham, and on one occasion Major Glenn Miller conducted his famous band there. Another unforgettable visit, arranged by Ken Bandy, was from the famous Windmill Theatre Dancers, although it appears that the majority of the audience in the camp theatre were WAAFs.

A photographic exhibition was held in February 1943 containing nearly 200 entries, which were judged by the well-known photographer Marcus Adam FRPS. Some months later, an arts and handwork exhibition was organised that included a large number of paintings executed by men and women of the Model-Making Section who were already artists of renown. They also decorated the camp theatre, as well as the officers' and sergeants' messes with giant murals.

On Sunday 16 May 1943, RAF Medmenham presented a concert in the Odeon Theatre, Marlow, as part of the town's 'Wings for Victory' week, a fundraising scheme to encourage civilians to put their money into government bonds. The concert was arranged and produced by Edward Wood and Sarah Churchill, who had persuaded some stars from London to visit and perform alongside the home-grown talent of army, navy and air force personnel.

The compere for the concert was Vic Oliver, Sarah's husband, for although they were living separate lives by this time, they were still on good terms. The Lynx RAF Medmenham Dance Band conducted by Stanley Lashmer-Parsons RNVR got the proceedings off to a tuneful start, followed by a song duet by two WAAFs. Next on the piano were Reynolds and Lashmer-Parsons, the nimble-fingered duo who entertained in the mess. 'A Spot of Magic' followed, presented by Lieutenant Davies of the Royal Engineers, after which LAC Noke performed an instrumental novelty on the double bass. Flying Officer McCormac gave a tenor solo from *Merrie England* and Sergeant Silverton was next on with 'Lightning Caricatures'. The first half of the concert ended with a song tableau by seven airwomen.

During the interval Group Captain Peter Stewart, the officer commanding (OC) RAF Medmenham, gave a short address before the second half started with the band playing 'Tunes from the Films'. The first visitor from the London stage was a film actress, Sylvia Saetre, followed by Jack and Daphne Barker, a husband and wife duo who had appeared in West End musicals. Vic Oliver entertained with his amusing mix of song, dance and humour, then the thirty-five members of the RAF Medmenham choir sang more pieces from *Merrie England* with the audience joining in the singing of *Jerusalem*. The concert ended with *God Save the King*.

Sarah Churchill was responsible for inviting several theatrical friends from West End theatres to entertain at Medmenham. Possibly the most famous of these was the Russian-born pianist Moiseiwitsch, who agreed to give a concert open to all ranks. There was concern that the thumped-out canteen piano would not be a suitable instrument for the maestro and Sarah asked Charlotte Bonham Carter for advice. She had a grand piano stored away, which, if transport was arranged, she was prepared to lend for the occasion. Another PI, Robin Orr, a composer and future professor of music at St John's College, Cambridge, agreed to tune the instrument. All those able to leave their duties crowded into the hall when Moiseiwitsch arrived and he expressed delight at the piano. Unfortunately, as Sarah recalled:

After a few crashing chords of Beethoven, a string chose to leave the piano and wave like a daddy-long-legs in the air. Moiseiwitsch did his best, but once you have one note out of order it is impossible to avoid it. He struggled valiantly with this difficulty, but whatever he tried, going rapidly to the softer tones of Schumann, the tentacle of that note would appear, beautifully illuminated by the harsh lights of the hut in which he was performing. He went red in the face at first and then became statuesquely calm. The concert ended, we naturally all applauded, he stood up and bowed and Charlotte swept onto the scene.

'Thank you Mr Moiseiwitsch, for ruining my piano'.

The tension broke as he shrugged and said the Russian equivalent of 'C'est la guerre'.[25]

Stella Ogle spent some her off-duty time saving works of art.

One morning I was walking down Bond Street delicately picking my way over the broken glass and debris from the raid of the previous night. As I approached the lower end where the picture galleries are, it suddenly struck me what an awful anxiety the owners must have in looking after their works of art in these raids. It struck me so forcibly that I went into the nearest one, which happened to be the Leger Galleries, and asked to see the proprietor. Rather surprised, they went and found Mr Henry Leger for me and I put forward my idea. The Officers Mess, well camouflaged and built of solid brick down at High Wycombe, could, in my opinion, be considered a safe haven compared to London and I asked Mr Leger whether he would loan some of his collection for the duration of the war. He accepted my ideas and the result was that a nice selection of minor works of art were sent down and eventually arrived at Bomber Command. There they looked very well and came to no harm, the only violation done to them being after one party in the Mess when someone stuck a label on the middle of the 'Rape of the Sabines' bearing the legend, 'Wing Commander Opie spends his gratuity'.

We were living in Phyllis Court at the time when it was the WAAF Officers Mess – Mollie Thompson was President and I was Vice-President. We replaced an old stag's head that hung over the fireplace with an 18th century portrait.

I absolutely hated those stags' heads, they were gigantic moose with horns and everything in a state of mouldering moth. The climax came one day when a crumbling bit of moth eaten fur fell off a moose's head into someone's soup. I organised some RAF friends and got them taken down and we put them in the Phyllis Court boathouse where, as far as I know, they went on mouldering away until the end of the war.[26]

With many young men and women in their twenties and thirties working and living close to each other, it is not surprising that a number fell in love. Some married from Medmenham and more were wed after the war. In true Medmenham fashion, many weddings were inter-service and international. Assistant Section Officer Pamela Dudding WAAF and Pilot Officer Robert Bulmer RAF claimed to be the first Medmenham 'alliance' and their air force example was soon followed by others. A regular interchange between RAF Medmenham PIs and RAF Benson PR pilots to discuss past and future sorties obviously had a social side too, as several WAAF PIs married pilots. Diana Byron met her pilot husband-to-be in the mess at RAF Benson and they were married in 1943. Mary Winmill WRNS married an army PI, and Section Officer Lavender Bruce WAAF married an RNVR PI in Medmenham church. Jean Fotheringham, a WAAF PI in the Night Photography Section, and Earl

Jean Fotheringham
WAAF and
Earl Hollinger
USAAF married at
Hambleden church,
in a nearby village to
Medmenham.

Hollinger USAAF, a PI in Second Phase, were one of the several international couples to be married in Hambleden church.

Corporal Pat Peat met her future husband, who was also an American, at RAF Medmenham during the presidential campaign in 1944, when she was busy encouraging US servicemen to vote:

> Well, there I am on a soapbox addressing these American soldiers, who are all art-ists in the Model Making Section, and telling them that they had to vote. And this man (Bill O'Neill) shouted out across the yard, 'I can't vote – I live in the District of Columbia.' I didn't know that – and they still can't vote in the District of Columbia, which most Americans don't know. Bill was impressed because here was a girl in a British uniform telling Americans to use their vote.[27]

Jeanne Adams married a medical officer in the Royal Navy, who was soon to be posted to the Far East:

> I was married in June 1943 from Medmenham and I hitched a lift to our wedding on a coal lorry. It was an almost entirely service wedding – even our bridesmaid was in uniform. My dress was made from lace curtaining, one of the few materials that was not rationed. Sophie Wilson, who lived in the same hut as me, sat and hand sewed

my underwear for the day, cut out of a parachute. Owing to shortage of sugar, our cake had a pretty top made of cardboard. On the night watch before our wedding, my friends and I made confetti with old maps and a punch. The maps had to be censored, just in case they carried classified information![28]

The unmilitary air that prevailed at RAF Medmenham did not sit comfortably with the RAF hierarchy, despite its efficient working in the production of intelligence and all its achievements. Periodically, attempts were made to bring some military conformity to Medmenham. Jane Cameron recalled:

> The Air Ministry, in its wisdom, decided that this Unit must be 'licked into shape' and sent down a Warrant Officer (Drill) to conduct this operation.
>
> We broke his heart and within three weeks had him on the run back to where he came from. The first crack in that hard heart was made on the first morning by a charming mediaeval archaeologist who had described his peace-time occupation on his official form as 'scraper of church walls'. (Dr Clive Rouse, the expert on medi-aeval wall paintings.) He was a tall handsome man and was chosen by the Warrant Officer to act as Adjutant of the parade and instructed in the commands that were to call us all to order. He was to call the male squad to attention first and then 'fall in' us women auxiliaries behind it. But the 'adjutant' was a well brought-up gentle-man who believed in 'ladies first'. Having listened to the shouted instructions very solemnly, he strolled towards us of the distaff side, swept his hat off and said: 'Good morning, ladies. Would you mind …'?
>
> As we walked back to our desks after this first drill, a Section Officer, one of the most individual members of the unit, said to me: 'Really, the impertinence of that young non-commissioned officer, trying to chase us all about as if we were – rabbits!'[29]

However, the determination to make RAF regulations prevail continued and in 1943, a new station commander, responsible for administering RAF Medmenham, was appointed. His predecessor, a 'laid-back' man who had recognised the neces-sity of independent thought in the PIs, had recently departed swiftly and under somewhat of a cloud. The new OC, a strait-laced 'regular' with instructions to 'sort out those academics and instil some much needed military discipline', was met at the main entrance:

> by a young and extremely comely WAAF officer, who introduced herself to me as my Personal Assistant. This came as a surprise since I was under the impression that PAs were the perquisite of Officers of 'Air', (that is to say General), rank and were in any case normal males of the ADC type. I took an early opportunity to enquire of her the nature of her duties which appeared to me to be of a rather personal nature, and not, as far as I could see, closely connected with my job as a Station Commander. I pointed out that I was shortly expecting my wife and daughter to

join me, who in the past had looked after such matters, and would, I hoped, continue to do so.[30]

Starting as he meant to go on, the OC's first order was for regular station parades and inspections. These would begin on the following Saturday morning and off-duty personnel of all services were ordered to attend. This caused a minor panic amongst those officers who had joined the RAF at the very beginning of the war without going through the normal training process. Many had thus never served in the ranks or 'square bashed' so they beat a hasty path to the Army Section, seeking instruction on how to march and recognise elementary commands. Saturday morning duly arrived and the Medmenham personnel marched on with varying levels of competency, one squad managing to appear from the opposite direction to that expected. Eventually they formed ranks and waited for the station commander to commence his inspection. Suddenly, a short figure bustled on to the parade ground, carrying an umbrella and a bulging string shopping bag – it was Charlotte. She stopped, breathless, in front of the bemused NCO in charge of the parade. 'My dear,' she said, 'I've found some tomatoes in Marlow. Isn't that wonderful!'[31]

6

WATCHING THE ENEMY

For much of the Second World War, Wing Commander Douglas Kendall was the Technical Control Officer (TCO) of the Allied Central Interpretation Unit (ACIU) at RAF Medmenham. It was a key post, of critical importance to the efficient running of a highly complex tri-service and multinational organisation. He was responsible for the tasking and allocation of resources needed for the PI work, handling requests from a multitude of customers, and for the quality of the intelligence produced from the unit.

RAF Medmenham was one of the first genuinely joint service units to be established in the Second World War, and certainly one of the most cosmopolitan. It accommodated men and women of the army, navy and air forces from Allied nations and the occupied European countries. They were a diverse mix of people, temporarily in uniform, drawn from scientific and artistic backgrounds, and who applied their specialist knowledge, skills and eccentricities to military intelligence use. With such an eclectic mix, Medmenham could have been fraught with rivalries or ill will that would have greatly diminished the achievements of the unit. The fact that it was not so was due in large measure to Douglas Kendall. Sarah Churchill wrote:

> It would not be possible to speak of all the inhabitants of Medmenham – or the 'Mad Men of Ham' as we were known locally – without mentioning our commanding officer, Wing Commander Douglas Kendall. He was brilliant, a wonderful co-ordinator with the Americans, kind, slightly shy, but he held his medley of personalities together. Many fascinating people passed through the station from all the services and all our allies.[1]

A mathematician and surveyor, Kendall was just 25 years old when he was appointed to head the ACIU in April 1941 and his pleasant character became a key feature in its smooth running. The senior officers, regardless of nationality, who were responsible for the actual interpretation, got on well with him

Wing Commander Douglas Kendall, the Technical Control Officer and in charge of all PI at RAF Medmenham.

and a flexible outlook made the acceptance of direct or unusual requests a simple matter.

Kendall also had the unenviable job of dealing with the Air Ministry, government officials and high-ranking officers of different nationalities who would all have liked to run the ACIU to their own advantage and prestige; he resisted them all and fought numerous battles on behalf of the PIs who he referred to as 'our team of individualists'. With a natural ability for deductive reasoning and a capacity for unending work, he frequently dropped in on one of the sections, day or night, to encourage all personnel coping with the huge amount of incoming photography, or pulled his stereoscope from his pocket to give an opinion to a young PI puzzling over a photograph. Thanks to him a pleasant and supportive atmosphere prevailed at Medmenham, described by Hazel Furney:

> There were so many interesting people there, of many nationalities. Everyone got on well together – there was no nastiness. It was all very friendly – and a lot of fun.[2]

A sortie of low, oblique photographs providing a panoramic view of an area could also reveal to the PIs at Medmenham some intriguing glimpses of everyday life in enemy and occupied Europe. While checking for signs of change in an area of interest they might see a football match in progress, hay-making in the fields or a fair in full swing in the marketplace of a small town. One day, while examining a batch of photographs of the transport systems in a particular part of Germany, Section Officer Dorothy Garrod found herself looking at a travelling circus. She was particularly intrigued by the elephants and followed their slow journey from town to town as subsequent sorties came in. A few weeks later there was a squeak of surprise from Dorothy's desk as, clearly visible in stereo on a photograph, a new addition to the circus could be seen in the form of a baby elephant.

Dorothy was working in the Third-Phase Communications Section, 'F', collecting information about the internal road, water and railway networks on the continent of Europe. Reports were issued on traffic concentrations and movements, as these were often the first signs of a planned enemy deployment, and if the nature of the troops and their equipment could be deduced, then the purpose of the deployment was established. Railway construction and the different types of rolling stock used for carrying chemicals or guns, for instance, all provided clues to enemy intent. The section also provided information on the location, layout and vulnerability of marshalling yards, depots, bridges and locks for targeting purposes. Assessments were made of the traffic interruption that followed Allied bombing attacks and the speed with which the facilities were restored to use.

Having spent several interwar years leading archaeological expeditions to the Middle East, in 1933 Dorothy Garrod had taken up the post of director of studies in archaeology and anthropology at Cambridge University. In 1939 she was persuaded to stand for election to the prestigious Disney Chair of Archaeology, at a time when women were still not awarded degrees and could not participate in university government at Cambridge. She explained her reason for standing to her fellow archaeologist and supporter, Glyn Daniel: 'I shan't get it but I thought I'd give the electors a run for their money.'[3]

She did get it, and so became the first woman to become a professor in any field at either Oxford or Cambridge universities, although it was seven years before her inaugural lecture could be given, due to the intervention of the war. She continued teaching at an increasingly empty Cambridge, all the while trying to enrol into the Air Intelligence branch of the RAF, but was consistently refused entry on the grounds of her age. She enlisted the help of two friends, Glyn Daniel and Hugh Hamshaw Thomas, both Cambridge academics and PIs at Medmenham, who knew that her archaeological background and knowledge of air photography made her an eminently suitable candidate for interpretation work. At last, under pressure, the Air Ministry discovered a rule that only applied to people who had served between 1914–18 and exempted them from the age restriction clause. On 5 May 1942, her fiftieth birthday, Dorothy Garrod reported for duty at RAF Medmenham.

Working alongside her in 'F' Section were Sarah Churchill and Robin Orr, who was the pre-war organist at St John's College, Cambridge. Two young Intelligence Corps warrant officers, Geoffrey Stone and Fred Mason, a Royal Navy lieutenant and a US army captain completed the team under the head of section, Captain Moody. Geoffrey recorded in a letter home:

I heard today about Sarah's experiences when she first joined the WAAF. Apparently there were three others with red hair in her group and they were often mistaken for her; in fact she claims to have had 'Sarah' pointed out to her on a number of occasions and says she always showed great interest in her 'other self'. However, she added that no one would treat her normally and used to push her to the back of queues just to show they weren't impressed. In fact, she says that she wasn't treated as an ordinary human being until she came to Medmenham.[4]

The YWCA hut near the hutted accommodation provided a welcoming and comfortable environment for men and women when they were off duty. The gramophone record recitals were always popular, with the music often being selected and introduced by Fred Mason, himself an accomplished pianist. Regular lectures, on a variety of subjects, could be attended by anyone at Medmenham and as the lecturer was invariably talking about his or her specialised interest, the quality was very high. With the numbers of archaeologists and explorers on the staff there must have been some exciting tales to listen to about 'digs' and the polar regions. At the beginning of 1944, Geoffrey recorded that Dorothy Garrod gave a 'lantern lecture' on the Lascaux Paleolithic cave paintings, which had been discovered by accident in the Dordogne region in 1940 after the German occupation of France. The details of the paintings had apparently only recently been smuggled out to England.

Another PI had an encounter with an elephant. Hazel Furney worked in another Third-Phase Section, 'L', Aircraft and Aircraft Industry:

I was cycling to Medmenham to go on shift one morning, turned a corner and came face to face with an elephant, part of a small travelling circus. I pedalled on to work thinking how I would surprise the other members of my section with my story of meeting an elephant. So when I went into our room I said, 'Guess what I've just seen on the way to work?' And another Waaf said, 'Oh, did you see that tiger too?'[5]

The head of the Aircraft Section was Constance Babington Smith. During the 1930s she had led a busy social life in London and trained as a milliner. It was when she went to live with her mother near Brooklands motor-racing circuit and flying club in Surrey – where, incidentally, Hilda Hewlett had flown her biplane in 1911 to become the first woman in Britain to gain a pilot's licence – that Constance was bitten by the aviation bug. While not wanting to be a pilot herself, she wrote verses about flying for publication in the magazine *The Aeroplane*, whose editor nicknamed her 'Babs'. Under that name she started writing articles on flying and visiting air shows, becoming intensely interested in all aeronautical matters. Constance was commissioned as an assistant section officer in the WAAF in 1940 and, having trained as a PI, worked alongside Jean Starling at Wembley, where she took particular interest in examining airfields and reporting any changes she observed:

Ursula Kay was a senior PI working in the Aircraft Section.

I was rather taken aback, however, to find that the aircraft themselves were normally reported rather as an afterthought, at the end of the statement on the airfield itself. Surely this was putting the cart before the horse – or rather the stage before the play that was being acted? But it was hardly for a WAAF who had been an officer only a few weeks to say so.

During the times when reconnaissance was held up by weather I used every spare moment to add to my knowledge of aircraft. I thought that before long I might be asked to interpret Italian aircraft, and I knew practically nothing about them. So I spent hours with Jane's 'All the World's Aircraft', and set down the main things I thought important. One of the civilian interpreters, Ray Herschel, was interested in aircraft too; and I picked up from him how to link the facts in Jane's with the tiny shapes on the photographs.[6]

At that time, Italy was poised to join Germany in the war against Britain, and as a result of her report on their aircraft, Constance was instructed to set up and head an Aircraft Interpretation Section. With the move from Wembley to Medmenham, 'L' Section came into being, initially as one desk in the corner of the big room occupied by Second Phase. After several moves, the Section found its final home in one of the towers of Danesfield House, occupying a spacious bedroom with adjoining palatial marble bathroom, large enough for three PIs and a clerk to work in, and overlooking the garden. Dorothy Colles was an early member of the Section before being posted overseas, Ursula Kay became a long-standing senior PI and from 1942 American interpreters joined the aircraft team. Charles Sims, who had been chief photographer on *The Aeroplane* before the war, became responsible for examining aircraft production in factories. When Hazel Furney joined the Section in 1942 she worked on identifying the many different German and Italian aircraft, searching for new types or modifications, complete with design characteristics such as their dimensions and function, and reporting when and where they were first seen.

With this information the Section built up a comprehensive dossier, constantly updated, on the state of the German aircraft industry, with the location of their factories and the types and numbers of aircraft built. This became particularly important from mid-1943, when it was realised that enemy aircraft factories were being dispersed to the eastern regions of Germany where they were at the extreme range of Allied bombers and, it was hoped, subject to fewer attacks. It also meant that new aircraft developments were more easily concealed from reconnaissance aircraft. An added twist to this dispersal programme was that the enemy left the original factories empty but intact, with the appearance of production going on, hoping that Allied bombs would be wasted on attacking them.

High priority was given to attacks on German aircraft assembly factories, where newly completed fighters could be destroyed before they became operational. In 1943, Constance became involved in behind-the-scenes work in the preparations for daylight bombing operations by Flying Fortress aircraft of the US 8th Air Force. She wrote:

> The work on aircraft factories that I shared with Charles Sims was at once injected with a sense of urgent responsibility. Those scraps of evidence that we pieced together like a jig-saw puzzle – a glimpse of a fuselage outside an assembly shop, the coming and going of lorries at loading bays, the floor areas of the workshops, the positions of the aircraft (which we found usually meant much more than mere numbers) – the meaning we found in all these things was going to be weighed against the lives of the Fortress crews.

It took months of patiently re-checking photographs of the German eastern borders that had been taken in previous years, and comparison with more recent sorties, before the Aircraft Section was able to provide the vital information on a new Focke-Wulf assembly factory constructed at Marienburg in East Prussia. On 9 October 1943, in a daylight precision raid, the USAAF successfully attacked the factory and put it out of action. By the spring of 1944 the enemy's aircraft production was seriously affected and Allied air supremacy over Germany was established for the first time.

Constance and her team were also responsible for identifying two revolutionary German-designed aircraft. Speed and the attainment of height and manoeuvrability in fighter and reconnaissance aircraft remained the essential qualities that enabled the Allied pilots to 'nip in and nip out' and retain the edge over their opponents. For some time the Spitfire could out-perform any other aircraft but by the end of 1943 the updated German Focke-Wulf fighter, the Fw 190, the prototype of which had been spotted by the Aircraft Section two years earlier, was challenging this claim. Fortunately a new, faster PR Spitfire was by then ready to go into service, and Allied superiority was retained.

In the summer of 1943, the Aircraft Section was instructed to watch for 'anything queer' on the photographs they examined of the experimental testing site at Peenemunde on the German Baltic coast, where secret weapons were being developed. Photographs taken in June in bright, clear weather helped to confirm the nature of these secret weapons, but Constance was far more interested in something else she had spotted on those same photographs: four little tail-less aeroplanes, which she considered 'queer enough to satisfy anybody'. These were measured and later identified as Me 163 rocket fighters, the only liquid-fuel rocket aircraft ever to fly operationally. They had a performance far exceeding that of contemporary piston-engine fighter aircraft, such as the Spitfire, taking off at a speed of 200mph and accelerating to pull up into a near-vertical climb to reach altitudes of 39,000ft in 3 minutes. When it began active combat in May 1944, it was a threat to all Allied operations, including the forthcoming Normandy invasion. Pictures of Constance at work show that she kept a wooden model of the Me 163 on her desk.

The early identification of the aircraft gave time for Allied air crews to be briefed on its attacking tactics and to prepare defensive measures. It was the Me 163's own impressive performance that limited its effective use as, having reached its slower-moving targets in a matter of seconds, it was then going too fast to fire at them accurately. It also needed a far bigger turning circle than any other fighter aircraft in order to return to the fray or return to base for refuelling, giving time for slower but more manoeuvrable aircraft to escape or vanish into a cloud.

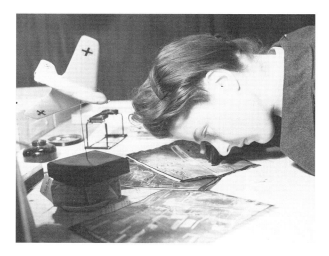

Constance Babington Smith, head of the Aircraft Section, with a model of the Me 163 rocket fighter on her desk.

At take-off, jet-propelled aircraft left pairs of fan-shaped scorch marks or long dark streaks on the ground and this distinctive clue enabled the Aircraft Section to locate other sites where similar marks were present. This led to their identification of the Me 262, a twin-engine jet-powered fighter considered to be the most advanced German aviation design in use during the Second World War. It could fly for 60–90 minutes with a cruising speed of up to 50mph faster than piston-engine fighters, including the Spitfire, and posed a very real threat to Allied operations in the last months of the war. At the same time Constance's team confirmed that Me 262s were being built in underground factories at Kahla. Fortunately only 200 Me 262s made it into combat due to fuel shortages. The Allies dealt with their threat by ground attacks and precision-bombing raids on the synthetic oil plants, which by then were the only means of German fuel production.

The long hours of all-absorbing scrutiny through a stereoscope were relieved by breaks in which the PIs could walk in the garden, gaze at the river or relax with a chat and a cigarette. One day of the week, though, was special at Medmenham because Wednesday was doughnut day! Suzie Morgan remembered:

> Every Wednesday the Americans used to get quite excited and form a long queue at the Red Cross kiosk where they could buy real doughnuts, made fresh on the spot, served with coffee. We Brits used to laugh that it meant so much to them but I suppose it reminded them of home.[7]

The Americans introduced many people to new foods and new ways of eating it. Myra Murden said:

> They were a lovely crowd. It seemed to us that they mixed all their food together but as they said, 'It all goes down the same way'. I remember how they toasted marshmallows on the fire which were really delicious.[8]

'Panda' Carter recalled that:

> The Americans introduced us to raspberry jam with bacon, and peanut butter with blackcurrant jam.[9]

Aircraft need airfields, and a Third-Phase Airfield Section was established early in 1940 at Wembley. With the move to Medmenham, the Section was designated as 'C' and headed by Section Officer Ursula Powys-Lybbe, a professional photographer before the war, with a studio in Cairo and later a successful business based in London. In July 1939, when war seemed inevitable, she gave up her business and joined the Auxiliary Fire Service in London, hoping to be usefully employed. Through the following Phoney War winter there was little for her to do so she resigned and went to stay with a friend who lived in Medmenham village. By a series of coincidences, she joined the WAAF, worked as a records clerk until her selection for PI training, and joined RAF Medmenham on 1 April 1941.

Airfield interpretation revealed not only the enemy's current status but also their future plans. The resources invested in airfield construction, with its associated buildings and communications, indicated an important strategic purpose. Early in the war, the Germans constructed standardised 'tailor-made' airfields, and PIs could deduce the function of the units based there – whether for bomber, mine-laying, fighter or transport aircraft – from the variety of installations in place. These distinctive clues could be applied to other existing or newly built airfields, landing grounds and seaplane bases in enemy or occupied territory. Regular monitoring ascertained if any airfield was being modified for a change of purpose.

Jane Cameron, the shy Scot who had worked in Coastal Command with a crowd of 'rumbustious' airwomen, was commissioned in August 1941, then posted to Medmenham. She wrote in her diary:

> I suppose people keep diaries – or begin to keep diaries – for all sorts of different reasons, so I imagine getting one's commission in the Women's Auxiliary Air Force is as good a reason as any other. Not that I ever imagined having a commission would be anything like this. When one is in the ranks of the WAAF, the 'officers' are a class apart. This is regardless of education or social standing in civilian life – everything. In the service, there are 'the officers' and 'the other ranks' and no matter how much of a social renegade one is, no matter how complete one's scorn of social custom, this becomes part of one's service mentality. One accepts the officers as a race apart.
>
> On my appointment, I came down from Leuchars to London in a dazed condition, by the night train, in the company of half a dozen sailors and drank beer with increasing solemnity all the way from Edinburgh to London. Occasionally I told myself that this was the last journey of this sort that I would make. This was the end of irresponsibility – that ruling characteristic of all rankers. From now on, I would be 'an officer'. It would be autre temps, autre moeurs. I felt a little sad about it all.

Jane Cameron worked in the Airfields Section at RAF Medmenham.

In London, I dumped my bags at a boarding house near Marble Arch and went shopping. That same evening, I stepped out of my boarding house on to the Edgware Road, an officer down to the second kid glove carried in the gloved left hand. At Marble Arch, an airman saluted me. I was now one of those 'up there'. I had left the ranks behind. I was overcome with melancholy.[10]

Despite professing a preference for ships over aircraft on her PI course, 'Jane' was posted to the Airfield Section, which seems to have been her choice:

I passed that course in the end, and I got the job I wanted in this comic unit, and now, after six months of it, I am beginning to feel that I know a little more about it. So much to learn, and such mentally exhausting learning too! We are now in a new Mess at Henley, (Phyllis Court) full of priceless people – Anne Whiteman, an Oxford Don-ess, Lady Bonham Carter, a charming and intelligent eccentric, Vyvyan Russell [sic] who has a face like Dolores – our Lady of Pain – utterly beautiful. Ursula Powys-Lybbe, the most modern of hyper-sensitive moderns, who has much of my own uncomfortable flair for seeing round all the mental screens behind which people hide their motives from themselves and the world. I love her dearly. Then there is Babs Babington Smith who I am only now beginning to know, due to her admitted façade of other worldliness which I privately think a little precious but which is none of my business and anyhow I like her in spite of it – I wouldn't like her if the otherworldliness were real, by the way.

A routine report on an existing airfield would include details on the dimensions of the landing area and the number, length and orientation of the runways with details on their serviceability – whether the surface of the runways was in a good enough state of repair to be operational or if there were obstructions and mines laid for demolition. The position of the fuel-storage tanks, the water supply and the ammunition storage were important, in addition to the number and size of the hangars, workshops and accommodation for personnel. Wireless telephony (radio) stations were always noted, as was the presence of a night landing facility called Visual Lorenz, which was a series of poles for carrying light cables that were sunk into the ground in line with the runway. The PIs could see this system clearly on photographs taken in daylight as the base of each pole appeared as a white dot. These were plotted for the navigators of RAF intruder aircraft, who would then home in on returning enemy bombers at the moment when the lights went on. Ursula wrote:

Our subject was as vital as any other at Medmenham, as we discovered, because we supplied information to the Air Staff, which could be used for the assessment of the order of battle of the Luftwaffe; the team being able to determine from the lay-out of an airfield under construction, the type of aeroplane likely to operate from it.[11]

Both Ursula and Constance battled with Air Intelligence departments at the Air Ministry, whose policy was to withhold information from other sources from the Medmenham PIs which would, on many occasions, have proved useful and time saving. Both eventually managed to visit the relevant departments and create lines of communication, although this was often dependent on the individual personality in post. Constance was consulted on aircraft development by several committees and was able to get her ideas across to them, although she became frustrated at the dismissive air or blocking attitude of some individuals, getting on better with the Americans, who listened to what she knew.

The Wireless Section, 'G', had started at Wembley under the leadership of a mathematician, Squadron Leader Claud Wavell. Its outstanding contribution was the complete unearthing of the enemy's offensive and defensive radio systems. The offensive transmitters acted as navigational aids to direct German air crew flying on bombing missions over Britain. The defensive system provided pre-warning of air raids in Germany and was later used to detect the first signs of invasion. The detection of the enemy's radar installations in occupied territory was of first-rate strategic importance. The first WAAF recruit to this work was Section Officer Vera Marsden, who had been a radio-location operator before training as a PI; she became an area officer responsible for reporting on radar installations in France. Her colleague, Section Officer Kay Henry, was similarly responsible for reporting on radar in Belgium.

It was not until they had failed to invade Britain in 1940 that the Germans recognised their need for camouflage, smokescreens and decoys. The Third-Phase Camouflage Section, 'E', was established with the move to Medmenham and head of section was Flight Officer Mollie 'Tommy' Thompson, a graduate

Kay Henry demonstrates the Altazimeter, an invention of Squadron Leader Claud Wavell, head of the Wireless Section. It was used to determine the height of aerial arrays on wireless transmitters from the angle of the sun.

in economics, who had joined the WAAF in 1939 and worked at Wembley. She was an expert on the subject, a regular lecturer at the PI school at Nuneham Park and advised the British camouflage designers. Section Officers Pauline Growse, an actress, and Kitty Sancto, who had studied at the Slade College of Art, also worked in the Section, showing the necessary keen eye for detail and ability to study each photograph with an open mind. Camouflage was in large measure ineffective against air photography, and in wartime often only served to emphasise the importance of the object being hidden. Ursula Powys-Lybbe wrote:

> There is an explanation for the apparent ease with which the interpreters could see through camouflage, both literally and figuratively, while a pilot might have been deceived. Camouflage was primarily designed in colour to blend with the background, so that aircrew would be unlikely to identify the target as they flashed by overhead with no time to search for it.
>
> Monochrome or black and white prints in front of the interpreters, meant that a range of neutral tone made it easier to define form, colour not being there to distract the eye, and also there was time for examination. If we had been faced with colour prints in those days, it might have been almost as difficult for us as for the pilot to find the target.
>
> The main guides by which camouflage could be detected were from tonal dissimilarity caused by differences in the surface of any material used, even though it might have been indistinguishable in reality because of good matching colours. Shadows and vague outlines would always show through netting, and anyway the structure or framework itself might produce strange shadows after a period of being subjected to weather and ageing.

Elaborate enemy camouflage was used in attempts to disguise factories, railway stations and oil-storage tanks as well as military targets such as gun pits, coastal barrages and ships. Sometimes the roofs of large buildings were laid out with dummy houses and trees to give the appearance of being part of the surrounding housing area. Water was the most important feature to try to camouflage, as it reflected in the dark and acted as a 'signpost' and a marker on target maps for bomber air crews. Larger items such as aircraft hangars and ships were difficult to camouflage, although disruptive painting on the hull of a naval vessel could break up the outline and make it hard for a PR pilot to recognise it.

Smokescreens were also used to protect important targets from day and night attacks and as soon as German radar stations detected approaching aircraft, they would be raised. These were a severe handicap to the Allied bomber and reconnaissance aircraft but by the latter part of the war, PIs had built up enough information on position, extent, density and pattern to make it possible for air crews to avoid or minimise the effects of the smoke pall. Decoys were also used by the enemy by simultaneously raising one smokescreen over a target about to be

The Camouflage Section. From left: Pauline Growse, John Bowden RAF, Flight Officer Mollie Thompson (foreground), head of section, and Kitty Sancto.

attacked and another over an open piece of countryside some miles away where bombs would fall harmlessly.

The Decoy Section, 'Q', worked very closely with camouflage and the Target Section that produced material for briefing bomber air crews. Helga O'Brien worked with the head of Section, Squadron Leader Geoffrey Dimbleby, searching for decoy fire sites, such as mock burning buildings, near to large industrial concerns. These, like the decoy smokescreens, were designed to lure the night bomber pilots away from the actual target. As well as sham factory sites and dummy oil-storage tanks, the Germans produced complete decoy airfields, with one in Norway even having a model aircraft on rails to make it appear more real.

Camouflage and decoys were, of course, also used defensively by the Allies to disguise their own industries, airfields and ports by building dummy airfields and pretend buildings in Britain. This was monitored to ensure its effectiveness by two ATS mapmakers at RAF Nuneham Park.

Joan 'Bo' Bohey was living in Dorset waiting to take up a teacher training place at Goldsmiths College, London, when the war changed her plans and she joined the ATS instead. At the end of her basic training at Aldermaston, all the 'artists' were picked out to train as draughtswomen, but Joan, whose main subjects at school certificate were geography and survey, was not classed as an 'artist' and was sent to be a clerk:

Joan Bohey ATS (left) with a colleague at RAF Nuneham Park.

I was filing papers one day when I came across the draughtswoman trade test requirements and thought, 'I could do that without even going on the course' and managed to get sent to an aptitude assessment where I got the highest marks ever! As a result I was sent on the three-month draughtswoman course at Ruabon in North Wales. I met Barbara Chandler there, who was a talented calligraphist, and she and I were posted to the Drawing Office at RAF Nuneham Park where we worked on map making. The photography came from RAF Benson or bomber stations and we dealt with all the English cover and the small amount of cover, usually taken by accident, of neutral countries such as Sweden, Switzerland, Greenland and Iceland.

Barbara and I were the only two ATS at Nuneham. Our work was so secret that every week we had to walk to the guard room by the gate to the station to collect our pay from an officer sent over from Oxford, but not allowed in! Standing in the guard room the two of us each gave our number, saluted, were handed our pay and signed for it.[12]

The English cover Joan refers to was used to test the adequacy of Britain's own protective camouflage and decoy system. She and Barbara marked out the camouflaged areas using the varying textures and tones seen under the stereoscope in the same way as the Camouflage Section at Medmenham.

The Industry Section, 'D', was one of the earliest Third-Phase sections to be set up, designed to gather information relating to the output of enemy war material. It worked closely with the Wild Section for measurements and production of plans used for monitoring and assessing industrial plants. These were used to identify new manufactories and assess industrial output, in the allocation of targets for the Allied bombing campaign, and for the Damage Assessment Section to

Charlotte Bonham Carter at work in the Ground Intelligence Section.

calculate the necessary time for an industrial plant to become operational again. Scientists, engineers and those with a specialised industrial knowledge, such as the oil geologists, were recruited to the Section as German oil production was always of crucial importance. While men predominated in the Industry Section, because at that time the majority of scientists and geologists were male, several women, including Ruth Langhorne, a geographer from Oxford University, Winifred Bartingale, who became a doctor, Celia McDonald and Anne Whiteman, an Oxford historian, all worked in the Section.

The storage and, later on, the production of oil was always a major part of the work of the Section. Oil-storage tanks were easy for PIs to spot but soon the enemy made it harder by constructing huge underground reservoirs concealed from sight with trees planted on top; fortunately the ventilators were still visible on photographs. With the failure to secure the oil fields in the Caucasus for their use, the main German source of oil came from sixteen synthetic plants constructed across Europe, which manufactured oil from lignite. These were subjected to Allied precision-bombing raids, however, which had a decisive effect on the German capability to continue the war.

The search for information on a new project or query from any section at Medmenham usually began in the Ground Intelligence Section, responsible for keeping all reports from ground sources, including an extensive reference library of maps, charts, guidebooks, periodicals, trade and telephone directories. There were also illustrated brochures, plans and handbooks of industrial processes produced by companies in pre-war Germany, which were consulted by the Industry Section in the search for oil plants. Early on, the ACIU was refused access to information from the interrogation of prisoners of war and agent's reports, as it was thought that interpreters would be biased and find on their photographs 'what they had been told was there'. In no other form of scientific thought involving logical deduction had it ever been suggested that those carrying out the work would be biased by being provided with supplementary information, nor was there any evidence that such a tendency had ever been shown by photographic interpreters. The imaginative use of ground information in conjunction with photographic evidence actually served to enlarge the scope of photographic interpretation and helped develop new techniques.

Anne Jeffery had graduated in classics and archaeology from Newnham College, Cambridge, and spent some years in Athens before war intervened when she enrolled as a VAD nurse before volunteering for the WAAF in 1941. Her keen attention to detail, visual memory and archaeological knowledge soon brought her to Medmenham, but it was found that her stereoscopic vision was lacking, so her time was spent on intelligence rather than interpretation. Anne worked in Ground Intelligence with Charlotte Bonham Carter and Flight Lieutenant Villiers David. He lived with his sister at Friar Park, in Henley-on-Thames, the same house lived in years later by the Beatle, George Harrison. There are as many anecdotes concerning Villiers as there are about Charlotte, including one that Ann McKnight-Kauffer recounted:

> When at last Villiers got rid of his Rolls Royce and chauffeur he got a motorbike. On the first morning he came to Medmenham on it, he found to his horror that he didn't know how to stop it. He did the circuit from front gate to house past the much-amused guards until his petrol ran out.[13]

There were many tennis and croquet parties held at Friar Park and sometimes Scottish dancing, when 'Villiers leaping about in red braces was a sight to behold'.[14]

Joan Bohey had good reason to be grateful to Villiers David for his hospitality, as it gave her an opportunity to meet her future husband, David Brachi, on social occasions. They had initially met through scouting, as Joan helped with the Cub pack in Marlow and David was associated with the Henley Scouts. Later on, when they started going out together, it had to be in secret, as Joan was an NCO and David an officer; such liaisons were not only frowned upon, but were against King's Regulations. For that reason Joan never wore her uniform when they met on a date, instead wearing a variety of civilian clothes gleaned from other women in her hut. They had very little space for storing personal clothing and usually uniforms were worn for all on- and off-duty occasions. Joan and David could meet at Scout and Cub functions and at several houses whose owners, Villiers in particular, were sympathetic to their plight:

> We used to go to Villiers David's house – Friar Park – where all the light switches and door handles were shaped like monk's heads, so you pressed down the monk's nose to turn on the light! He and his sister had bought the farm next door so there was butter and cream at meals which was such a treat.[15]

It has often been noted that RAF Medmenham resembled more of an academic institution than a military establishment, with men and women recruited from widely diverse civilian occupations. The early, informal recruitment for the RAF of suitable, academically qualified colleagues at Wembley was successful and was formalised under Wing Commander Hamshaw Thomas at Medmenham. The WAAF selection system was also successful in picking out potential women PIs, and not only the obvious choices with qualifications and experience in photography, archaeology, art and geography. Historians and English graduates were also among those recruited, as were the women who had shown at a selection board that they looked at and examined a subject in depth, seeing more than the superficial view.

Although the comprehensive collection of men and women working alongside each other at Medmenham were experts in the widest variety of specialist subjects, all had a common characteristic: none took things at their face value and all questioned whatever they saw on the photographs. Searching for clues under the stereoscope, examining something unusual and then following it up until the answer was found became second nature to them. From 1940, as soon as WAAF regulations allowed, women were employed on the same work as men and were recognised as being equally capable. They were given responsibility for decision making in all aspects of intelligence production at Medmenham.

7

MILLIONS OF PHOTOGRAPHS

Squadron Leader John Saffery DSO DFC flew PR Spitfires from RAF Benson in 1943–44 and commanded 541 Squadron. He married Margaret Adams, a WAAF PI who worked in Second Phase at RAF Medmenham. He wrote graphically about flying at high altitudes while on solo photographic missions:

It is the climb through the tropopause into the stratosphere which is like crossing the bar from the shallows into deep water. The climb up has been a matter of constant change. The continually falling temperature, successive layers of cloud, varying winds, the appearance of trail, and the turbulence or vertical movements of the air are liable to be felt to a greater or lesser degree all the way up.

There was always the fear of passing out with very little warning if anything went wrong with the oxygen system, and to guard against this I used to keep a fairly elaborate log because I reckoned that if I could write legibly I must be alright. Nevertheless until the arrival of pressure cabins we were a bit slow witted from lack of oxygen I think.

The cold, the low pressure and the immobilising effect of the elaborate equipment and bulky clothing in the tiny cockpit had the effect of damping down and subduing all the senses except the sense of sight. One became just an eye, and what one saw was always wonderful.

On a clear day one could see immense distances, whole countries at a time. From over the middle of Holland I have seen the coast from Ostend round beyond Emden, and from the neighbourhood of Hanover seen the smoke pluming up from burning Leipzig. I've seen the Baltic coast from above Berlin and from over Wiesbaden seen the Alps sticking up like rocky islands through the clouds. On such days, which are rare in Europe, it was more like looking at a map than a view.

After 1942 the cabins were heated and a temperature of slightly above freezing was maintained so that we flew in battle dress with thick sweaters, long woollen stockings, double gloves and flying boots, but electrically heated clothing was not necessary. But the air temperature outside was 60 or 70 degrees below and if, as occasionally happened, the cabin heating failed, the cold was agonising. Everything in the cockpit became covered with frost and long icicles grew from the oxygen mask like Jack Frost's beard. Most alarming of all, the entire windscreen and blister roof was liable to frost up so that one could not see out at all except where one rubbed the rime off with a finger to have a frenzied peep round through the clear patch before it froze over again. At such times one felt the air was full of Messerschmitts.[1]

Only the PR pilots operated at such heights for long periods. In mid-June 1944, shortly after D-Day, John had to bale out of his Spitfire into the English Channel where he spent a day 'bobbing about' until he was picked up by a passing motor torpedo boat.

The photographs that the PR pilots took were mostly 'verticals', taken directly above the target from cameras fitted through portholes in the floor of the aircraft. These could also be used in sequence to provide a run of stereo pairs for intelligence gathering or as smaller-scale photographs for map making. Cloud was the greatest handicap to obtaining good photographs. The most successful pilots were those who appreciated the need for meticulous flight planning and good meteorological briefing. Photographs could also be 'obliques' taken sideways from the aircraft or, less commonly, to the front or rear, and these provided a wider view of an area. Low-level obliques were used to take pictures of targets which would otherwise have been obscured by cloud or for which information could not be obtained by any other means. This was known as 'dicing' and the elements of surprise and speed were essential. It was therefore very dangerous and carried out by only the most experienced pilots, producing some of the outstanding photographs of the war.

Great advances in camera and film technology took place during the Second World War, largely due to work at the Royal Aircraft Establishment, Farnborough. Longer lenses, designed for high-flying aircraft, provided better spatial definition and showed more ground detail. Improvements in film emulsions increased sensitivity and resolution, while better camera mountings in aircraft eliminated the effects of vibration. The end result of all these advances was a reduction in the effect of film grain and a clearer picture when viewed by PIs through a stereoscope.

As soon as a PR aircraft returned to base, the photographic personnel took charge of the film for immediate processing, followed by First-Phase interpretation. Pamela Howie was a photographic processor at RAF Benson, dealing with the film from 1 PRU sorties.

Pamela, aged 19, had received her call-up papers in the summer of 1942, so left her job as librarian in Boots the Chemist's library in Kendal, and enrolled in the WAAF at Carlisle where she was rated medically A1, despite having had asthma for several years. She reported to RAF Bridgnorth in Shropshire for kitting out and quickly learnt a thing or two about communal living:

An aerial view of RAF Medmenham provides a good example of a vertical photograph.

At lunch on returning from the tea queue I found my knife and fork missing. Nobody had seen anything so armed with spoon and mug I went to the Corporal who said, 'You only get one issue so you will have to steal them back again!' At tea-time I found a knife just lying on a table so snatched it![2]

When her group of WAAFs were despatched to Morecombe for basic training, she teamed up with a girl called Doris who had fainting fits but, like Pamela, had been rated medically A1. Their first parade was held on a very hot July day and Pamela had to keep rescuing Doris when she fainted, which brought on her own asthma. They were both brought before a medical board who discharged Doris as medically unfit but decided that Pamela could stay in the WAAF, although with a downgraded medical status of C3, which meant that she could not be posted abroad.

Pamela liked the drilling but hated physical training, which she considered to be degrading as it was held in a big bus garage open for all to see, and the WAAFs had to strip down to shirt and knickers. She learnt how to salute:

> Longest way up, shortest way down. Right arm up and extended out to the side, then bent at the elbow and the top of the index and middle fingers to touch the right temple, fingers rigid, palm facing forwards, then curl the fingers forward and down, turn the whole wrist now like a fist down in a straight line to your side, to the count of up 2,3, down 2,3. We were told we were not saluting the individual but the King's uniform.

She worked as a clerk at three different RAF stations, continually putting in requests to be trained for a trade, and was at last posted on to a three-month photography course at RAF Farnborough. It was a comprehensive mix of theoretical lectures on light and optics, and practical work on the pinhole camera, types of lenses, light and chemical changes, followed by developing and filters. The WAAFs learnt how to load film into an aerial camera and practised installing and retrieving it from an aircraft:

> We were taught about processing, camera maintenance and how to load film in the dark. I passed the first photographic test with good marks of 50 out of 60.

Later on they absorbed information on air pressure and electrical circuits. Other subjects were about night photography, mechanical faults and stereoscopic harmonisation, which ensured the correct overlapping of photographs to produce stereo pairs. They also learnt about all the chemicals used and how to title each negative to show when and where it was taken.

Having passed their final exam, ACW1 Pamela Howie and her friend Nell were posted to RAF Benson, the very busy PR station close to Medmenham. There was the constant noise of reconnaissance aircraft, Spitfires and Mosquitoes, revving up and taking off. Pamela wrote:

> We were kept busy developing, printing and titling the films ready to go to the interpretation office for inspection. Recently a fantastic aerial shot of our airfield had been taken. I would have dearly loved a print to take home and show Mum, but I realised that had I been searched on one of the railway stations by M.Ps (military police), they may have thought I was a spy, it just was not worth the risk, pity though.

Instead Pamela wrote and described RAF Benson to her mother:

The main gate which leads out to Wallingford and Oxford is near the guard room and where the Alsatian dogs are kept. The other two normally unmanned gates are at either end of the camp, the first one after coming in the main gate leads to Mrs Crane's café, back inside that gate and to the right is the sick bay, (trust me to know that), somewhere nearby are the officer's quarters and a lone Spitfire aircraft on display, which when they decided to move it, a wheel ran over one of the aircraft hand's toes. I happened to be nearby and heard his blood curdling screams. Nearby is the parade ground and further on the cookhouse, NAAFI and YMCA … Station Head Quarters, clothing store etc. Further over still are the hangars for the planes and the aircraft runway … on the further side of our billets the roadway continues to the other gate leading to our photographic section and the village, Henley and eventually Reading.

The summer of 1943 was exceptionally hot:

It was such a shame to be working most of our time in dark rooms, when it had been such a brilliant hot summer. Outside our section was a septic tank and that plus the chemical smells of hypo etc were sometimes overpowering. I'd noticed a rash appearing on my hands, so reported sick, and was told, 'You have metol poisoning'. We'd been warned of this on the course, but nobody was over worried as they claimed that only one in a hundred got it, of course the odd one out just had to be me. I was given a special cream and gloves to wear at night, and my job now could not have anything to do with chemicals, so I was moved to the titling section with Grace.

We all worked shifts, the worst one being 4 o'clock in the afternoon until 8 o'clock the next morning. Then we went for breakfast and often felt too tired to sleep. The other shift was easy by comparison. I actually preferred the night shift for if flying was cancelled due to bad weather we were allowed off early, and got a really good breakfast in the cookhouse, generally of bacon and egg. But we got crafty and said we were from MT (motor transport), as the cooks didn't like us, they considered photographers snobs for some reason.

Pamela describes how important accuracy was:

Aerial films were very large and had to be wound by means of handles across a long bench. Our job was to put on each negative frame all the relevant data, but most important of all was to title the first piece of blank film 'START' and then when we came to the end we put 'END'. The data included the number of the unit, the sortie number (the single operational flight of the aircraft), negative and serial number, date and subject.

Our work was tiring and exacting and you could not afford to make a mistake as Grace did one day. To explain – when you were on the 4 pm to 8 am shift, by about 2.30 in the early hours you were working like an automaton. Later around 4.30 am you were wide awake again, but between those times you were at your most vulnerable.

On this particular night Grace had put 'END' on both ends of this aerial film by mistake due to being so tired. It had been spotted once it reached the interpretation office, whose job it was to assess from our photographs what areas had to be bombed again and what damage had been done to targets already bombed. The punishment – poor Grace was put on a charge. I could have wept, she was my best friend.

It was the Japanese attack on Pearl Harbor on 7 December 1941 that convinced Pat Peat, a US citizen, to join the WAAF, and later on she worked in the Photographic Section at RAF Medmenham. Pat had graduated from the Art Institute of Chicago in the summer of 1940, with a Merit Award of $500 and a determination to follow her younger sister Betty, who had already joined the WAAF. Their father was a Canadian veteran and their mother came from Northern Ireland and both were peace campaigners following the First World War. Pat and Betty never went to school, being taught instead by their parents as they travelled to lectures and meetings across America. In 1937 their father, Mr Harold Peat, who owned a leading lecture agency in New York City, was engaged as Winston Churchill's agent for a planned lecture tour across America in the autumn of the following year. Subsequently, due to the political outlook in Europe in 1938, Churchill had to cancel this tour.[3]

When President Roosevelt declared war on Germany and Japan in December 1941, a friend of the Peat family wanted Pat to join the US Women's Army Corps to recruit volunteers, as she had presence and speaking experience. Not wanting any person to plan her life for her, Pat immediately went to the British Consulate in New York City and enrolled as volunteer 301 in the WAAF, and soon followed her sister to England. In 2009 she said their mother and father were 'devastated' that both daughters had decided to serve in the WAAF:

> I was born in Chicago Lying-In Hospital and I'm a US citizen. I didn't go over to Britain on a passport – nobody even asked about them back then. There wasn't any ferolderol – I just signed up. I went over to England on a Swedish tugboat with an American Army Medical Unit whom we seldom saw. We were in convoy to Liverpool and I think it took a week and a half.[4]

Pat joined an all-female group of trainee photographers at the RAF School of Photography in Blackpool and considered that they received excellent tuition. Each day started with a march from their billets to the sea front, usually whistling the popular tune *Pedro the Fisherman*, where they drilled and Pat could see her favourite donkeys on the beach. They learnt how to install and quickly retrieve the cameras from aircraft, how to develop the film and carry out some initial examination then print the photographs. They were also taught how to process film in the field using two buckets, with developing fluid in one and water in the other, in the event of a conventional processing unit not being available. Once they had passed the course they were sent to a bomber airbase for practical experience. Pat remembers how young the pilots were – just 18 or 19:

WAAFs in the Photographic Section using pantographs to reduce plots to the required scale, watched by Margaret Hockenhull.

The planes were the size of a Boeing on the airfield I was sent to. To be alone on an airfield but 'in charge' of the processing and having to look for signs of Fire, Track or Combustion (FTC) on the photographs, which were the accuracy indicators of the bombing raid, was a responsible job. The FTC showed whether the pilot would be credited with the flight or not. Bernard Babington Smith came to explain why this initial analysis at the airfield was important to night photography. Oh yes, I learned one more thing at this bomber base and that was how to make the tea with milk. And later on I learned how to tell fortunes from the tea leaves!

Pat was then posted to work at RAF Medmenham, which she loved:

Danesfield House had beautiful gardens. It was hard work there but intelligent humanity. All my free time was spent visiting relatives and sketching – I filled up four sketchbooks while I was there.

The Photographic Section had started life in the old stables of Danesfield House, moving later to Nissen huts, which provided the necessary space to house the

Photographic reproduction on a large scale in the processing unit.

machinery and deal with an ever-increasing workload. Film from aerial cameras was processed into negative form at PR bases, such as RAF Benson, and then brought to Medmenham for the production and duplication of positive images for the Second- and Third-Phase sections on site. The section had the most up-to-date machinery to work with, much of it non-standard RAF equipment, and included continuous processing machines and the latest type of duplicators and multiprinters with an automatic exposure control. There were rectifying enlargers for producing a run of photographs called a mosaic; machines that could handle the extra-large prints, called photographic skins, needed in model making; and Rotaprint machines that produced target maps. The Photographic Section became the equivalent of a large and efficient commercial photographic organisation operating on a 24-hour basis with three shifts. By the end of the war the Photographic Section had produced over 19 million photographic prints and Rotaprints, and duplicated thousands of sorties. Pat remembers:

> From 10am the negatives from the film that the reconnaissance pilots had taken started coming into the section and they were processed and printed. We all knew that if we didn't do our work properly we would be putting pilot's lives at risk because they may have to repeat the sortie.

Winston and Clementine Churchill paid an official visit to RAF Medmenham in 1943. Section Officer Sarah Churchill was in attendance.

The tanks used for processing were made of teak and lead lined – they were large enough for two people to stand side by side. We worked in dark red lighting and once the prints were run off they were taken off to the main building.

People specialised in different ways, some did photographic mapping. I was always a processor and was promoted to Lance Corporal.

RAF personnel, with a high proportion of WAAFs, made up the photographic workforce. Mary Tate was one of four WAAF officers in charge of up to 100 photographers on each shift, responsible for ensuring the required quality of photography for interpretation. Sergeant Sorrell was the senior WAAF NCO photographer at Medmenham and probably the first in the RAF. An efficient negative library was established to store the intake of sorties from the PR squadrons, other commands and the USAAF, which were all filed to assist in quick retrieval. In 1944–45, when the Allied advance through France and Belgium was under way, Section Officer Maddison was posted to 2nd Tactical Air Force (2 TAF) to take charge of the negative library located near Brussels.

Many distinguished visitors came to visit the Section including the Prime Minister on one occasion. His daughter Sarah visited the Section too and, remembering that Pat's father had once been Winston Churchill's lecture agent, she invited Pat and two friends to lunch at 10 Downing Street:

The three of us decided to buy ourselves new service caps for the occasion so we did that first of all then took a taxi to 10 Downing Street. We went upstairs to the dining room and I sat next to John Churchill, the younger brother of Winston.

Pat described herself as a solitary sort of person, not gregarious: her interests lay in exploring the countryside with her painting materials and visiting art exhibitions at the Tate Gallery in London. She enjoyed visiting relatives too, and met a whole new set of cousins in Belfast. On their off-duty days in the summer time, Pat and several colleagues went to pick peas for local farmers.

Within 24 hours of the prints being received, all operational sorties were plotted on to maps to show exactly where and when each photograph had been taken, essential both for immediate interpretation and for any future sorties. Plotting was always a predominately female occupation. On 1 May 1940, ten WAAF officers, four sergeants and six ACW2s had been posted into RAF Heston, which at that time was the base for PR aircraft and the processing of film. None of the WAAFs had previous experience of air photography and most had been formerly employed on administrative duties. Two duty watches were formed, the night watch dealing with the urgent sorties that covered the invasion ports three times a day, while the day watch dealt with sorties received from PR bases elsewhere in UK and Gibraltar. In 1940 the plotters dealt with ten to twelve sorties per day, with each aircraft carrying one or two cameras; by 1944 that number had leapt to more than eighty sorties each day with each aircraft fitted with four or five cameras.

Millicent Laws was one of the first WAAF officers to serve at Heston, which she describes as 'the most bombed airfield in the Battle of Britain', where the plotters worked in trenches making frequent dashes to grab more maps from the map store. She moved with the Section to RAF Benson on Boxing Day 1940 where, due to shortage of space, the Photographic and Intelligence Sections were set up in the village of Ewelme. By this time the numbers of plotters had been reduced

The Plotting Section. Front row from left: Elspeth Macalister, Margot Munn, Pauline Kraay, Jo Gidney. Second row: Jan Magee, Diana Ashcroft (second in command of section), Betty Rumball. Back row centre: Jeanne Adams. Back row left: head of Section Flt Lt Beetham.

Pauline Growse draws maps out of the extensive map store.

so the shift system was abandoned and the Section worked as long as there was work to be done and took time off when things were slack:

> The plotters and PIs were billeted in an old house in the village whose owner had taken up a post in Motor Transport, leaving his butler and housekeeper to look after us. I shared a room with Elizabeth Weightman who was a PI seconded over from the AOC at Wembley.[5]

In September 1941 three WAAF officers, including Millicent, were transferred to Medmenham to build up the Plotting Section and airwomen, several of whom had been tracers and artists in civilian life, were moved from other duties to learn the skill. The 8- and 16-hour shift system that Pamela Howie disliked so much at Benson also operated at Medmenham, with a WAAF officer in charge of each shift. The section came into being in the former library of Danesfield House but soon outgrew that space and moved to a splendid room that in earlier days had been the ballroom. The volume of photographs continuously increased and long hours were worked to keep up to date with the plotting. In 1944, in preparation for the Normandy invasion and in the search for V-weapons, the number and urgency of PR sorties mounted, and over 8 million photographs were plotted at Medmenham.

Plotters used a pen called a stylograph, rather like a black ink fountain pen which marked with a pointed nib, and a stereoscope. With a 'plotting square' made from pieces of metal hinged to form adjustable squares or rectangles, and a pair of proportional dividers to hand, plots could be transferred from one scale to another. A sufficient supply of maps of different scales had to be held as during a busy spell up to eighty map sheets a day would be used. The only aid to identification the plotters had was the pilot's trace, on which he recorded his course during the flight.

Even when the trace erred in accuracy and cloud obscured a large part of the picture, the WAAF officer plotters at Medmenham became so expert at recognising the smallest dots of land or coastline, that they averaged a rate of plotting over 100 prints per hour.

Jeanne Adams was posted to RAF Medmenham early in 1942 as a plotter and spent six months in the ranks to learn the nature of the job. Her pay was 18s 2d per week. Jeanne returned to Medmenham after being commissioned and passing her PI course. She explained her work:

> Our 'customers' were numerous and came from the War Office, the Admiralty, the Air Ministry, the service commands, the overseas commands and other secret services. All our reports were sent directly back to our 'customers'.
>
> The work of PI was important, secret, demanding and at times, very exciting. When you are given the photographs you had no idea what you might see. We watched shipping movements daily, we studied air fields old and new, aircraft, marshalling yards and railways, ports and beaches. At one time I think I could identify any port from Norway to the South of France at a glance.
>
> I was a plotter in the Plotting Section which is where the photographs were located on the maps. This was done with a stereoscope and we used a set square to get the right scale. Usually the photographs were accompanied by a sketch from the pilot showing the targets he had covered. It was easy for the plotters if it was accurate but sometimes because of bad weather or the pilot being lost they were difficult to place. Sometimes the cameras would be switched on because the pilot saw 'something that looked interesting down there', but did not know what it was and occasionally, because of the weather, where it was! This could, at times, take all

Jeanne Adams plots a sortie on to map sheets by marking the locations where the photographs were taken.

night to find, just a railway line with a wood beside it, or a dot that looked like an aircraft on a tiny strip of runway somewhere in Germany. After being plotted the photographs were passed on to Second and Third Phase.

All this usually began to happen between 2am and 8am which was hectic and rather like being in Fleet Street. We all worked a long watch of twelve hours either by day or night. But between work there was lots of fun and the biggest bonus for a WAAF was that there were always more men than women, so that finding a partner for a mess dance was never a problem![6]

Jeanne mentions pilots taking a photograph of something that caught their eye and 'looked interesting'. One of the PR pilots' instructions was never to return to base from a sortie with unused film, as a chance glimpse of something unexpected or unusual could provide a clue to enemy activity. One of the 'Points to Remember', quoted below, was in the operational notes handed to all new PR pilots in 680 Squadron:

REMEMBER that you are a RECONNAISSANCE PILOT. Keep your eyes open
for all types of enemy movement, shipping, aircraft, tanks, MT, etc. both on your
way to and from the target area.
REMEMBER that from the height at which you operate appearances are
deceptive. When you see anything you decide to report, note it's POSITION,
DIRECTION OF MOVEMENT and NUMBER and ALWAYS TAKE
PHOTOGRAPHS.

IT'S YOUR JOB![7]

Elspeth Macalister was still languishing as a clerk at RAF Duxford:

I was bored, bored, bored. I shared my tiny bedroom with the dirtiest girl on the camp, a cook, she never washed. She had a different man in bed with her most nights – I learnt quite a bit about sex. She stole everything of mine that she could lay her hands on, money, ornaments, even my mother's photograph.

In desperation I wrote to the Air Ministry and pointed out that I had joined up to do photographic interpretation and would they please post me to a proper station ie Medmenham. I got my posting there within a week. On arrival I had to report to Wing Commander Hamshaw Thomas and while I was waiting, the transport arrived from Phyllis Court and out tumbled some WAAF officers who I recognised from Cambridge, including my three fellow recruits – Ena, Sophie and Lou. And they expected me to salute them!

I was allocated to the Plotting Section. Our job was to see what route the PR pilots had followed and whether they had covered the target. Each pilot had a flimsy piece of tracing paper which showed his route. These were invaluable and we worked with countless maps. First job was to see where he had crossed the coast as

Personnel of all services drawing previous photographs out of the print library to compare with new cover.

the cameras were always switched on there. Then we had to follow his route marking the photographs in black squares, each relevant square picking out landmarks, such as churches, canals etc – challenging but fascinating work. Not being artistic, at first I made an awful mess with my mapping pen and black ink and my plot would be a puzzle of inexplicable black lines.

I made some of my very best friends on my shift. I loved the countryside – the smooth flowing Thames, the woods so beautiful in all seasons, lovely Henley, friendly Marlow, discreet little villages – we all had our bikes so we could explore. I always enjoyed night duty and having 24 hours off-duty ahead. We would rush up to London and probably see two plays, getting free tickets from the YWCA – London theatres were thriving – we ate in Lyons Corner House. How often we puffed up those steps at Paddington station to get the last train to Maidenhead and transport back to Marlow as being late meant being on a charge.[8]

In 1943 ten of the plotters, including Elspeth, made their way to an officer training unit in the Lake District for their course in preparation for being commissioned:

In due course the final exams came up and London tailors appeared to measure us for our new uniforms should we have passed. I chose Austin Reed for my first uniform, but not for my second when I saw they had written by my measurements, 'Thick Thighs'. Our new uniforms came while we were on leave. I wore mine down to Cambridge and met a squad of new recruits marching along St John's Street. The command 'Eyes Right' was given so there I stood, taking my first salute.

1 Danesfield House Hotel in Buckinghamshire. During the Second World War this was RAF Medmenham, the headquarters of Allied photographic interpretation.

2 The gardens and River Thames in 2011.

3 'The Airwomen's Mess', sketched by Mary Harrison:

'For breakfast, sausage with baked beans,
For dinner, camouflaged with "greens",
For tea, it finds itself in batter,
By supper – Oh, it doesn't matter.
The Eternal Sausage.'

STEREO PAIR — 60%
OVERLAP.

4 A cartoon, 'Stereo Pair – 60% Overlap', drawn by Flight Lieutenant Julian Phipps, a PI at RAF Medmenham.

5 Camera loading into a PR Spitfire painted in distinctive 'Camotint' colour. A re-enactment in 2011.

6 Above left: The Wild A-5 stereo-comparator, used for calculating exact measurements.

7 Above right: 'WAAF Methods of Travel':

'I wonder if you've ever tried
When going for a lorry ride
To climb into it "dignified"
I did and darned near died.'

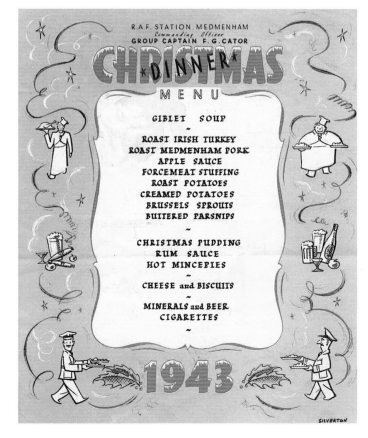

8 Right: The Christmas dinner menu 1943, at RAF Medmenham.

9 Pantomime programme for a production at RAF Medmenham.

10 Section Officer Diana Byron (Cussons), who worked in Second Phase.

11 'WAAF on Parade', illustrating the inconvenience caused by a broken suspender.

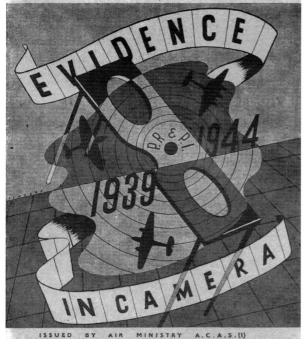

12 *Evidence in Camera* booklet. Produced weekly, it selectively publicised some of the best reconnaissance photographs taken during the war.

13 & 14 An imaginative programme design for the revue *Out of the Blue*, which had an all-female cast.

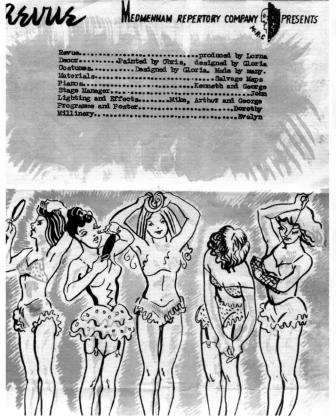

15 Above: A V-1 flying bomb in flight, otherwise known as a Doodlebug.

16 Right: The Medmenham Club was formed in 1946 'to preserve wartime friendships'. The lynx at the centre of the crest represents the keen-sightedness of the photographic interpreter.

17 An aerial view of Danesfield House in 2000, under reconstruction, showing the extent of the grounds and its proximity to the river.

18 Pat Peat (O'Neil) at home in Maryland, USA, in
August 2009, displaying her sketch of Studley Priory
in Oxfordshire, drawn in 1945 before she sailed
home for demobilisation.

19 Margaret Price (Hurley) and Xavier Atencio,
a 'Disney Legend', were both PIs at RAF
Medmenham. They met again in California, USA, in
December 2010.

20 A Medmenham Club reunion in the gardens of Danesfield House Hotel, August 2010. Len
Chance (a PI at Wembley and Medmenham), Suzie Morrison (Morgan), Hazel Furney (Scott), Myra
Murden (Collyer), Lavender Bruce (Westwood) and Elizabeth Johnston-Smith (Hick).

Telephonists at the RAF
Medmenham and RAF Nuneham
Park exchanges linked the
many sections of the stations.

After plotting, the photographs were passed to the PIs for examination and analysis, and then filed in the print library where 2½ miles of shelves were stacked with many boxes of photographs, ready to be retrieved for comparison purposes at any time.

The WAAF largely staffed the Library, Signals, Communications and Typing Sections. The teleprinter operators were the essential link in co-ordinating the work of the interpreters at Medmenham and the reconnaissance operational sorties, the teleprinter being the means by which an immediate signal could be sent with the highest priority. The telephonists who manually connected over 300 extensions on the switchboards also played a vital part in linking all the different sections at Medmenham and Nuneham Park. The typing pool frequently had to tackle reports from sections that ran into many pages. One, when completed, covered over 37ft of manuscript. Fine weather meant the typists faced an in-tray overflowing with top-secret and priority jobs and an average of 100 copies of each report to be rolled off the duplicators. Filing clerks ensured that papers and photographs were kept efficiently to ensure quick retrieval. All these essential support services relied on the accuracy and efficiency of the WAAFs who operated them and by all accounts they did an excellent job.

When the Press and Publicity Section, 'J', was formed in May 1940, its function was to select suitable material for the press and for exhibitions. Photographs of a spectacular or topical nature were chosen from current sorties being flown if they were thought suitable for reproduction in the daily newspapers and weekly magazines. These provided a great boost to wartime civilian morale in Britain

Shirley Eadon in the Press and Publicity Section prepares photographic material for inclusion in *Evidence in Camera*.

and overseas – and if some photographs did find their way into enemy territory they would provide encouragement to the people of occupied lands and excellent propaganda for the Allied cause. In some cases where good comparison could be made it was possible to provide the press with 'before and after' photographs of raids. There were also numerous requests for photographs to illustrate books, pamphlets and government publications.

Margaret Price had an unexpected beginning to her war. Her husband had already joined the RAF and on 1 September 1939 four little girls aged 6 and a helper arrived at her house:

> They were from the Royal Soldier's Home in Hampstead – my evacuees. After ten months they left to join all the other children from the Home and I decided to join the WAAF and was posted to HQ Coastal Command in Northwood to be a teleprinter operator.
>
> Ten months later I applied for, and passed, the PI course then joined 'J' Section at Medmenham. I also became assistant entertainments officer in my spare time. My husband of seven years was killed in early 1942 – he was training to be a night fighter navigator. [9]

One aspect of Margaret's work was to select the photographs for albums covering important and interesting incidents of the 'Air War'. These were prepared at intervals for special presentation to His Majesty the King; Prime Minister Winston Churchill; the Chief of the Air Staff; the Secretary of State for Air; and Mr John Winant, the US ambassador to Great Britain.

One of the most remarkable and successful publications of the Second World War was called *Evidence in Camera*, which was a legal term for testimony given in secret, and an appropriate title for a magazine that provided confirmation by photographs taken covertly. Although it may seem contradictory for a secret establishment such as the ACIU to publish a magazine full of operational photographs, it had the lowest security category of 'Restricted' and fulfilled a valuable purpose. Shirley Eadon explained how it came into existence:

> I was posted to Medmenham in 1942 with several others after passing my PI course. The officers' mess was an enormous Nissen hut like Paddington Station and that was where we were sorted out to work in the various sections and I ended up in 'J'. Group Captain Peter Stewart was the station commander – he was a rebel, wickedly mischievous and great fun. His greatest wish was to produce a weekly publication of some of the brilliant photographs taken by reconnaissance pilots flying solo and unarmed. Their results were seen by so few and he wanted more people to see these marvellous photographs. At that time the Air Ministry issued a dreary document – AMWIS – 'Air Ministry Weekly Intelligence Summary'. It had a dark red cover, no illustrations and very few readers among the aircrews of Bomber Command for whom it was intended.[10]

Constance Babington Smith relates how Group Captain Stewart first got the idea for a picture magazine. Visiting HQ Bomber Command one day, he sat for a while after lunch in the anteroom:

> He glanced idly round the room, and then suddenly caught his breath. He had just noticed that Air Vice-Marshal Saundby was deep in the 'Illustrated London News' and that all round the room the picture magazines and the illustrated papers were being looked at, while most of the other papers were lying untouched. What photographic intelligence needed was promotion. The raw material was flowing in every day; all that was wanted was the right presentation to make it really interesting.[11]

Shirley continues:

> Peter Stewart pushed things along relentlessly against much murmuring and dire prophecy of breach of security from higher quarters. We pressed on and produced a mock up of No. 1 Evidence in Camera in an attractive blue cover designed by one of the many artists on the station and containing full page photographs and brief captions.[12]

The mock-up of the proposed magazine was sent to the chief of the Air Staff, who replied, 'Excellent. Proceed':

> Eventually, in September 1942 we produced and circulated the first edition, the printers generously carrying the cost – it was a member of the printing firm who chose the title. So, with a touch of individuality and dash, characteristic of many another Air Force operation, the first number was launched from the banks of the Thames, like a new missile.

Copies were distributed to all RAF establishments and a number of naval and military units. It was an immediate success and there could be no withdrawal. The Air Ministry took over financial responsibility and 'Evidence in Camera' became an official publication showing selected air photographs taken on operations by the combined Allied Air Forces and aimed at the pilots. Each week the publication had a different cover design and cartoon frontispiece.

Winston Churchill obviously inspected it from time to time and reprimanded us on one occasion for using the German word Muenchen in a caption instead of Munich. Quite rightly I think.

The co-editors, Flight Lieutenant Howard Simmons (head of section) and me, Section Officer Shirley Eadon, remained unchanged throughout until it came to a close in March 1945. I feel really lucky having had such a wonderful job.

Shirley described RAF Medmenham as a 'bunch of nuts' – they were all distinctive characters and individualists. She recalled that Charlotte Bonham Carter, carrying her trademark umbrella and breakfast remnants, used to take a shortcut to work across the playing fields to avoid having to walk up the long drive. One day the groundsman confronted her and told her that she was wearing out the grass. Charlotte replied that she paid her RAF Medmenham station sports' subscription but never played games, so walking on the grass was the way she got value for her expenditure.

The possibility of enemy gas attacks on civilians was one of the earliest concerns of the British authorities, stemming from the terrible effects of the use of gas in the First World War. It was believed that the enemy could release gas in some form from aircraft over the civilian population. Consequently, at the outbreak of war everyone was issued with a gas mask in a case, which had to be carried at all times no matter where the individual was. Gas tests were part of basic training for armed forces personnel, followed by regular practices.

The procedure was that a group went into a sealed room and put their gas capes and masks on, after which a gas pellet was released and the order was given to remove masks. The occupants had to hold their breath and move outside in an orderly fashion to the fresh air where everyone did lots of coughing. Pamela Howie disliked the practice as it brought on her asthma. Pat Peat had a nastier experience during a test when she was hidden behind a tall man in the sealed room and the pellet was released before she had her mask on correctly. As a result of the gas spraying her face she lost her sight for six months and spent that time in hospital having autohaemotherapy – fortunately she recovered.

The gas practices at Medmenham were carried out monthly at 8.30 a.m. on a Saturday morning. Squadron Leader Geoffrey Dimbleby was responsible for observing and checking that everything went according to plan on these practices and that all personnel conformed to the rules. On one occasion he saw what appeared to be an animated gas cape making its way across the parade ground, when everyone was supposed to be in the shelters. He wondered who it was, and then saw that it was carrying a little wicker shopping basket!

8

A New Purpose for Photography

The Bombers

Whenever I see them ride on high
Gleaming and proud in the morning sky
Or lying awake in bed at night
I hear them pass on their outward flight
I feel the mass of metal and guns
Delicate instruments, deadweight tons
Awkward, slow, bomb racks full
Straining away from the downward pull
Straining away from home and base
And I try to see the pilot's face.
I imagine a boy who's just left school
On whose quick-learnt skill and courage cool
Depend the lives of the men in his crew
And success of the job they have to do.
And something happens to me inside
That is deeper than grief, greater than pride
And though there is nothing I can say
I always look up as they go their way
And care and pray for every one,
And steel my heart to say,
'Thy will be done'.[1]

Sixty-three minutes after war was declared, a Blenheim reconnaissance aircraft and a small bomber force took off from RAF Wyton in Cambridgeshire to carry out Bomber Command's first photographic sortie of the Second World War. The Blenheim was the first British aircraft of the war to cross the German coast. The brief was to confirm the location of enemy warships north of Wilhelmshaven, which had been photographed the day before by one of Sidney Cotton's pilots. The aircraft returned 4 hours later with excellent quality photographs confirming the numbers and location of the ships. The subsequent loss rate of the Blenheims, however, when carrying out further photographic sorties from Wyton, and later in France, proved conclusively that they were too slow and unresponsive for effective reconnaissance purposes.

The Air Ministry turned to Sidney Cotton, and the Heston Special Flight was quickly formed. Using the fast, manoeuvrable Spitfires for reconnaissance sorties enabled pilots to reach the target in the shortest possible time, take the required photographs and out-fly enemy aircraft on returning to base. Although the photography the Spitfires brought back was small scale and could not be examined with the conventional apparatus available at that time, the single Wild A-5 survey machine at the Aircraft Operating Company was able to exploit it and Wembley soon became the central point for photographic interpretation services. HQ Bomber Command retained its own separate Interpretation Section, however, and the first female PIs of the Second World War, who had been recruited and trained at Heston, moved there and soon afterwards were enrolled into the WAAF. They were soon to be involved in a contentious interpretation event that was, unfortunately, the forerunner of other similar incidents.

Early bombing strategies were an inexact science, lacking the advantages of the navigational aids and target sighting devices that improved accuracy later on. A few hours after a bombing raid, a reconnaissance aircraft flew over the area and the photographs obtained were analysed to establish the accuracy of the bomber's navigation to the target area, and the overall effectiveness of the raid in achieving strategic target bombing priorities. The difficulties experienced in achieving accurate navigation, the camouflage and decoys that could mislead air crews, and the enemy ground and air defences, often resulted in bombs missing the target by a wide margin, and sometimes being dropped in the wrong area altogether.

During the six months of the so-called Phoney War, when President Roosevelt's bombing truce prevented any bombing on mainland Europe, only one British attack took place on German territory. In March 1940 Bomber Command was ordered to carry out a reprisal raid for a German attack a few days earlier on Royal Navy vessels at anchor in Scapa Flow, in the Orkney Islands. During that attack, enemy bombs had been dropped on land, killing one civilian and wounding seven others. On 19–20 March, forty British bombers attacked the chosen target of Hornum, a seaplane base on the German island of Sylt. The air crews returned from the raid reporting a completely successful operation, and an overjoyed government and press immediately publicised the total destruction of the enemy base. However, when the post-attack photographs were examined at Bomber Command a few hours later, the PIs could find no sign of damage and not even one bomb crater. The reaction was total disbelief by all those who, understandably, needed to show that Britain had the capacity to inflict damage on the enemy. After all, the air crew had reported having seen the bombs falling, followed by

Stella Ogle and an RAF colleague at Pinetree assess the extent of bomb damage after a raid.

fires and widespread damage and surely that was proof enough. Some reports state that orders were then given that the PIs be locked in their room with the photographs until they did 'find' the claimed destruction. The press were clamouring for photographs but the report remained the same – no bomb damage was to be seen. Even after PIs at the Air Ministry confirmed their colleagues' reports, the recriminations and anger against them continued. It was not until a further photographic sortie was flown several days later, and the new photographs analysed, that it was found that the bombs had fallen on a Danish island many miles away and the actual target had been missed completely.[2]

Stella Ogle, a WAAF officer at Bomber Command, wrote:

We were constantly being pressurized by the Station Commander to publish glowing reports of glorious successes. If the interpreters found no trace of damage or craters, they were accused of minimising the results, and our unfortunate officer in charge received hell – no one believed our reports, and our reputation was nil. The worst of it was, so often no damage existed, and bomber crews had to be told the truth. Can you imagine our feelings?

To begin with, they hated taking night photographs as operating the cameras meant just one more headache during a period of great danger, and they always had the thought of carrying with them in the aircraft a large amount of flammable material in the form of film, which they would be unable to discharge in an emergency. The photographic flash was the responsibility of the bomb aimer, and the method of launching the flash was primitive. They might have to consult outdated maps of, for example, miles and miles of featureless Dutch polder-country made up of interminable canals, and trace their position by some group of willows, or a kink in a dyke, and desperately try to plot craters by the bomb flashes. Half the time they

were lost, as navigational aids and bomb aiming devices were of the crudest. It was
tragic when they managed to stagger back with dead or wounded only to be told
that they had been nowhere near the target by what they considered to be a bunch
of idiots. We longed to be able to see successful results and hear their relieved and
excited remarks.[3]

In September 1941 the small group of male and female interpreters who worked
at HQ Bomber Command moved to RAF Medmenham to set up a new Third-
Phase Damage Assessment Section, which was identified by the letter 'K'. Its
function was to identify, assess and calculate the extent of the damage caused to
the enemy by each bombing raid. Subsidiary to this was assistance in establishing
the accuracy of navigation of the aircraft and assessment of the disruption caused
to German industrial output permanently or temporarily. Even a short-term clo-
sure was worthwhile if it disrupted the production of essential equipment. The
Industry Section, which monitored manufacturing rates of output, was also supplied with an accurate appraisal of the time required for the enemy to restore
normal production.

Stella Ogle and Pat Donald met on their PI training course and joined 'K'
Section together, remaining life-long friends. Pat said:

> I had done a secretarial course before joining the WAAF in 1941. After basic training
> I was posted as a clerk (general duties) to RAF Kinloss, a Coastal Command station
> on the Moray Firth, in Scotland. I was then posted to RAF Medmenham as a clerk/
> typist and fell foul of an obnoxious WAAF corporal who once put me on a charge
> for being late on duty. However, soon afterwards I was recommended for a commis-
> sion and PI training and was quietly pleased to note that the corporal remained a
> corporal![4]

The Damage Assessment Section took over a large first-floor room in one of the
towers of Danesfield House; two large bay windows gave them plentiful light and
provided splendid views of the gardens and river. American PIs joined the Section
in 1942, giving a welcome boost to numbers as the bombing campaign intensified.

Allied bombing was used as a strategic weapon aimed at the total destruction
of the enemy's means of production on the one hand, and of their cities and
population morale on the other. By the spring of 1942, the British build-up of
large numbers of bombers and the development of longer-range aircraft marked
the start of increased-scale raids over specific industrial targets, especially in the
Ruhr and in major strategic cities. From August 1942, when the American heavy
bombers joined the bombing campaign, the US 8th Air Force attacked by day and
the RAF raids continued at night. New navigational electronic guidance devices
began to help in attaining greater accuracy in reaching and destroying targets.

PI played a significant part in each phase of an operation. In the planning phase
all sources of intelligence would be used, including air photography from an

A post-attack photograph of a raid on Cologne, 28 October 1944, shows smoke from areas still burning and the extent of the burnt-out buildings.

increased number of reconnaissance flights. The interpretation of these photographs could result in reports from several different PI sections at Medmenham, all providing intelligence for effective planning. Air photographs were also used in the targeting material essential for exact navigation by bomber air crews. Photography taken during and after the attack would show if the navigation was accurate, if the bombing objective had been achieved and would show the extent of the disruption caused.

In May 1944 the Damage Assessment Section moved to High Wycombe Air Station, code-named Pinetree, to join the HQ USAAF 8th Bomber Command. This relocation provided greater space, availability of photographic materials and numbers of personnel. Pinetree was based in Wycombe Abbey, which had been a private girls' school until it was commandeered in 1942. The premises reputedly caused some hilarity among the incoming US personnel who found various instructions, designed for the recently evacuated girl pupils, still stuck to the dormitory walls, one of which stated: 'Ring if mistress required.' The British PIs at Pinetree became part of a US unit under the command of an American officer, with the same friendly co-operation prevailing between the different nationalities working together as there was at Medmenham. While the US personnel at Medmenham had to endure British food rationing, the British PIs benefited perhaps from getting American-style rations. Pat recalled:

> I was amazed at the amount of food available at 'Pinetree' and resented any complaints of British food by US personnel. There was always chicken and ice cream served on Sundays. I remember that the Carol Gibbons Orchestra and the Glenn Miller Band came to play.

From the beginning of the British bombing campaign in 1940, cameras were installed in aircraft on daylight raids in order to bring back a record of where their bombs had fallen. Constance Babington Smith wrote of the long-standing attitude towards photography in Bomber Command:

> Photographs were considered as a useful adjunct to bombing, but not a vital necessity. The camera was regarded somewhat as a motorist regards his mileage gauge. It's nice to know how far you've been, and sometimes very useful too. But you certainly do not expect your mileage gauge to turn round and accuse you of having lost your way almost every time you've been out. When the photographs began to do precisely this, it was very natural that many of those whose work it affected jumped to the comforting conclusion that something must have been wrong with the camera or the photographs or the man who wrote the report.[5]

When the RAF switched to night-bombing, a new technique was needed to obtain a similar record of where bombs had been dropped in the darkness; one of the leading pioneers in this field was Constance's brother, Bernard Babington Smith. For many months he worked on the principles of this new branch of interpretation. Constance wrote:

> He used to explain to me that any lights which showed in the darkness below the camera while the shutter was open appear on the photographs as streaks, because the exposure was often as long as five seconds. And unless the aircraft were flying straight and level the streaks would naturally undulate according to its movement – in other words they were an exact record of all the manoeuvres it had made. They were also, of course, a record of the many different kinds of light that go with an air attack: the fires and the bomb flames: and also the tracer, the heavy flak and the searchlights of

the defences. But Bernard did not confine his analysis to individual photographs: he soon became interested in working out the relationship between photographs taken by several bombers on the same raid, allowing for the different headings and evasive actions of each, so as to calculate the progress of the fires on the ground.

Early in 1942, the Night Photography Section, 'N', was formed at Medmenham, with Bernard as head of section, to carry out the detailed interpretation of the photographs taken by the night bombers themselves. It was housed in one of the recently erected huts and one of the first PIs to join the Section in February 1942 was Assistant Section Officer Lady Dorothy Lygon. Always known as 'Coote', she was described as forthright, with a quick intelligence and sense of fun. She was a close friend of Evelyn Waugh, the author, and devoted companion of Dorothy's beautiful sister Mary, who had been photographed by Ursula Powys-Lybbe before the war. 'Coote' herself was plain and wore thick-lensed glasses, having been very short-sighted from childhood. This raises the interesting question of how someone with such seemingly poor eyesight qualified for a job that entailed spending a 12-hour shift looking at minute objects through a stereoscope. Douglas Kendall, in charge of all PIs at Medmenham, wrote:

> One of the prime requirements of a PI was excellent eyesight and we kept a well known eye surgeon at Medmenham to deal with the eye strain associated with the job. Curiously enough, although the interpreters spent many hours per day with their eyes glued to stereoscopes, their eyesight, far from deteriorating, improved.[6]

The muscles of the eye become more efficient with regular exercise, and this was provided by daily use of a stereoscope. Several other wartime PIs found that they could throw away their spectacles and photographs of 'Coote' later in the war show her without glasses.

Elizabeth Johnston-Smith worked in the Camouflage Section for some months and heard that there was a section concerned with night photography. She was interested and approached Bernard Babington Smith and soon joined 'N':

> This was in 1943 and by that time all the night bombers were equipped with cameras on board which worked on an open shutter principle. Earlier on, not all aircraft had cameras – only the most efficient crews carried them and there were large discrepancies between the films and the claims made by the aircrews. Bomber Command was concerned and Winston Churchill tasked Professor Lindeman (the Prime Minister's Chief Scientific Adviser) to look at the problem and new navigational aids such as Gee, Oboe and H2S were introduced. The creation of the Pathfinder Force (PFF) was very valuable as they used target indicators to guide the bomber force to the target.
>
> At Medmenham we got all the films of the raids from Bomber Command – they came to us in metal canisters. Bernard allocated a raid to each one of us to work

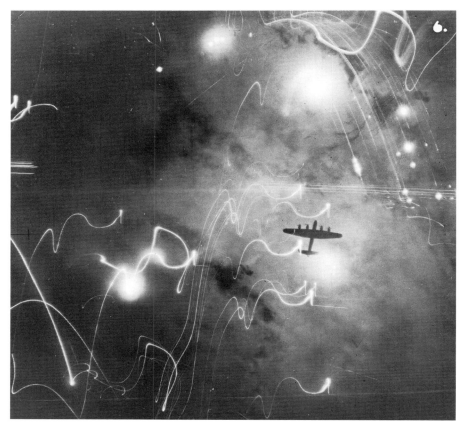

A night photograph of Hamburg taken during a raid on 31 January 1943. The different markings of light denote fires, flares, searchlights and anti-aircraft fire from which the overall progress and accuracy of the raid could be determined. A Lancaster bomber flies below the aircraft taking the photograph.

through and from that we could work out how the operation had progressed. You saw on the films the run-in, and on the first frame you could see the marker flares that were dropped, then on the next frame, which was a bombing frame, you got the photo flash which was supposed to coincide with the bomb drop. This didn't always happen because the bombs dropped later than the photo flash went off, but in many cases from the photo flash and the bomb flame you could pick up ground detail and this was very valuable because you could then start to plot where that particular aircraft had been.

From the films from other aircraft in the raid you could link up a whole pattern of the incendiary drop and the subsequent fire patterns and how the high explosives went. Then from the ground detail you could work out how the whole raid progressed. The frame that followed on from the bombing sequence was useful because apart from the evasive action which the aircraft took, that picked up search lights,

Jean Fotheringham and Loyalty Howard organise the cans containing the film from one night-bombing raid for interpretation.

flak, tracer, decoys, smoke screens and high explosive bombs – not particularly of that aircraft but maybe of others. So, as you gained more information from the films, you had a whole big trace and you could work out exactly where each aircraft had been. These were sent to Group HQ and then to Bomber Command.[7]

Elizabeth mentions the new electronic navigational aids devised and the Pathfinder Force formed to fly over the target and drop brightly coloured indicators to guide the following bomber aircraft to the correct position for bombing. By using colour film in conjunction with black and white when filming the raid, PIs were able to differentiate between normal and incendiary fires and detect decoy fires.

Decoys, often large and ingenious, were used to deflect navigators in the bombers from the correct route to their target. Navigators relied on visual landmarks that marked a particular point on their maps, and water was the most effective because it reflected light in total darkness. Flight Officer Loyalty Howard had noticed that bombs destined for the Krupps Works at Essen in the Ruhr were consistently dropping 6 miles from the target. She studied many comparative sorties and found that a whole lake had been drained by the enemy and instead of using this as a visual landmark for Essen, the navigators had been duped into using a bend in the river which was 6 miles away and this was the reason for missing the target.

Loyalty Howard was a geographer and a WAAF operations room plotter through the Battle of Britain before coming as a PI to Medmenham. In a unit where women did exactly the same job as the men, Loyalty was a respected second-in-command of 'N' Section. An RAF colleague in 'N' recalls that of all the many high-level military officers who visited the Section for information, only one, Field Marshal Jan Smuts, the Prime Minister of South Africa, spoke patronisingly to her.

Cloud is the enemy of the reconnaissance pilot and the photographic interpreter. Surprisingly, the average annual number of absolutely clear days across the whole of Europe is just thirty. Elizabeth described another innovation:

Pam Mitchell, Elizabeth Johnston-Smith and Loyalty Howard worked in the Night Photography Section.

There was often ten tenths cloud over the target making it impossible to distinguish if the bombing was accurate. Bernard worked out a way of plotting on cloud patterns so that with just the smallest glimpse of ground detail below it was possible to fix the location. It all related to how quickly the clouds were moving and the speed of the aircraft and proved successful.

Susan Bendon carried out First-Phase interpretation:

I was posted to the Photographic Intelligence (PI) unit at Bomber Command Headquarters, a vast underground garrison hidden in the beech woods at Speen, near High Wycombe. Our small PI area was adjacent to the much larger intelligence area where numerous personnel were always on duty. We were visited by many of the grandees of the day, among them famous scientists and inventors. Frank Whittle, inventor of the jet engine, came one day soon after I arrived there, was interested in my work and took time to tell me about his. At the end of our talk I gave him my considered opinion, which was that I doubted whether a jet engine would ever be realised!

Our work was to report on the results of bombing raids on Germany. There were cameras installed in bomber aircraft which, visibility allowing, photographed the ground far beneath as each bomb was released. The results of the early bombing raids on Germany up to 1941 had been disastrous, targets rarely being hit and the loss of aircraft was huge. A Pathfinder Force (PFF) was formed to overcome these catastrophes. Equipped with highly sophisticated electronic equipment, by flying in advance of the bombers and planting brilliant flares right on the target, their purpose was to enable the bombers to drop their bombs spot on, regardless of poor weather conditions. In February 1943 H2S Radar, a means of 'seeing' through blackness, became available and this further improved the success of PFF's operations.

From May to August 1942 there were frequent 1,000-bomber raids mainly to the industrial area of the Ruhr, our principal target area, where the majority of Germany's ammunitions were produced, principally at the vast Krupps factories.

Susan Bendon worked in the underground headquarters of Bomber Command near High Wycombe.

PFF was led by a dashing Australian, Group Captain Donald Bennett, later pro-moted to Air Vice Marshal. Although acknowledged within the RAF as a spectacular advance in tactics, many at Bomber Command were wary of Bennett's boasts after almost every sortie, that his squadron's flares had been dropped bang on target. Reports from underground intelligence forces operating in Germany, sent to head-quarters by devious, secret means, usually came through about a week or ten days after a raid and occasionally cast doubts on Bennett's claims.

In PI over the years of reviewing aerial photographs of German territory, one became totally conversant with its 'design' – from a height of around 30,000 feet, looking down, the ground resembles a patchwork quilt, every field being a specific stripe or rectangle and it seemed that through sheer familiarity I was able to recog-nise the patterns of the vast Ruhr area like the back of my hand.

There were usually only two or three of us on duty in PI and every morning after a raid, at around 5 am, Air Chief Marshal Arthur Harris, the head of Bomber Command, would phone in for a report on the night's results, as by then the bombers would have returned and both their and the PFF photographs would have been rushed by motor bike to us, the latter from their base in RAF Wyton in Cambridgeshire. There was always tremendous haste to view them under the stereo-scopes we used to give a three-dimensional view of the ground.

One night, in spite of the weather men telling everyone that conditions over the Ruhr were 'ten-tenths cloud' a 1,000-bomber raid on Essen went ahead, relying on the Pathfinder's skills to achieve the desired results. As usual we received the photographs in the early hours – there used to be hundreds of them – and they were all completely black, just solid midnight cloud. Towards the end, having all but given up, in the corner of one I spotted some miniscule stripes, all together far less than a quarter of an inch across. Something made me pause and enlarge them – they could easily have been scratches on the photographic paper but somehow they rang a chord. In those days I did have a so-called 'photographic memory' and there was a hint of familiarity about them. Frantically I started to go through the hundreds of reference photos that formed our 'maps' of the Ruhr and eventually, Eureka! – I matched them to an area just outside a tiny village, 15 miles east of Essen. When 'Bomber' Harris phoned I told him exactly that. Simultaneously, Bennett's report came through that his flares had been 'bang on target'. Then all hell broke loose.

One must remember that this was a frenetic, desperate time for everyone involved in the war – the crews were used to so many of their comrades being shot down over enemy territory night after night and almost every one of them left letters for their nearest and dearest, to be sent in the event of their non-return. Bennett went berserk when he got wind of my report and although he had been on duty throughout the night, he instantly rushed from his base at Wyton to Command HQ to seek out the idiot who had reported such nonsense to Harris.

He came into our sub-basement unit where he found me and would have torn me limb from limb – his six-foot-plus towered over me, he beat the air (would have done so to me had I not by that point been surrounded by several officers from

WAAF and civilian draughtswomen produced target maps for Bomber Command at nearby Hughenden Manor. Kathlyn Williams is second from right.

Intelligence), screamed at me and reduced me to floods of tears – I too had been on duty for about 20 hours which was normal for that time – it was dreadful, but one did feel a little for him in his anguish.

About ten days later, underground intelligence reports filtered through and confirmed that on the night in question, 1,000 bombers had dropped their entire bomb loads in the middle of fields, 15 miles east of Essen.

Bomber Harris was an exceptionally powerful man – his ruthless wartime tactics, the devastation they caused in Germany – Dresden, Hamburg, Berlin and so on and the hundreds of thousands of civilians killed in those raids – are criticised to this day. He did not like Bennett anyway, thought him too pleased with himself, and he would not tolerate a member of his staff being humiliated by such a vain bully. And so the very last thing in the world I would ever have wished for occurred.

Harris summoned Bennett to the Intelligence department and, in front of the entire department plus many others who sensed there was some sport brewing, made him unreservedly make a deep, supposedly humble apology to me. It was excruciating to observe the ridiculous 'theatre' being performed, to see Bennett being humiliated in that way and I simply did not know where to look or what to do. But that was Harris's way of 'encouraging the others', making sure that no-one messed with his inner team.[8]

In October 1941, about 100 RAF, WAAF and civilian personnel with their commanding officer, Major Quaife of the Royal Engineers, moved into another requisitioned red-brick Victorian mansion sited on the brow of a hill overlooking the beautiful Chiltern countryside. This was Hughenden Manor, the country home of the nineteenth-century Prime Minister Benjamin Disraeli, and its wartime purpose was to provide a secret, secluded unit for the production of targeting maps, graphics and other briefing materials for bomber air crews carrying out raids over enemy and occupied Europe. The unit was code-named Hillside, and it was conveniently situated about 10 miles from Medmenham, from where it received air photographs; 4 miles from Bomber Command at High Wycombe where the completed maps were sent to; and equally close to HQ 8th USAAF at Wycombe Abbey.

Precise navigation was essential to ensure the effective bombing of a target. The target folders and briefings handed out to bomber air crews before each mission started contained all navigational information available to reach the target area, the identification of the actual target and the return flight. Maps and photographic illustrations were of great importance to this process. Reconnaissance sorties would have been flown by aircraft from RAF Benson and other PRUs to photograph the route to the target, the approach to the area and the target itself. Interpretation reports from Medmenham could include input from several sections to ensure the most up-to-date information was provided for air crews, for instance if new enemy defensive flak positions had recently been identified on the bombers' route in and out. Mosaics (photographic maps) were produced and details of any decoy site designed to lead the attacking force astray from the target were included. All available recognition data on the target and a target map showing the bomb-aiming points were included in the target folders.

The RAF and WAAF personnel at Hillside produced these target maps for Bomber Command. Most of the men and women had drawing, art or design in common. Kathlyn Williams was one of those who, having joined the WAAF in her home town of Gloucester, was sent to the Royal Engineers unit at Ruabon in North Wales to train as a cartographical draughtswoman. She joined the half dozen or so map-making WAAFs at Hillside and described how they worked:

> We came in past the police post in the Entrance Hall – they knew all of us but we still had to show our passes. Then to our own workroom (originally this had been the drawing room) where we worked in silence, painting on 'Kodafoil' with a brush and a large jar of water to hand. We had to get it right – we were told to be accurate to 'within a hair's breadth'. We painted using ox-blood and had to remember to cover it over when we went to lunch otherwise it would be smothered in flies when we returned.[9]

The 'Kodafoil' that Kathlyn refers to was Kodak Bromide Foil-Card, which had a thin layer of aluminium foil sandwiched between two sheets of lightweight photographic paper. It was stable and used where a very high degree of dimensional accuracy was required, such as the draughtswomen's instruction to draw 'within a hair's breadth'. Cartographical modifications and additions could be made to it by hand using pencil, ink or a brush.[10]

Another WAAF remembers that in 1942 they prepared target maps for the beginning of the 1,000-bomber raids, which led to the loss of many lives and devastation: 'It contrasted with the tranquil setting of Hillside.' Only one bomb fell near Hillside, destroying the Disraeli window in Hughenden church.[11]

ATS women Joan Bohey and Barbara Chandler assisted the WAAFs at Hillside in 1945 by working on target maps at Medmenham. Joan explained:

> The maps covered an area of 15 miles around the target and were painted as a picture the pilot would see in moonlight as he approached. Trees and woods were painted black, bushes were stippled grey, roads, hard surfaces and still water (canals) were painted white and moving water stippled white. The target was painted orange.[12]

When the target maps were completed they were delivered to Bomber Command and then sent on to the relevant RAF bomber stations for briefing purposes and included in the target folder for each aircraft flying in the raid.

Kathlyn Williams recorded that:

> At the end of the war we were invited on a trip in a Halifax bomber to see the results of our work. We all piled into a lorry and were driven to RAF Waterbeach in

A WAAF map clerk issues target maps and material to air crew (plus a dog) before the Dambusters Raid on 16 May 1943.

Cambridgeshire where we were given fish and chips for lunch. We were briefed and given enormous parachute packs, then staggered out with them with bandy legs to the plane, but we were not told how to use them. We were told however that sick-bags should only be emptied over water. Another WAAF and I found ourselves in the nose of the Halifax lying among the wires. The weather forecast was good and as we flew we saw fluffy clouds and got glimpses of chateaux and gardens down below. First we were taken to the Moehne Dam to see where it had been breached, then to Cologne where the roof of the cathedral was intact but chaos all around. Then we turned for Holland where whole farms and villages were submerged and at Dunkirk we could still see the bomb craters in the sand. It was uncanny and we returned to Waterbeach with mixed feelings.[13]

What were the thoughts of the different groups of women who worked every day on material designed to ensure greater accuracy of bombing the enemy, who prepared the maps the bomber pilots would use on attacks, or who saw through a stereoscope the effects of a 1,000-bomber raid on a city? Pat Donald, while working in the Damage Assessment Section, remembers seeing the photographs taken after the breaching of the Ruhr dams in May 1943 when millions of tons of water poured through the holes blown in the Moehne and Eder dams. While realising the necessity of the raid in disrupting the enemy output of materials for the manufacture of armaments, she and Stella Ogle voiced their misgivings to each other about the loss of so many civilian lives in the valley below. The head of the Model Section recalled the sadness felt by model makers at the loss of women and children in the farmsteads that they had recently fashioned. Personnel from all sections at Medmenham were instructed to visit 'K' Section to view the spectacular dams photographs. This seems to have been the only occasion when PIs viewed photographs in a section other than their own. Elspeth Macalister, a plotter, remembered:

One of the most exciting nights of my life was after the bombing of the Moehne and Eder Dams by Guy Gibson and his Dambusters. I was on duty when the photos came in that night and we had all the top brass standing round our tables and pinching the photos we were trying to plot.[14]

Sarah Churchill worked in the Damage Assessment Section for some months in 1943 prior to accompanying her father to Teheran for the conference between himself, President Roosevelt and Marshal Stalin. Throughout the negotiations, Stalin pushed hard for the USA and Britain to open a second front in Western Europe to relieve the pressure on Russia. The western nations were intent on pursuing their strategic-bombing operations to weaken German industrial output before embarking on an invasion. Sarah's time in 'K' Section undoubtedly affected her thoughts, for it was she who wrote the poem at the beginning of this chapter. Churchill himself visited Medmenham informally on many occasions to enquire about specific cover and got to know a lot about interpretation. On an official visit in 1943, accompanied by Mrs Churchill, PIs in each section were surprised to hear him clearly explain to her what could be seen on the photographs, showing a detailed knowledge of their subject and an appreciation of PI techniques.

When hostilities ended, several other women PIs were taken on flights over what had so recently been enemy territory. Susan Bendon wrote:

> The day after VE Day, on 9th May 1945, Squadron Leader Morris, who had been in charge of PI at Bomber Command throughout my time there, drove us to Elsham Wolds airfield in Lincolnshire where we were taken up in a Lancaster bomber. We were flown to the Ruhr so that we could actually view the territory we knew so well from photographs, exactly as experienced by the bomber crews.
>
> My years at Bomber Command were dramatic and hugely rewarding. We participated in momentous events including the bombing in May 1943 of the German Moehne and Eder Dams, when for days on end everyone was on duty, taking an occasional nap at the desk. The 'Dambusting' operation was made possible by the invention by Barnes Wallis of the bouncing bomb – he often came to our PI unit. The raid was led by Wing Commander Guy Gibson from RAF 5 Group and was an amazing success, causing catastrophic flooding of the Ruhr valley. I prepared an album of the entire sequence of the raids for King George VI and was Mentioned in Despatches. And finally, there was the invasion of Europe and the subsequent vast battles, in every one of which the bombers played a vital part.[15]

Kathlyn Williams, the WAAF from Hillside who had worked to produce accurate maps for bomber air crew, voiced her thoughts following her flight over Europe at the end of the war:

> With our paintbrushes we had helped to kill people we did not know. At one point I had considered becoming a conscientious objector. With every target, in my mind I had put my hands together and prayed that no children would be killed. In a discussion with a major from Sandhurst Military Academy, a kind and humane man, I was told

A photograph taken by a reconnaissance aircraft the day following the Dams Raid, showing the breach in the Moehne Dam with water flooding into the valley below.

that, 'You have to protect the things you believe in'. So I continued to paint. As a result I now have two medals and know there are facts of life I shall never understand.[16]

A model maker, Mary Harrison, was also troubled by her role in the bombing campaign and wrote a poem that is reproduced in the next chapter. Jane Cameron, the quiet, introspective Scot, wrote:

I have come to understand, I think, why the war years meant so little to me. I did not live those six years. They lived me.

We have the evidence of the pyramids, the works of Michelangelo, the music of Beethoven and many other things to prove that man is a constructive, creative animal and the creative instinct is the dominant one in any artist, however minor. Except for a few months, my war years were spent in the main Photographic Intelligence Unit. The earliest of these years were spent in gathering from aerial photographs information about every kind of enemy activity on the continent of Europe. Every shipyard, wireless station, railway yard, airfield, every installation of every kind was closely examined and recorded in minute detail with one end in view, their future total destruction. This work ran counter to my deepest instinct and instinctively, I think, I developed a resistance to it, a resistance of non-thought, a mental opting-out. I turned into a pair of keen-sighted eyes peering through a stereoscope at enemy-occupied territory and a hand holding a pen that recorded what the eyes saw.

When the war entered the phase of Allied attack, the protection afforded by non-thought became even more necessary, for we at the Unit were among the first to see on photographs the destruction of the Ruhr Valley by the floods of the broken Moehne and Eder dams, the ruins of Dresden and the liberated victims of Belsen, human beings reduced by beasts to bestiality.

When I was demobilised in the autumn of 1945, I went home to 'The Colony' for a short holiday and among the trees of the moor I faced the fact that I, in my small way, had been as bestial as the beasts of Belsen. I had been caught by the weather of the world and had let myself 'obey orders', just as the guards of the concentration camps had done. It was a sickening wounding experience in self-discovery and there was no comfort in the excuse that the Nazi will to destroy all that stood in its path could be overcome only by the destruction of Nazism. The fact remained that I had behaved counter to my deepest, and I think, my best instincts.

At that time in 1945, I could have put none of this into words. It seems to me now that I was in a state of shock for my only conscious need was to get away from my family, from everybody I knew and do something, anything that would occupy my mind in a constructive way. The desire to write had left me. This was my invisible war wound and it took a long time to heal.[17]

Many years after the war, Elizabeth Johnston-Smith and Pat Donald, the two youngest members of 'N' and 'K' Sections, considered that they 'just got on with the job in hand'. The Allied strategic urban bombing campaign and Air Chief Marshal Sir Arthur Harris will continue to be controversial subjects for many years to come and historical hindsight will attempt to provide acceptable alternatives. However, if Germany was to be defeated, it was considered necessary not only to destroy their industrial and armament capabilities, but civilian morale also. For the last nine months of the war enemy missiles were fired indiscriminately at the civilian population of Britain for that very reason. The air crews of Bomber Command, of whom nearly 55,000 were killed in action or died while prisoners of war, had done what was asked of them and had also 'just got on with the job'.

9

MOST SECRET

As Dorothy Garrod stared through the twin lenses of her stereoscope at images of a desert landscape, she must have recalled her days in Palestine some ten years previously when she had been searching for evidence of Neanderthal man. Now, in the autumn of 1942, she was searching the terrain of North Africa for signs of defences and obstructions that might impede the progress of an Allied amphibious invasion. Dorothy was working in a newly formed 'Most Secret' section at Medmenham called Combined Operations or 'R2'. This section was to be permanently engaged on the production of PI reports required for future commando operations, and later on small operational landings in France and Belgium.

By this time America had entered the war, bringing with it much-needed armament and manpower resources. The desperate days of 1940 and 1941, when Britain stood alone against the Axis domination of Europe, had become a time when the Allies could plan for a return to the enemy-occupied countries of Europe, and ultimately to Germany itself. The first Anglo-American operation of the war was to be an invasion of North Africa, with the prime objective of seizing the French colonies of Morocco, Algeria and Tunisia, then controlled by Vichy France, and so to deny these territories to the German Afrika Korps under the command of Field Marshal Rommel. A rapid eastward advance through Tunisia would follow, enabling the Allies to push enemy forces towards a planned joint pincer movement with the British Eighth Army, pursuing Rommel's troops westwards from Egypt. If successful it would push the German and Italian forces out of all the North African coastal countries for good and, with their departure, the Mediterranean Sea would be under Allied naval control, making the planned invasion of Sicily in 1943 an achievable objective.

The invasion of North Africa, code-named Operation Torch, was planned for 8 November 1942 under the leadership of US General Dwight D. Eisenhower. Time was short for all the preparations that had to be made and a huge amount of photographic intelligence material, essential for planning and briefing purposes, was needed. The numbers of special reconnaissance sorties immediately increased,

Cartoon of Combined Ops attempting to mend a broken world. While Lieutenant
Commander Philip Hayes checks its condition and Robin Orr takes notes, Sarah Churchill
applies a soothing hand and Dorothy Garrod prepares to remove an offending part.

intensive work was directed towards the production of maps and models of the
area, and interpretation reports on enemy dispositions and defences were ongoing.

When 'R2' was formed at RAF Medmenham in August 1942, Douglas Kendall
put together the small PI team responsible for producing most of this material. The
team was inter-Allied and inter-service with representatives from all three services,
including American and Canadian PIs. Head of section was Lieutenant Commander
Philip Hayes, a very tall, fair-haired Royal Navy officer. Two PIs from Second Phase
joined the team: Robert Bulmer, an architect in pre-war days and Robin Orr, an
organist and composer at St John's College, Cambridge. These two men had become
very experienced in carrying out detailed interpretation of pinpoint locations used
for landing agents on mainland Europe, and were to provide similar knowledge for
Allied commandos seizing key ports and airfields in North Africa.

Other members of the team included two Cambridge archaeologists, an actress
and American and Canadian army PIs. The archaeologists were Peter Murray
Threipland and Dorothy Garrod, both familiar with the patient searching necessary for examining the landing sites at Casablanca, Oran and Algiers. Terrain
models were built by the Model-Making Section and the area reports produced

by 'R2' showed the topography including details of roads, railways, ports, airfields and industries. Information on wireless telegraphy and direction-finding aerials, seen on air photographs, was aimed at the disruption or destruction of enemy communications. These reports were of considerable size and were fully illustrated, specifying every defensive aspect to be encountered.

Dorothy was described by friends as short and upright, wearing her thick, crisply wavy hair short. She was one of the two people at RAF Medmenham entitled to wear the General Service ribbon of the 1914–18 war on her tunic as she had been an ambulance driver in France for the last two years of that conflict. She gave an impression of controlled energy of mind and body, had a pleasant, quiet voice and even under pressure imparted an air of repose. In addition to her wartime experiences in France, she had travelled rough in remote places for archaeological digs in the 1920s. On her first dig in Palestine, her Arabic was fluent, her command absolute, and despite protests, she employed local women to dig the site because they worked harder than the men.[1] Glyn Daniel described Dorothy as easy to get on with: a generous, lovable, outgoing person who was interested in people. She enjoyed her work and the company of other staff at Medmenham, just as she had enjoyed the excavations before the war. Ann McKnight-Kauffer wrote:

> Did you ever go to one of the parties Dorothy Garrod gave in her hut with peaches from her Cambridge garden in an old pie dish from the Mess and sprinkled over with a liqueur brandy given by Charlotte Bonham-Carter? We passed the dish round and dipped in our teaspoons and told more and more funny stories. The prime one concerned a dig in Turkey which was diverted to Albania and involved the requisitioning, by mistake, of the Lunatic Asylum.[2]

The actress in the Combined Operations team was Sarah Churchill. In 2010 one of the Canadian army PIs on the team recalled her kindness:

> When I was stationed at Medmenham they organized a big dinner and dance weekend and I arranged for my wife to join me. (I met the love of my life on 28th June 1941 at the Palais de Dance in Kingston-on-Thames and we were married on 22nd August 1942 in Kingston.) Jean arrived by train on Friday evening but in her rush to greet me, left her suitcase on the train. It was never recovered and you can imagine our embarrassment arriving to check in at the Compleat Angler in Henley sans luggage! However, despite raised eyebrows, we managed. I informed Sarah of our predicament and she met us at the door of Medmenham and took Jean under her wing making her feel at home despite the loss of her best dress and high heels – impossible to replace in those times. Sarah was a great lady and did not deserve her later experiences.[3]

By the evening of 7 November 1942 the intense work and rush at Medmenham for Operation Torch was over and Sarah had 48 hours' leave to visit her parents:

Chequers was near enough for me to go over on my leaves. Sometimes, I would go on a borrowed army motorcycle – so heavy that I had to have a hand to get me started. Luckily, there were regular van deliveries between the three RAF stations in the area and I could hitchhike most of the way to Chequers. On arrival, I would normally go straight up to see my father as, being in uniform, I did not have to dress for dinner. On one special occasion he was in his bath, floating full length with an enormous sponge strategically placed.

'Come in, come in. What have you been up to?'

'Just the usual routine.'

'Ah.'

He yelled for Sawyers, his valet, who wrapped him in an enormous Turkish towel. I waited discreetly while drying and dressing occurred. Then came the final touch, combing his hair and then brushing it with two ivory hair brushes. He used to part the two or three remaining hairs across the dome of his head with meticulous care, splash on some cologne and then we would go down to dinner.

On this particular evening, while this elaborate hair-dressing procedure was taking place, he said, 'At this very moment, sliding stealthily through the Straits of Gibraltar under cover of darkness, go 542 ships, for the landings in North Africa.'

I couldn't resist it. I said, '543.'

'How do you know?'

'I've been working on it for three months.'

'Why didn't you tell me?'

'I believe there is such a thing as security.'

He looked at me with what I feared would be a blaze of anger at my impudence. Instead, he chuckled, and we went down to dinner where he told the story delightedly. Later, when Mrs Roosevelt came over to England to see how women were faring in the services, my father proudly repeated the story to her. Mrs Roosevelt, a remarkable woman of whom I became very fond, returned to America to give her account of English women's work in the war machine and she recounted this story to illustrate the importance of security, even between father and daughter. It went down very well, I am told, but not for me. I was summoned to the Air Ministry for a carpeting for breach of security![4]

The landings on the North African beaches were successfully carried out, French resistance minimal, and after consolidating their forces the Allies moved into Tunisia. General Montgomery's success at El Alamein forced the Afrika Korps to retreat westwards and, after fierce fighting, it was eventually trapped between the Eighth Army and the Allied troops in Tunisia. With the Afrika Korps' surrender, a major step had been taken towards the Allies' return to the European continent.

Mention has been made of terrain models being built as part of the preparations for Operation Torch. For centuries, detailed models, built to scale and showing fortifications and features of the landscape, had supported military operations. Early in 1940 a model-making workshop was formed at the Royal Aircraft

Doreen Davidson and two colleagues work on a terrain model.

Establishment in Farnborough after representatives of the army, navy and RAF met to discuss intelligence gathering for commando raids. The three-dimensional models, built to precise scale and detail, were invaluable when briefing troops prior to an operation; they could inspect the terrain, landmarks and obstacles they would encounter so they became familiar and 'fixed' in their mind's eye.

The Model-Making Section, 'V', moved to Medmenham in 1941, setting up their workshops in the stables off one of the courtyards. A number of suitable recruits had to be quickly found as very few professional model makers, who were normally employed by architectural or legal firms, were available. Craftsmen recently called up for war service in the RAF suddenly found themselves transferred to model making, while more candidates were found among the staff and students in art schools. The result of this targeted recruitment drive was the creation of a unique collection of highly talented artists, sculptors, engravers, illustrators and others who formed the core of the model makers. As the value of the models was recognised, it was not long before more model makers were desperately needed. Earlier manpower sources had run dry so the suggestion was made: 'Well then, what about woman-power?' After the establishment shockwaves had receded, the recruiters set off to find suitable female model makers from other sections and in art schools; the first two to arrive at Medmenham were Thea Turner and Gilly Porter. Only WAAF personnel were recruited for this work and their numbers were never large, amounting to a total of two officers and twenty-one other ranks.

The Air Ministry initially had difficulty in accepting that artists of all sorts could adapt to military discipline and, even more importantly, keep their work absolutely secret. They also pondered over which trade group to place them in, as they were dealing with a new 'trade'. Eventually, despite their exceptional skills with their hands, the model makers were designated as Pattern Makers Architectural (PMA),

Section Officer Helroise Hawkins
works on a model in 'V' Section.

which was a Grade V trade and paid 2s 6d per day with little expectation of promotion. This decision affected the WAAF personnel too and very few of them were promoted and even fewer were commissioned. It was not until September 1944 that the trade was upgraded and they became officially known as model makers. Some 'top brass' never got used to artists working in their individual creative way, paying scant attention to military duties and failing to behave 'like real soldiers'. Prior to the North African landings, some officers had been dismissive of the use of models but their practical value proved decisive and General Eisenhower was quoted as saying: 'Each of these model makers is worth a hundred men!'

In 1942, three officers and 150 enlisted men from the Engineer Model Making Detachment of the US Army Corps of Engineers joined the RAF model makers. They must have brought a whiff of glamour to Medmenham as a number of them had worked with movie companies in Hollywood. Joe Hurley was still a student at art school when he was launched into the film industry with Columbia Pictures as a sketch artist. Joe met Margaret Price from the Press Section at Medmenham and they married in America after the war. The American men who joined the Model Section (there were no US women model makers) had to adapt rapidly to new duties, strange surroundings, extra training and tight security. However, they got on well and worked side by side with their British counterparts; they liked the local people and countryside and their unit got the loudest cheer from the people of Henley in a 'Wings for Victory' parade in 1943. Getting accustomed to wartime British food may have been a problem, but as a US model maker wrote:

> One compensating factor was the presence at Nuneham, Phyllis Court, and Medmenham of several hundred Waafs. They came in quite a variety of ranks, shapes, sizes, and dispositions. Friendly relations, friendlier relationships, and even some marriages flourished. But anyone foolish enough to presume that the women were primarily for decoration or dalliance was in for a rude shock. The hard realities of several years of war had made it abundantly clear that women could do a lot of jobs, including model making, and do them superbly well.[5]

Mary Harrison had been a student at Nottingham Art College before joining the WAAF in 1940. She became a clerk (special duties) and worked as a plotter in the operations room at RAF Watnell, in Nottinghamshire, the HQ of 12 Group Fighter Command, and was about to be promoted to sergeant when she read a notice in Routine Orders about a model-making course. The specified entry requirements for applicants were for architectural artists, artists and sculptors, and all those who had completed at least two years at art college. Mary had not studied for two years, but said she had, and was accepted – but her sergeant's stripes were forfeited. In the summer of 1943 Mary arrived at the model-making school at RAF Nuneham

Mary Harrison became a model maker in 1943.

Park, by which time some of the first British model makers had been detached to set up similar units in Egypt, Italy and India. Seven other WAAFs, twelve RAF and five US army personnel joined Mary on the four-week course and on the first day were put to work learning practical carpentry, modelling with plaster of Paris and painting. Mary enjoyed all these subjects but struggled with the maths necessary for constructing to scale. In her diary she commented on how accurate she had to be and the fiddly nature of the small-scale jobs, but on 30 July she recorded:

Finished my model. Everyone worked terribly late and we were caught by the duty NCO and officer – expect there will be a lecture about it!

Sure enough there was: 'Got a ticking off by the CO this morning about last night.'
    Mary passed the course and was posted to RAF Medmenham where the WAAF modellers lived, being transported each day to work at Phyllis Court in Henley:

The whole gang went to the Dog and Badger to celebrate. We got a late pass and went to the village Hop – amusing time watching the Yanks teach the locals how to jitterbug.[6]

Mary found the work suited her and enjoyed the relaxed atmosphere of a shift when

At first glance this picture looks like a vertical photograph. It is, in fact, a photograph of a model of the St Nazaire naval base, built for briefing on the raid in March 1942 and demonstrates the detail provided by the model makers.

the very pleasant US and British sergeants were in charge. In her spare time she enjoyed swimming and boating on the river and discovered the Dutch Café and the cinema in Marlow. After two months she summed it up: 'I do like it here!!'

Model making required long hours of detailed work and single-minded concentration. A model of a port, for instance, would include the individual dock layouts, road and rail links, buildings, cranes, ships and boats, all built to scale with added details of cargoes and crates. Distinctive features such as the shape of a roof were included, and the whole model was painted in the colours of the real structure. Everything exactly matched the scene the attacking force would see and encounter, whether by air, land or water. Ordering models was usually one of the first actions to be taken when planning an operation; consequently the model makers would know when and where it would take place months or even years before it did. Despite the relaxed working atmosphere prevailing in the Model-Making Section, security rules were strict and there was not one breach or inadvertent slip of the tongue.

Obviously there could be no personal attribution or signature on any of the models sent out from the unit, but at least one small mark of individualism was made. Bill O'Neill, an American who later married Pat Peat, did manage to incorporate the initials 'US' into a tree pattern on one model of a Romanian target. Mary also remembered working on models for the Pacific invasions, which were planned to start once Europe was liberated. There was great concern about the landing craft to be used due to the strength of the waves breaking on Pacific shores, so a model of the beaches was constructed. When this was uncovered for a large number of admirals to inspect, sitting on a rock was a tiny mermaid, made by one of the model makers. No comment was made but at the end of their discussions the admirals thanked the Section and asked that the mermaid remain in place when the model was delivered to them.

One of Mary's brothers was serving with the RNVR on Russian convoys and the other was in the Royal Armoured Corps. When their mother, who lived alone, had an operation, Mary was granted fourteen days' compassionate leave to return home to nurse her. However, this was not long enough and Mary was asked if she wanted a temporary release from the WAAF until her mother regained her health. She accepted this and had to return to Medmenham to complete the process:

> Kit inspection, a medical and bags of red tape before finishing. A soldier on the train from Grantham asked me to marry him!!

One month later she returned to Medmenham and got back to work. Having forfeited her sergeant's stripes to become a model maker she started working for her trade tests to become an ACW1. On Christmas Day 1943:

> Had a marvellous dinner – I went in fancy dress as a gypsy. Then we went to the Hare and Hounds and on to a dance.

Mary settled back into Medmenham, enjoying the work and finding her colleagues very congenial:

> Nice sort of a day. I was working in the American room and with the wireless going
> and the sun streaming in, it was very pleasant.

When off-duty Mary enjoyed the occasional ENSA show, gramophone recitals in the YWCA and lectures on such diverse subjects as 'The Temples of Ancient Egypt' by an archaeologist PI and 'How a Disney Film is Made' by one of the Disney animators. Two of her fellow WAAF modellers, Mary Oliver and Joy Jarvis, kept their art studio in Marlow throughout the war and this was used by several fellow artists. Mary also remembers Chantry House in Henley where WAAFs could go to read and have a little peace and quiet. She was, however, not too keen on WAAF discipline and bureaucracy:

> Ticked off today by a WAAF officer for collecting the form for new shoes on the
> wrong day. Only just missed a charge and have got to forfeit two late passes. Stupid,
> trivial business.

A few weeks later:

> Got into a row for talking on Pay Parade and had my hand slapped by the Flight
> Sergeant. I had to laugh which didn't improve matters.

Two WAAFs model a town
area using plaster of Paris
for the buildings.

Three days later:

> Ticked off about putting my hat on in the Mess. The pettiness of those who have
> nothing else to do makes me sick.

Mary enjoyed working with the American model makers. Although they once
went on strike over the unappetising food at Medmenham, they willingly shared
their superior US rations and cigarettes with their British colleagues. On one
occasion Mary offered one of her British wartime 'Robin' cigarettes to an
American who was so appalled at the taste of it that he kept her supplied with US
cigarettes for the rest of the war.

The section regularly made models of fjords for Norwegian forces flying in and
out of their home country with agents, couriers and saboteurs – with the objective
of disrupting and harrying the German occupying troops. Mary worked on one job
where the pilots fly a few feet above the water in the confines of a narrow fjord with
no room to alter course. The enemy guns were mounted on either side of the fjord
to trap the aircraft between two walls of anti-aircraft fire. The PIs and modellers
calculated the guns' field of fire with the greatest precision in order to determine
the exact bearings for the pilots to fly on without deviation and avoiding being hit:

> After the raid the Norwegians came to thank us. The Section also received letters
> from bomber pilots saying how useful our models were.

In fact there were many messages of appreciation from troops of all three services
who had benefited from having had a detailed preview of their target. Nothing
else at that time could give troops and air crew such accurate visual information on the terrain of an area, or particular features they would encounter when
attacking an enemy-held position.

Geoffrey Price in the Naval Section wrote:

> The use of scale models enabled us to plot raids by my section on cargo vessels in
> the Norwegian fjords. These ships made their runs only by night and during daylight
> hours anchored up under the cliffs in the fjords where the water is deep. This made it
> difficult for the rocket firing Beaufighters and Mosquitoes to attack at low level and
> pull away due to the steep mountains. Models were therefore made of these anchor-
> ages so that the pilots could have a good view of the position of the valleys in the
> hills and plan their approaches and escape routes.[7]

Mary's brushes with authority continued:

> A party of us went to the Hare and Hounds to celebrate Bessie's birthday. Coming
> back we were caught cycling more than two abreast by Flight Lieutenant Deeley and
> the five of us have got to report to his office tomorrow.[8]

The next day: 'Deeley was a pig and put the five of us on three hours gardening.'

The gardening turned out to be digging an uncultivated plot of garden. Mary shared a hut with eight other modellers and a few photographers; Nancy Hayes was their WAAF corporal. A few months later, for a crime unspecified, Mary was put on a week's fatigues, which entailed her getting up at 6.30 a.m. to sweep the hut, scrub the lavatories and swill the floor before going on duty. Although a modeller friend helped out, by the middle of the week Mary was certain she was getting housemaid's knee and resorted to locking herself in the lavatories to get a smoke in peace: 'More ruddy fatigues. How I hate it. A wretched officer gave me some advice today – I suppose the old fool thought I was a regular ACW.' The last day of fatigues arrived: 'Celebrated by cycling into Marlow and saw "Spider Woman".'

However much Mary enjoyed working in the Model-Making Section, she was very aware, in a similar way to the PIs who worked to improve the accuracy of bombing raids, of her personal contribution to every operation carried out. Mary wrote this poem after being shown post-raid air images of a German city and remembering those air photographs from which she had worked when building the model:

My Hands

Do you know what it is like to have death in your hands
        when you haven't a murderer's mind?
Do you know how it feels that you could be the cause
        of a child being blind?
How many people have died through me
From the skill at my finger tips?
For I fashion the clay and portray the landscape
As the fliers are briefed for their trips.

Do these young men in blue feel as I do
The destruction
The pain.
Let me cover my eyes as you cover the skies
Let me pray it can't happen again.

Don't show me the pictures you take as you fly,
They're ruins and scape – little more.

Is all this part
Of the madness we choose to call War?
If there is a God up above who listens to all
Does he know why this has to be.

Did he give me my hands just to fashion the plans
That my own land may always be free?[9]

Model makers and PIs needed exact measurements for their detailed reports and
accurate models. 'Almost' or 'nearly' were not words used in 'W', the initial letter
chosen to designate the Photogrammetric Section, quite appropriately as the
Swiss-built Wild plotting and measuring machines were at its centre. For the first
eighteen months of the war the only operable Wild A-5 stereo-comparator in
the country had been the sole means by which small-scale photography could be
examined; this machine was moved from Wembley to be installed at Medmenham
in 1941. The need to acquire another A-5 became critical as the only similar
machine in UK was owned by Ordnance Survey and had been so badly damaged
in bombing raids on Southampton in 1940 that it was unusable. Such was the
importance placed on its repair that a Cabinet-level decision was taken to smug-
gle the machine back through enemy territory to the Wild factory in Switzerland
and to set up a clandestine operation to return it repaired to Britain. This was the
machine used in 'W' Section at RAF Nuneham Park. The two machines were
used throughout the war in every type of reporting that required high levels of
accuracy in measurement, three-dimensional calculations and volumetric assessments. High-quality optics and transparent imagery allowed the operator to see
landscape and objects in three dimensions and greatly magnified. Detailed measurements could be obtained, and by the use of complex mechanical linkages and a
plotting table, highly accurate plans could be drawn.

In the spring of 1942, Sophie Wilson, Lucia Windsor and Ena Thomas were
coming to the end of their geography and surveying degree course at Cambridge
University, which had included use of a Wild A-6 comparator. The department was
visited by the head of 'W', on a recruiting mission for trained surveyors to work at
RAF Medmenham, but found that the Royal Engineers had already signed up all
the male students. It was pointed out to him that the three women had completed
exactly the same course, and they were instructed to join the WAAF on deferred
service until their degrees were finished. In August 1942 they duly reported
for duty at Medmenham where it was found that although their degree studies had made them highly competent in operating the Wild machines, they had
not attended an official PI course. They were, incidentally, the three new officers
whom plotter ACW2 Elspeth Macalister, very recently a fellow Cambridge student, reluctantly saluted. Sophie takes up the story:

> When we arrived there was a panic on in 'W' Section and it was decided that the
> work required for the North African landings was more important than doing the
> PI course first. I cannot tell you how much aggro this set up amongst the Waafs who
> were there already! So, Lucia, Ena and I went straight into the Section and I spent
> from August to early November making contoured maps of parts of North Africa
> from which the Model Section cut their basic contours. However, once that was all

over we were sent off one by one to do the course and I went off to Nuneham Park
in March 1943.[10]

The 'W' Section PIs converted small-scale reconnaissance photography into information, plans and maps, referred to as 'mathematical intelligence', and used by all
other sections when the maximum precision of measurement in all three dimensions was required. By the time Sophie, Lucia and Ena joined the Section, the extent
of photographic coverage over occupied or enemy territory was so great that it
could be claimed that anything that moved, that was built or attacked in Europe
had already been photographed by Spitfire or Mosquito reconnaissance aircraft. The
photographic intelligence provided on enemy intentions helped to turn the tide of
war in the Allies' favour and enabled them to take the initiative against the Germans.

One of Sophie's first jobs was in preparation for the famous Ruhr Dams Raid
in May 1943, for which she calculated the depth, volume and level of water in the
German dams as well as for those in the practice areas. These had to be taken at
different times of day and month in order to determine the optimum date and
time for the raid to take place. Strict security ensured that she was not told the
location of the photographs she was making her calculations on. However, her
memories of the Lake District, where she had been brought up, caused her to
think frequently how similar the photographs were to Derwent Water, which was
subsequently revealed as one of the sites used for the air crews' practice raids.

Although others disliked the long hours of duty Sophie soon got used to the
12-hour shift pattern that meant getting up four times in three days. She lived in
one of the accommodation huts in the woods and her workplace was one corner
of the cellars beneath Danesfield House which she described as:

> A bit like the Ladies Lavatory at Waterloo Station – all white tiles. It was reached by
> a narrow, twisting staircase from one of the courtyards. One day I was rushing down
> to go on duty and collided with a bearded man with red staff tabs on his uniform
> coming up – I nearly knocked him over. In the tight confines of the staircase I some-
> how managed a salute and found out later he was Field Marshal Smuts.

Sophie contoured many target areas to provide accurate heights, sometimes calculating the declination and altitude of the sun to show how it would fall on a
particular target area as the pilots were on their approach flight. Her contouring
work was also used to ensure that heights were correct on models being built for
the briefing of pilots. Nowhere would accurate measurements be more vital to a
pilot than in the life or death situation of attacking a pinpoint target of a single
building located in a busy city centre in well-defended enemy territory. Sophie
remembered one particular job where she calculated the height of all low-flying
obstructions within a mile of Gestapo headquarters in The Hague in Holland. Her
work was in preparation for one of the most remarkable low-level precision raids
carried out in an enemy-occupied country in Europe.

The Dutch underground organisation had contacted London to ask that the five-storey high Gestapo building in The Hague be destroyed. The reason for this request was that the records of all Dutch civilian identity cards issued were kept in the building and from these the Gestapo could identify members of the Dutch Resistance. The building was in the centre of The Hague, and the number of obstacles and constrictions to the aircraft's approach along a busy city street were many. One can imagine how closely the air crews scrutinised the model, the pinpoint maps and the recognition charts. On 11 April 1944 six Mosquito aircraft took off from Hampshire and flew, at a height of just 50ft to avoid detection by enemy radar, to The Hague. They circled the city then banked and flew straight along the Scheveningsche Weg to drop their bombs, then climbed steeply to exit the target site. One of the Mosquitoes was equipped with cameras and the photographs showed a spectacular success: two of the bombs had gone through the front door of the building and two more through the windows on either side:

> So accurate was the bombing that it is reputed that a number of civilians waiting in line for bread across the street were left unharmed. Indeed, no Dutchman outside of the building itself was killed.[11]

The building and most of the records were destroyed and Dutch officials were able to fake the remaining ones thus saving the lives of many brave resistance workers. Sophie summed up the work she did: 'You had to get it right; lives depended on what you did.'

Sophie's friends Lucia and Ena moved over to the map-making part of 'W' Section, which was based at RAF Nuneham Park. After they had finished the maps for North Africa, they did the same thing for the Sicily and Italian invasions. Soon they were preparing up-to-date maps and plans of many French, Belgian, Dutch and German towns as part of the build-up for the Normandy invasions. They also created detailed maps of Germany that were then printed on to silk scarves and supplied as escape maps to air crews in the event of them being shot down.

All sections at Medmenham dealt with secret material: for strategic planning, for shorter-term tactical information or for gathering material on the enemy's capabilities. Sophie described the security at Medmenham as 'not obtrusive' but any lax security or 'careless talk' would have been disastrous. Pat Peat recalled that the photographers, if questioned about their job, had been instructed to reply that they worked in the cookhouse. Clerks who typed up the secret reports were instructed to answer similar queries by claiming that they worked in 'Maintenance Command'. The head of the Model-Making Section reported being approached one day in a hotel bar in Marlow by a civilian stranger asking questions about 'the photographic establishment up the hill towards Henley'. He claimed to have seen WAAFs on a bus with chemical stains on their fingers and had noticed a Kodak yellow van making deliveries. Was it an enemy agent or a check by British security?[12]

Fine drawing and annotation for map making in 'W', the Photogrammetric Section.

A new station commander arriving at Medmenham in 1943 to take up his post commented:

> In view of the Unit's intelligence function, I was rather surprised at the absence of a perimeter fence and other security measures, other than a main gate on to the Henley to Marlow road, with an RAF Police Guard House. The Officers' Mess and Quarters together with the other Ranks' Messes and Quarters were nearby. The whole layout had a somewhat casual appearance, intentional as I afterwards discovered, since this, and the security of the actual operational buildings, was thought to provide better all round security than wire fences, gates, lights and the like. At any rate, I never heard of any case of a breach of security. Bearing in mind the wide variety of occupations and professions from which the interpreters and other experts were drawn, their standard of security consciousness was extremely high.[13]

However, why was a conspicuously large white mansion standing on a prominent plateau above a noticeable curve in the River Thames chosen as the location of RAF Medmenham and its secret work when it was apparently such an easy target from the air? The answer was that no attempt was made to camouflage it or make it to appear different – it did not arouse suspicion because it looked normal. Danesfield House was but one among hundreds of substantial English country houses across the south of England, many of which were requisitioned by the services during the Second World War. It was normal too to have Nissen huts built in the grounds, filled with servicemen and women and vehicles coming and going. Danesfield House, Nuneham Park and Hughenden Manor were just three of many similar properties and so avoided close attention.

There were, of course, security checks on all staff entering and leaving Medmenham through the main gates, and servicemen and women were apprehended for not having the right pass at the right time – again, it was normal. The Second World War had an impact on the whole population, for they had all faced the threat of invasion and the battles had been conducted in the skies above them. Many had lost relatives and friends, many had been bombed out of their homes, most lives had been disrupted and there was much suffering – it was a personal war. Signing the Official Secrets Act was taken seriously. The PIs worked in their own sections and did not enquire about what others did elsewhere. Day by day they saw the effects of war in the photographs they examined. Many had worked on reconnaissance bases and had been there when a pilot failed to return from a mission. In these cases, they were losing a personal friend whom they might have been talking to the night before.

When the war in Europe ended, the head of the Model-Making Section circulated a letter to all personnel who had worked there. An extract reads:

> Your loyalty and devotion to duty has been outstanding. Your sense of responsibility and security has been unsurpassed. The latter has brought forth many expressions of admiration from other members of the Station who have only recently learnt of the true nature of the work upon which you have been engaged for so long.
>
> The making of models for the briefing of vital operations on land, sea and in the air has put you very much 'in the know' as to the exact spot where and, to a certain extent, when the next blow at the enemy was to be made. Not once did you break the trust that had been placed upon you.[14]

PIs and model makers felt the responsibility they held for the safety and life of each soldier, sailor and airman for whom they provided information. Sophie's words – 'You had to get it right; lives depended on what you did' – echoed the thoughts of everyone at Medmenham.

10

FURTHER AFIELD

Joan Bawden's wish to be posted overseas was granted. After six months' service at Medmenham she was in the first group of WAAF PIs to be posted overseas to RAF Heliopolis, near Cairo. Joan and her four colleagues, Letitia Robinson, Elizabeth Hemeltyk, Diana Orlebar and Margaret Perkins, arrived on 12 March 1942, having sailed from Liverpool two months previously on board the SS *Otranto*. The long voyage in convoy had been enlivened by four days ashore in Durban, frequent parties and dances on deck in the tropics and the presence of an RAF squadron en route to the Middle East. Only sea sickness early on and a German Condor plane following the convoy for some hours off the West African coast gave them cause for concern. The WAAFs joined the newly formed Middle East Interpretation Unit (MEIU) under the command of Squadron Leader Idris Jones. They worked on air photography of North Africa and the Mediterranean taken by No. 2 Photographic Reconnaissance Unit (2 PRU), based at Heliopolis.

A further contingent of six WAAFs from Medmenham soon followed, including Honor Clements, who had initially worked at Bomber Command, and Dorothy Colles, one of the first WAAF officers at Wembley. It must have been a strange return for Dorothy, who had spent the first twenty years of her life in Cairo, where her father was a professor at the university before the family had returned to England. She attended Epsom School of Art before joining the WAAF in July 1940 and, after a few months as a clerk, was selected for PI training and worked in the Aircraft Section at Medmenham before her posting to Egypt. On the voyage out, having been forbidden to draw any portion of the ship for security reasons, she turned to portraits instead, hoping to supplement her pay: 'I have drawn nine portraits as commissions so far but have only been paid for three,' she recorded in a letter home. 'Cairo is very much as I remember. Hot and dusty and full of smells and flies', she wrote in one of her first letters on arrival, followed quickly by a telegram to her mother: 'Have parted with appendix unexpectedly.'[1]

No. 2 Photographic Rencconnaissance Unit used Beaufighter aircraft to fly daily cover of the Western Desert and the Mediterranean, which were areas of intense military action at that time. Fierce fighting along the North African coast from Benghazi to Tobruk and El Alamein had been shifting backwards and forwards since 1941. Although part of the Italian fleet in the port of Taranto had been destroyed or crippled in a Fleet Air Arm torpedo attack in November 1940, some remaining vessels were still a threat. Malta had fought and survived determined German and Italian attacks. The strategic planning for the Allied landings in North Africa in November 1942 was well advanced with air reconnaissance providing information for engagements on land, sea and air. Longer-term planning for the Allied invasion of Italy in 1943 was also under way and part of Dorothy's work was on models for the landings in Sicily.

As the work of the MEIU increased the numbers of PIs grew to a total of 300 men and women.

In June 1942, Field Marshal Rommel started the German breakthrough eastwards from Benghazi along the coast towards Egypt. By 21 June he had taken the Libyan port of Tobruk, capturing tens of thousands of British troops, and reached the Egyptian border. The British forces retreated to El Alamein, only 60 miles from Alexandria, and there was a very real threat that Cairo would be overrun. Evacuation plans for all non-essential personnel at Heliopolis, including the WAAF PIs, were prepared. The PI unit was sited alongside the very busy airfield at Heliopolis, where each day the PR planes returned with film showing the most recent enemy dispositions. The interpretation of these photographs was vital work and provided immediate information for British Eighth Army tactical decisions as well as planning for future operations.

On 19 June, Dorothy had her first flight in a Lysander aircraft taking photographs. She wrote home: 'I cannot tell you how incredibly, utterly intoxicating flying is.' Twelve days later Dorothy had her second flight, but this time she was on a stretcher in a Beaufighter, being evacuated to RAF Ramleh, near Jerusalem in Palestine, having been admitted to hospital earlier with an infection.

The British defensive positions at El Alamein successfully halted Rommel on 1 July, the same day that the WAAF PIs made their hurried departure from Heliopolis. Orders that all secret documents that were not required should be destroyed resulted in the air above the various headquarters being full of charred paper. The MEIU worked as usual through the morning, then at midday Joan and the other WAAFs were instructed to return to their quarters to pack up essential personal items hastily and prepare to be flown away to a safer place. Many things had to be left behind as the lorry soon arrived to take them back to the airfield. The PRU Beaufighters, designed to carry a crew of two, were used to fly the WAAFs away a few at a time, to join Dorothy at RAF Ramleh. Joan, Diana Orlebar and Margaret Perkins clambered into one aircraft and somehow squeezed themselves and their luggage into the limited space. Joan wrote:

> Warby, the blond, beautiful Unit's Ace was our pilot. We took off and flew over Ismailia, the (Suez) Canal, the desert and along by the sea to Lydda. It was a wonderful

trip. I stood up in the back looking at the beauty of the clouds and thought – this is living.[2]

'Warby', to whom Joan refers, was Flight Lieutenant (later Wing Commander) Adrian Warburton DSO and Bar, DFC and two Bars – he was later awarded a DFC (USA). A charismatic 24-year-old, 'Warby' was a PR pilot who always got his photographs, and had perfected the art of dicing, once returning from a sweep so low over the Italian fleet in the port of Taranto that part of an enemy ship's radio aerial was caught in the tail wheel of his aircraft. Suzie Morrison, who worked in Italy later on, said of him: 'He was such a glamorous chap and we all fell for him.' 'Warby' was killed in April 1944 while flying alone over Germany. His body and plane were not located until 2003, when he was buried with full military honours at Durnbach Military Cemetery, near Munich.

Dorothy and Diana had another adventure later on while serving at Heliopolis, this time on a Royal Navy destroyer going on exercise with several WRNS officially on board. The two WAAFs managed to go along too, unofficially, thanks to one of the ship's officers, Diana's brother, but their short trip turned into two days spent at sea, as the ship was diverted to search for a bomber crew afloat in a dinghy after ditching their aircraft.

As the WAAFs were unable to do any interpretation work at RAF Ramleh, they swam, socialised and visited Tel Aviv, Jerusalem and Haifa. Joan met her future husband again and Dorothy recovered enough to visit Transjordan and Amman. After this unexpected, peaceful interlude of three weeks, they returned to normal duties at MEIU providing intelligence for the invasion force in Algeria, and increasingly on Italy. The German advance had been held at El Alamein, although there were still air raids on Cairo and Heliopolis. At the end of October 1942 General Montgomery led the Allied force that defeated the enemy at El Alamein, starting the Axis power's retreat from North Africa. The North African landings, code-named Operation Torch, began on 8 November.

At the beginning of 1943 in England, WAAF PIs were being interviewed for their suitability for posting to North Africa. Hazel Furney:

A contingent of interpreters was destined to go there and that included ten of us WAAF. We were all interviewed at the Air Ministry. I was chosen as they needed an 'L' Section (Aircraft) person. We knew the WAAF interpreters already in Cairo had a slightly dizzy reputation, so we all went looking as frumpy as we could with our hair tucked up, caps pulled down. They weren't, in fact, too keen on Suzie and me as we were too young. However, they were persuaded that we were needed, so to our joy we were all off. Of course, we couldn't say where we were going, just as we could never tell anyone what we did.

One lovely Spring day, my mother, sister-in-law and her two children came down to Medmenham with a picnic, which we had on the river bank. My mother said, 'You'll remember this lovely English scene when you're somewhere hot and dry'.

What she didn't know, and nor did I, was that when I got back to Medmenham, it was all go; five of us were flying out from Benson that evening in an American Flying Fortress. We landed in Cornwall and were given beds until dawn and then we were off on our great adventure.

We flew to Gibraltar, not a luxury flight, no seats, but I found a lovely ledge in the nose where the navigator was, and lay there. The landing was sensational; flying in on my stomach.

Gibraltar was an exciting place. There were hundreds of aircraft there, bombers, fighters and transport as well as naval ships. We were taken in Jeeps to the Rock Hotel for lunch and gasped at the sight of stalls selling oranges, lemons and bananas along the way, things we hadn't seen for ages. We had a drink with the crew, then lunch when, before the dessert, which was a lovely chocolate confection, they told us our transport had arrived. Ann Whiteman, who was our senior officer and an Oxford don, marched us all out, leaving the crew, who were in no hurry. We found it hard to forgive that, after so much rationed food![3]

They flew on to Algiers, with pavement cafés and shops to enjoy, but perhaps the best sight of all was the Eighth Army soldiers, khaki shirts and shorts bleached white by the desert sun, triumphant after their victory at El Alamein. The five WAAFs were much feted and photographed by the Eighth Army News as the first servicewomen to arrive there. A WAAF officer had been sent ahead to arrange accommodation for them but had failed to do so:

We were put temporarily into a rather sleazy hotel near the Souk – Lothian Nicholas complained that cockroaches were trying to eat her gas mask, which we all carried everywhere, and they had kept her awake. Peggy Thorpe and I, returning from work late at night, walked into our room to be greeted with a cry of 'Ahha' from a Frenchman who was in bed! We finally moved to a villa above Algiers.

Suzie Morrison's first application to go overseas had been turned down because her 'hair was too long and her skirt too short'. However, after an expensive hair-do before her second interview, she was accepted and flew out to Algiers with the second group of WAAFs on 27 May 1943, again landing at Gibraltar for refuelling and breakfast, when they 'gorged themselves on the bowls of oranges in the Mess'. Their arrival in Algiers brought the WAAF PI numbers to ten and included Dorothy Lygon from the Night Photography Section, Celia MacDonald from Industry, Vera Marsden from Wireless and Radar and Angus Wilson from Damage Assessment.

They were based at an Anglo-American unit, the North African Central Interpretation Unit, at Maison Blanche, near Algiers, where the US president's son, Colonel Elliott Roosevelt, was the commanding officer. It was agreed by those PIs who worked with both the president's son and Sarah Churchill, the Prime Minister's daughter, at various times during the war, that the latter displayed all the positive qualities expected of a leader's offspring, while the former did not.

WAAF PIs in La Marsa, Tunisia, explain their work to an American visitor, sitting next to Anne Whiteman and Suzie Morgan. Standing from left: Hazel Furney, Peggy Thorpe, Lothian Nicholas and Sibeal Maguire.

The PIs worked at night after the flights had landed and the films had been processed. Suzie worked on Second Phase and Hazel on aircraft identification, as at Medmenham. Breakfast at 3 a.m. was American style and they got used to being served sausages and bacon with maple syrup, probably making a pleasant change from the night-time fare offered at Medmenham.

A few weeks later the group moved eastwards to La Marsa, near Carthage in Tunisia, where they lived in a convent; the males at one end of the building and seven nuns at the other, with the WAAFs in former nuns' cells above them. They worked in a nearby seminary, where Hazel found a page of a German aircraft recognition book, showing all aspects of Spitfires, left behind by a hastily retreating enemy PI. The unit experienced extremes of climate, from heavy snowfalls to a sirocco when the heat was so great that the photographs rolled up as they tried to interpret them. The flying forces at La Marsa became more international during 1943, when 60 Squadron South African Air Force joined the RAF's 682 Squadron, which included Canadians, Australians and New Zealanders as well as Polish and Czechoslovak pilots; American and French squadrons were based nearby. Although there were parties to celebrate the capitulation of the Italian forces on 8 September, the intensity of work for the invasion of Sicily and mainland Italy meant that the PIs rarely got time off:

Life was pretty spartan, we never had hot water and the food was not great, but there was a hotel in Tunis we could use to dine and dance. We hitched everywhere, not a problem due to the ten of us being the only females around. We swam in the sea a lot and occasionally went to the local Turkish Baths, which was very entertaining – men in the morning and women in the afternoon – who did all their washing of clothes, babies etc while there.

We were visited by Air Marshal Tedder, General Alexander and President Roosevelt. Churchill came on his way back from Teheran; he had pneumonia and was not seen but Sarah came to visit us.[4]

Hazel Furney, who worked in the Aircraft Section, investigates a crashed German aircraft at Foggia Airfield, southern Italy.

In December 1943 the WAAFs were flown in Mitchell bombers to San Severo, in Apulia, southern Italy, the HQ of 336 PR Wing, landing at one of the eleven satellite airfields of Foggia, recently captured by the Eighth Army. Hazel had discovered the tenth of these airfields on photographs she had analysed at La Marsa, and by coincidence it happened to be the one on which they landed. In fact, the PIs knew all the details of the town of Foggia, as well as many other areas, having provided detailed targeting information for air crews. They also assessed the extent of post-raid bomb damage and provided tactical information for advancing Allied forces. Hazel was an expert on aircraft recognition, and found it particularly interesting at Foggia Airfield to climb inside the wreckage of some of the German planes, which she had identified earlier on photographs.

Forty miles north of San Severo, the Allied forces were encountering enemy resistance and the PIs worked in their office at a local college to the background sound of gunfire. Hazel and other WAAFs lived in a nearby block of flats where they also had their mess:

> One night an officer with a dozen or so Canadian soldiers arrived quite late. He explained that they had been fighting non-stop for two days and could they come in to sleep on the floor until morning. I went to make some tea, and when I came back they were all flat out in their sleeping bags on the floor – they had been fighting at Ortona.[5]

Dorothy Lygon, 'Coote', with the Night Photography Section at San Severo, Italy.

The town's opera house became an officers' club, where they danced in the evenings to a gramophone or an occasional band, and once an operatic company came from Naples to perform *Rigoletto*. The WAAFs were never short of escorts from the PR squadrons for dances and visits to restaurants, where they were warmly welcomed by the local Italian population. Despite these pleasant interludes, the harsh realities of war were always apparent to them in the number of aircraft losses and the many casualties. Mosquito aircraft at San Severo had enough range to reach Poland and Romania to photograph the synthetic oil plants and underground factories, so they worked all hours. Hazel wrote:

> Once we had stopped the Italian cook flogging our rations and serving us very poor quality pasta, we fed better but still no hot water – just lots of cockroaches in the bathroom. We slept three or four to a room on camp beds, lined with layers of newspaper to keep us warm. We got airmen's woollen vests to augment our pyjamas and we all took to wearing an odd assortment of clothes in place of uniform.

In 1942 Suzie Morrison had been working at RAF Wick, on the north-east coast of Scotland, where she met a PR Spitfire pilot who had just flown in from RAF St Eval. Over lunch she told him that she had interpreted the photographs he had taken of German battleships off the French coast. Their next chance meeting was at a dance in Algiers and after a whirlwind courtship, Suzie was married on 9 February 1944 to Squadron Leader Jimmy Morgan DSO, the commanding officer of 682 PR Squadron based at an airfield near San Severo. Suzie wrote:

> I had to ask permission to marry from my Commanding Officer, Group Captain Fuller, as it was the first Allied wedding in Italy. He then sent a signal to the Commander in

In February 1944, Section Officer Suzie Morrison married Squadron Leader Jimmy Morgan in the opera house at San Severo. He was the commanding officer of 682 PR Squadron and the wedding cake was suitably adorned with a model Spitfire.

Chief Air Headquarters at Caserta, who replied, 'Permission granted provided it is not brought to my notice.' That meant I did not apply for a marriage allowance, and carried on with my duties as usual. I did, however, have to alter my marriage licence from age 21 to 20, as I had added a year on to my age when I joined up in 1940.[6]

Their marriage took place in the opera house and Suzie managed to find enough material locally and a dressmaker to make her own dress and four pale-blue ones for the bridesmaids. She even arranged for a traditional iced wedding cake, suitably adorned with a model Spitfire, to be served to the guests. Their CO, Colonel Roosevelt, let one of his pilots fly the newly weds in a P-38 Lightning for a four-day honeymoon in Malta. Suzie wrote:

A few months later, on 4th June 1944, my husband was responsible for taking some very important photographs, the day that Rome fell to the Allies, after heavy bombing. He flew the reconnaissance sortie twenty minutes after the bombing to prove to the world that the Allies had not destroyed the ancient sites in the city.

As the Allies advanced northwards, some of the PIs moved from Cairo to San Severo, including Dorothy Colles, who often disappeared into the countryside

The start of the WAAF sack race at San Severo. From left: 'Coote', Honor Clements, Peggy Thorpe, Lothian Nicholas, Angus Wilson, Celia McDonald and Suzie Morrison.

with her painting gear and produced enough pictures for an exhibition in London after the war. Dorothy Lygon, 'Coote', was able to spend some time visiting Evelyn Waugh, the novelist, in hospital in the nearby town of Bari. Waugh had been badly burned in a plane crash while on an assignment with Randolph Churchill to make contact with the partisans in Yugoslavia. 'Coote' had been one of Waugh's closest friends since his first visit to her family home of Madresfield in 1931. When he was sent to Rome to convalesce, she spent her leave there looking after him.[7]

The following extract from a captured German Divisional Order dated July 1944, and subsequently published in the British Eighth Army news bulletin, confirmed the effectiveness of the reconnaissance and interpretation work carried out by the Mediterranean Allied Photographic Reconnaissance Wing:

> Enemy Aerial Reconnaissance detects our every movement, every concentration, every weapon, and immediately after detection smashes every one of these objectives.

In January 1942, Wing Commander Glyn Daniel, the Cambridge archaeologist, was posted to India. His instructions were to organise PI training for as many army and RAF officers as possible and to set up an interpretation unit, based on the Medmenham model, to work with PR squadrons flying reconnaissance cover in support of British troops fighting the Japanese in Burma. The unit became the Command Photographic Interpretation Centre (CPIC), the HQ for PI in preparation for defeating the Japanese once the war in Europe was won. In February 1942 Singapore was overrun by Japanese forces and surrendered, causing several PIs who were in transit to the Far East to divert to India and form the nucleus of instructors. CPIC had truly palatial buildings to work in as they were allotted Hyderabad Palace, the Delhi residence of the Nizam of Hyderabad, which housed all the Far East Third-Phase sections, a Model-Making Section, and a PI school.

Early in 1945, WAAF personnel were posted to work in India as part of the shift of emphasis from the European theatre of war to that in south-east Asia. They had quite an effect on their male counterparts as Glyn Daniel recalled:

> The WAAF other ranks arrived first and naturally caused a big stir among the airmen. Within a week of their arrival one of my sergeant photographers came to see me and asked for permission to marry one of them. She was a very nice girl but I counselled a short delay to which they agreed, and after a month I gave her away in St James's church in Delhi.
>
> Then the WAAF officers arrived and people began going down like ninepins. I posted one WAAF officer, Elspeth Macalister, who had read archaeology at Cambridge, to 'Trader' Horne's office: he had complained for some time of being overworked. A shy man, he immediately moved his desk out onto a draughty veranda, but in a few weeks they were engaged to be married. I proposed their health at their marriage back in Cambridge after the war.[8]

What Elspeth did not know at that time was that 'Trader' had asked Glyn spe-
cifically that no WAAF should be posted to his section, as they would disrupt
the work.

In December 1944, Elspeth and five PI colleagues had set sail from Liverpool to
Bombay, followed by a three-day train journey to Delhi, giving the WAAFs their
first sight of India:

> Small villages, wells, simple ploughing with camels or oxen, women in brightly col-
> oured garments complemented by luminous peacocks. We stopped at numerous
> stations and at meal times disembarked to be fed at the station café. At night when
> the train stopped at a station, brown arms would stretch towards the windows of our
> carriage to see if anything could be purloined. Eve Holiday lost her uniform as she
> had hung it rather conspicuously on a dodgy hanger. As her other uniform was in
> her trunk in the guard's van, she had to arrive in Delhi in her WAAF striped pyjamas!
>
> We had all served for several years at Medmenham in different sections; plotting,
> communications, Second Phase and bomb damage. At CPIC I was allocated to the
> Shipping Section. The head of this Section was a handsome Army officer, Capt JET
> Horne; the staff consisted of two naval officers, five RAF officers and me.[9]

The Shipping Section produced reports on the Japanese navy and Malayan port
installations in preparation for Operation Zipper, the planned invasion of Malaya,
which would be the prelude to the defeat of Japan. One of Elspeth's tasks was to
make a mosaic, a detailed map made of runs of photographs, of the Mekong River
at Bangkok.

Although it took rather more than the 'few weeks' claimed by Glyn Daniel for
Elspeth and 'Trader' to become engaged, before long they were spending their
days off together, exploring Delhi on their bikes and enjoying dinners at the
Imperial Hotel. Later on they visited Jaipur and Kashmir together:

> Of course in those days it was not done for single girls to go off with single men. It
> was assumed they would, of course, sleep together. I had a letter from Mum forbid-
> ding me to go and Trader's mother kept it very dark. We took no notice and went
> ahead with our plans.

And sure enough, they were 'cut' and snubbed by Europeans making just that
assumption on all their travels. When the war ended, so did their journeys, and
'Trader' returned to be demobilised in Britain, but that was not the end of
their story.

Glyn Daniel himself was not immune to the WAAF effect on CPIC, for he
also met his future wife in Delhi. Ruth Langhorne had read geography at Oxford
University and worked in the Industry Section at Medmenham before travelling
to India. Her first meeting with Glyn had, in fact, been earlier at Medmenham
when he lectured to WAAFs on CPIC, and Ruth had been unimpressed by 'a

Elspeth Macalister WAAF (left) and Christine Guthrie WRNS arrived in Delhi in 1945 where it was cold enough to wear blue uniform. 'Trader' Horne is second from left, back row.

slightly bland man playing down the difficulties of life in India'. However, she did volunteer for India as travel at government expense seemed too good an opportunity to miss, and before long she and Glyn were planning their own wedding. With the Japanese surrender in August 1945, Glyn, like 'Trader', found himself unexpectedly heading back to civilian employment in England, while Ruth stayed on in Delhi for another six months as commanding officer CPIC.

Ann McKnight-Kauffer had spent some time in the Night Photography Section at Medmenham learning about H₂S, a navigational aid using radar in the aircraft, and went to India to promote its use and interpret any photographs obtained. She lectured first in Delhi and was then detached to Calcutta, but could not create much interest for the system among the British, although the Americans were more enthusiastic. Ann also flew to Ceylon (now Sri Lanka) and wrote:

I was flown from Dum Dum (Calcutta's airfield) via Vizagpatam and Bangalore to Raturalana, near Columbo. It was a long and bumpy journey through the monsoon, but made immortal by the view northwards up the toe of India from over the islands at sunset.

From Raturalana I went by car to Columbo and thence in Lord Louis Mountbatten's (Allied Supreme Commander in South East Asia) conference train up the dark mountain way to Kandy (the location of Air Headquarters). Dinner of bacon and eggs was served on the train and of all the strange coincidences I found myself hailed by Tommy Tilling of 'K' Section from Medmenham who joined me for the feast. I think he was a little surprised that I was being summoned to Kandy and so was I![10]

Eve Holiday had been in First Phase at RAF Benson and went to work in First and Second Phase at 347 (Reconnaissance) Wing at Bally, near Calcutta, where she became the senior WAAF PI:

The interpretation was very different from Benson, and although we had been briefed a bit in Delhi we had to learn as we went along. Most of the cover was over

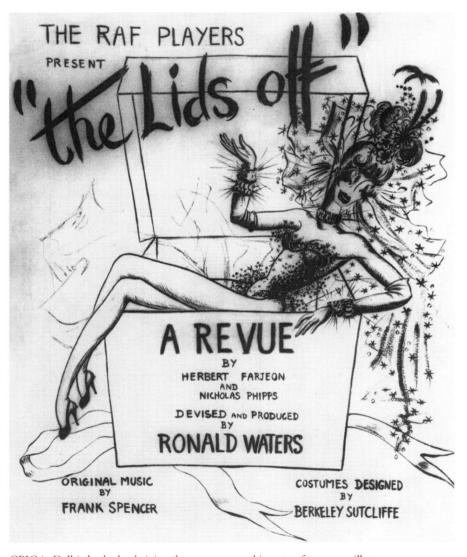

CPIC in Delhi also had a thriving theatre group as this poster for a revue illustrates.

jungles and rivers, and a sort of 'Guerrilla Warfare Interpretation' was needed. You
had to watch for elementary signs of human habitation – trees being cleared, track
activity, smoke from fires. I remember searching sortie after sortie for smoke.

The Japanese, knowing that the Allies would avoid upsetting locals by attacking
temples, habitually used them as ammunition dumps; so you had to watch the track
activity very carefully. The normal worshippers used straight, well established paths
to the temple, whereas the Japanese soldiers cut corners with consequent track activity. On the rivers, sampans were often used as gun positions, and we got to know
when they were converted.[11]

During the war, the Prime Minister, Winston Churchill, made several overseas
journeys to meet the other leaders of the Allied nations, accompanied by his wife
or daughters. Sarah wrote:

One day in November of 1943 I was summoned to the commanding officer and told
by him that I could accompany my father on an important journey.

The RAF station at Medmenham was quite near to Chequers, and whenever I had
forty-eight hours' leave it was easy for me to get over there. I hurried there now, and my
father told me that a conference between the President of the United States, Stalin and
himself had been arranged at Teheran, that the President, despite his health and physical
handicap was making the long journey and that Stalin had finally been lured from his
lair. My father and the President were to meet in Cairo before the conference in Teheran.
I was to accompany my father as one of his aides-de-camp … I walked on air.[12]

The first Conference
of Allied Leaders
was held at Teheran
in November 1943.
Section Officer
Sarah Churchill
stands behind Prime
Minister Winston
Churchill, President
Roosevelt of the
USA and Marshal
Stalin of the USSR.

Sarah sailed with the conference delegation on 12 November aboard the battle-ship HMS *Renown*. First stop was Gibraltar:

> It was dark when we anchored at Gibraltar. The Rock rose from the sea in solitary
> splendour, surrounded by a necklace of lights, the first I had seen since the blackout
> had begun in 1939.
>   My duties were mainly to see, along with others, to my father's comfort and
> wishes, to relay messages, and to drape myself silently along the coat racks in the
> ante-chambers of the conference rooms with other ADCs assigned to similar duties.
> I did not have any 'ideas above my station'.

A week later they were in Malta awaiting the arrival of the president and his party. The Prime Minister was unwell before the ship had set sail from England and welcomed the chance to rest, while Sarah was looked after by the RAF:

> I was taken on a flight in a Mosquito, then perhaps the best and fastest aircraft of the
> RAF. I remember we flew around the whole of Sicily, over all the bits I knew so well
> from sitting at a desk at Medmenham gazing at photographs. It was an unbelievably
> exciting experience. I knew it so well, I didn't need a map. The only unfamiliar
> aspect, of course, was the colour – I only knew it in black and white, and it was all
> lovely pink earth. We flew around the slopes of Etna, which was capped by snow
> and cloud, and then back to base, chasing a Walt Disney sun that refused to set. I
> confess that the flight made me feel a little sick. As we twirled about Etna, dropping
> and climbing some hundreds of feet, my ears hurt and that awful feeling in the joint
> of one's jaw, as if everything was turning to water, overcame me. I had to use an
> immense effort of will and concentration not to shame myself or my uniform.

Churchill's health did not improve as the voyage progressed to Cairo followed by the flight to Teheran. Sarah noted that:

> This was the conference at which, among other things, 'Overlord', the invasion
> of France, was planned. It was the first meeting of all three leaders. Everyone was
> relieved and surprised at the genuinely mutual facility of expression between the
> three of so vastly different temperaments.

The conference was over in four days and the return journey started, but at Tunis Churchill became seriously ill with pneumonia, causing great concern. Sarah was described as a pillar of strength to her father and diplomatic in her dealings with everyone else, always ready to listen and talk. She managed to visit her PI colleagues at La Marsa, near Tunis, to exchange news of Medmenham. A period of convalescence in Marrakech was necessary for the Prime Minister and it was 18 January before he and Sarah arrived back in England. Returning to work in the Communications Section, she brought presents of oranges for her colleagues, regaling them with tales of Teheran and the people she had met, especially 'Uncle Joe' Stalin, whom she imitated very well.

Sarah acted as ADC to her father again:

> I was still at RAF Medmenham in January 1945 when one afternoon I received a message which told me that I was to accompany my father on another journey. As before, secrecy and excitement prevailed. There was the last-minute rush for prosaic but necessary things like my laundry. I had to invent another story to explain to my friends my sudden departure.

A second conference had been arranged between the 'Big Three' – Roosevelt, Stalin and Churchill – at Yalta on the Black Sea. The Prime Minister's party departed on the night of 29 January by air for Malta and, once again, Churchill was unwell:

> Though my father had an amazing constitution the heavy injections before these trips sometimes made him feel ill, and once again he was to start out on a journey not feeling his best. At first the plane was very cold, so all the heating was turned on and in a few minutes we were screaming for air. My father asked for a thermometer. His temperature was up and it subsequently rose to 102 degrees during the night. My heart sank and I thought, 'Oh Lord, here we go again', but there was nothing to do but settle down. Nobody slept much.

An 8-hour car journey over appalling roads followed from the airport to Yalta where the conference was held in the Lividian Palace. With victory in sight, the discussions of the Big Three centred on the shape of Europe when Germany surrendered. Her father's health caused worries, and he was evidently brooding deeply on the horror and suffering in the world. Sarah wrote to her mother:

> Last night just before he went to sleep Papa said: 'I do not suppose that at any moment in history has the agony of the world been so great or widespread. Tonight the sun goes down on more suffering than ever before in the world'.[13]

Sarah and her father arrived back in England on 19 February 1945.

Two months before Sarah's trip to Yalta, Helena Ewen in Second Phase had been making plans to see her parents:

> I came to England in 1937 when I was in my early twenties – and later joined the WAAF after my application was much vetted. My parents stayed in my home town of Lille, in NW France, and during the whole war I had no news from them. I could only send them a monthly Red Cross message of 25 words, wishing them well and saying I was in good health and living in the country! I was very keen to go there as soon as I could, so when I saw a possible opportunity, I jumped at the chance. An

Helena Ewen managed to make an unofficial visit to her parents living in Lille, northern France in 1944.

American officer came to Medmenham in November 1944 from Dijon, General Leclerc's HQ – sent by him and other Allied heads to get the latest positions on the German Army, who, after being on the retreat appeared to be planning another assault from the East. I contacted this American to whom I proposed that, being a PI, I could explain better than he to the General, the latest covers we had for him to take back the following day.

He was very reluctant to include me in his trip and added that he would not take any responsibility for me if I did go. I went to our CO, Wing Commander Kendall, to explain. I also told him that I was due seven days leave. He emphasised that I could spend my leave as I pleased, but added that I had to be sure to return on time for duty; he would not sponsor my trip nor take any responsibility. I was keen – nothing could stop me![14]

American friends at Medmenham gave Helena boxes of candy recently received from the USA, and she bought 7lb of coffee beans, leaving just enough space for a change of clothes and a toothbrush in her bag. The next morning she set off with her companion to RAF Northolt and they flew to an airfield just north of Dijon:

I was longing to put my feet on French soil after so long – and I thought also that I would celebrate with a glass of French wine! But there had been lots of floods that year so we landed on a metal grid. The end of my hopes of stepping onto French soil, as we were immediately picked up and placed in a waiting Jeep!

The papers were safely put away at HQ and I went to the Mess for dinner. I remember we had turkey, such a luxury after our meagre fare in England. But I could not get a glass of wine, (only several bottles!), so I went out and found my way to the Grand Place and went into the largest café, typically French with a long mahogany counter and pewter top. All eyes were on me – who was this woman soldier in RAF uniform, dropping in and speaking French? Everyone gathered round me, bombarding me with questions. The first was, 'Do you know Churchill?' I said no, but I knew his daughter! This was true as Sarah and I often shared a Good Night milky drink together at the end of a shift!

Next day Helena presented herself at the HQ and, after explaining the photographs, was asked about her wish to get to Lille. The Americans gave her a travel pass, which helped considerably with getting a flight to Paris, where she stayed overnight in the Hotel Georges V, requisitioned for the accommodation of British officers, and had another turkey dinner. In the morning she caught a 'Micheline', a two-wagon train, to Lille. The journey was slow, sometimes travelling at walking pace, as they went over Bailey bridges very recently constructed by the Royal Engineers in the Allied advance through France. At Lille, the travel pass ensured a lift to her parents' house:

They, of course had no previous knowledge of my arrival; nor that I was in the Forces. When my emaciated father opened the door he screamed for my mother and I cannot describe the delight and crying that followed. I poured out on to the kitchen table my hoard of real coffee, purchased only a few days before in Reading. My father took some to the local café and sold it on the black market; that money would enable them to buy meat for a while.

The next morning I found a Jeep to take me to Brussels as I knew a detachment of PIs from Medmenham was working there and they would help me get back to England, and so they did.

That evening the Mayor of Brussels was giving a reception for British troops who had delivered the City from the enemy in the previous fortnight or so. There was a big banquet and I was asked, as there was a great shortage of women! It was a wonderful evening and I remember being taken to the house of the Rothschilds which had a round ballroom where they were giving a Ball. Being the only woman in uniform I had plenty of partners, although my WAAF service shoes kept slipping on the floor.

Next day, with great relief, I got a plane, a Hudson I think, back to England. We landed on grass at Croydon airfield and from there I travelled back to Medmenham having accomplished my dream of seeing my parents. I reported for duty on time and incidentally saw Wing Commander Kendall in the Mess, who gave me an understanding smile.

11

D-DAY AND DOODLEBUGS

In the summer of 1942, Ursula Powys-Lybbe was detached from Medmenham to work at General Headquarters (GHQ) at Norfolk House in St James' Square, London. This was the centre for planning Operation Torch, the code name for the invasion of North Africa in November 1942, and preparations for the future invasion of France, Operation Overlord. She was attached to the 21st Army Group and soon encountered several former Army Section colleagues from Medmenham. Ursula found herself the only officer wearing an air force blue uniform among all the brown army ones:

> 21st Army Group needed information about airfields and landing areas for the moment when the troops were to go in. I was asked to submit preliminary reports regarding the selection and suitability of certain specific areas for landing gliders and dropping parachute troops. The reports would then be passed to the geologists for their opinion on the terrain, and receive the final assessment from other experts.[1]

Ursula's work on landing areas for gliders and dropping zones for parachutists was just one small, but vital, part of the overall preparations for Overlord, which called for extensive intelligence input from all sources. One of the first orders to be implemented, more than two years before the invasion, was an increase in the number and frequency of photographic reconnaissance flights, with a corresponding increase in the volume of photographs being delivered to Medmenham. Tens of thousands of PR sorties were to criss-cross north-west Europe collecting information specific to the invasion, while the routine flights continued. Photography was one of the most efficient means of gathering intelligence for the planning of the largest amphibious invasion the world had ever known.

Since the fall of France and the failure of the German plan to invade Britain in 1940, both sides knew that at some point an Allied invasion of France would be launched, followed by an advance through the Low Countries and into Germany. By 1942 several major events made it possible to envisage and plan for a future invasion. The entry of the USA into the war against the Axis powers in December 1941, and their decision to prioritise the defeat of Germany before dealing with the Japanese domination in the Pacific, was crucial to any plans for a European invasion. The huge resources of US industry and manpower were essential for the planning and implementation of all Allied operations. The reverses inflicted on German forces following their invasion of Russia in 1941, had resulted in large numbers of troops being moved from Western Europe to reinforce the Eastern Front. The successful North African landings at the end of 1942, the first Allied operation, provided the springboard for a subsequent invasion of Italy and an advance northwards to the southern German territories.

The raid carried out on 19 August 1942 against the German-occupied port of Dieppe acted as a rehearsal for the future invasion of Normandy. It was designed to test the feasibility of capturing and holding an enemy-occupied port for some hours using combined ground, naval and air forces. In the event, none of the major objectives of the raid were achieved and accounts from prisoners revealed that the enemy had foreknowledge of the attack. While the Dieppe Raid provided valuable lessons in the planning of Overlord, it graphically illustrated how difficult the Allied invasion of Europe was going to be.

All Medmenham sections were involved in intensive long-term interpretation in the preparations for Overlord, but none more so than the Army Section. As a deterrent to invasion, the German forces had constructed a massive armed fortification, known as the 'Atlantic Wall', stretching along the north coast of France and

'B6' Army Section PIs examine the plan of the underground aircraft factory at Kahla, on the border of Czechoslovakia. Standing: Helga O'Brien (left), Geoffrey Orme and Sarah Churchill.

This low-level oblique photograph of defensive devices on a Normandy beach in 1944 reveals rows of stakes and 'hedgehogs', some mined, concreted into the beach. The two horses and dray were used for transportation on the sandy terrain.

the Low Countries. PR squadrons carried out repeated photographic sorties of a 30-mile-wide swathe of coast, from Holland to the French–Spanish border, providing information on the state of enemy defences that the invading Allied forces would have to overcome. Army PIs undertook the long-term task of examining all these photographs to locate and plot every existing gun installation and flak battery, updated with details of all enemy reinforcements. This was of vital importance for briefing air crews and indicating targets for Allied bombing raids. In addition, as described in Chapter 4, the PIs of the army sub-section, 'B6', including several WAAFs, located nearly 400 underground factories and depots constructed throughout mainland Europe from France to Czechoslovakia.

A key issue for the invasion was the selection of a suitable amphibious landing area. There were two possibilities: the Pas de Calais, which included the ports of Calais and Dieppe, or Normandy around Cherbourg. Photography was a prime source of information in the final choice of landing beaches and PIs examined the whole coastline of northern France, recording depths and tide levels at different times of the year, an enterprise in which even family photographs of children paddling at French holiday resorts before the war proved useful. The difficulty of moving tanks and tracked vehicles on pebbled terrain had been a major concern at Dieppe. For Overlord the expertise of several Medmenham PI geologists was called upon to examine samples of the Normandy terrain of sand and gravel, and to determine where beach landing craft could safely discharge heavy armoured vehicles. Dieppe had also shown the vital need to detect the beach and underwater obstructions that both landing craft and troops would encounter. Particular PI attention was paid to plotting these hindrances and traps in the form of stakes, spiked 'hedgehogs' and tripods, and also to the detection of the belts of mines buried in harbours and beaches.

The landing had to be of sufficient strength to set up a strong bridgehead before the enemy had time to react and bring up reinforcements. Normandy had no sizeable port equipped for oil-storage or discharge facilities and ensuring continuous fuel supplies was crucial. PLUTO – Pipe Line Under The Ocean – was the answer. Oil would be carried through a flexible hollow cable laid on the bed of the English Channel from Dungeness on the Kent coast and Shanklin on the Isle of Wight, to Normandy. This solution provides an example of the role of the Allied defensive camouflage detection that Joan Bohey was examining at Nuneham Park. The concrete mixers needed for construction work were located in the ruins of the Royal Spa Hotel in Shanklin, and every time a lorry came along the front, men were detailed to brush out the tyre marks in case enemy aircraft came over to take photographs. Further along the coast the pipeline was hidden from view in the shingle of Dungeness beach: 'The effectiveness of this camouflage was tested each week by aerial photography, courtesy of the RAF, and no changes were ever visible.'[2]

Two prefabricated military harbours were towed in sections across the Channel with the invading armies, and were assembled off the coast of Normandy. These 'Mulberries' provided all necessary port facilities, including piers and roadways. The American one was destroyed in a storm early on but the one at Arromanches, named Port Winston, which was built, operated and maintained by the Royal Engineers, saw heavy use for eight months, despite being designed for only three.

'Bunny' Grierson, carrying out First-Phase interpretation at RAF Benson, remembered D-Day and an early sight of these structures:

> How did we, as a team of 15 or so UK and US interpreters, react to the news of the Second Front – at last? We all worked together at Ewelme, as necessity arose,

The Mulberry Harbour in place.

very flexible, no-one having to explain their movements. In spite of watching the increases in enemy defence, the day by day, week by week, month by month, waiting had all became a background to me; until we started a lottery which went on for some weeks – 'winner takes all'. I chose 9th June, my brother's birthday, and won, being the nearest to the 6th!

Shock – I heard it at breakfast in the Mess. There, and down at Ewelme later, I remember quiet, and hoping for news; as far as I remember that is all we were hoping for. Joy came, as I was lucky, I had no-one close likely to be part of the invasion force, at that time. Where was it? As we met up, any more news was shared. I wasn't the only one feeling quiet, and any new news was shared, even what was heard on the radio; some with hope, some with fear. In spite of all this, still a sort of quietness. You saw people talking in groups, no secrets, anything new spread by word of mouth, eventually getting a wider picture by radio.

But we had film to work on, another sortie somewhere, I can't remember. But I do remember the hope and purposeful determination to get on with our work.

Some time later, perhaps a day or two, we had some photographs which were sent straight to us to see. They were low obliques of platforms, at all angles along the edge of a long beach. There were various floating connections attached to the structure. The harbour became news later – it was called Mulberry.[3]

The construction of airfields was a top priority as soon as a beachhead was established. In the months before the invasion, Medmenham PIs identified suitable sites from air photographs where airstrips could be quickly set up. In addition, an estimation of the enemy's air strength was made from coverage of all the Luftwaffe bases in France. Just two days after the invasion, Allied aircraft were operating from airstrips built since D-Day, and within three weeks thirty-one squadrons were able to transfer to airfields built in north-west France. By 12 June the Mulberry harbours were constructed and operational. The Communications Section had produced comprehensive and updated reports on all transport routes leading to Normandy. In the early months of 1944, an Allied systematic bombing campaign started, which destroyed much of the means by which the enemy could reinforce the area.

The first Normandy terrain models were started late in 1942 and built on a scale of 1:25,000, about 5 miles to 1ft of model, showing the pattern of rivers, roads, railways and towns. These were soon followed by an order for a single model of the entire Normandy coast and going a few miles inland, on a scale of 1:5,000, about 1 mile to 1ft, which included the finest possible detail for combat briefing. It became the largest and most accurate model in military history. Every road, path or track had to be painted in by hand to a precise width and colour, complete with hedgerows, trees, houses and other buildings, all copied in detail from air photographs. It took the model makers eighteen months to build and the work on its construction had to be fitted around all the other requirements for current operational demands. These included models for the V-weapons search and for specific D-Day operations such as the model for Pegasus Bridge, the site of the first glider landings in Normandy.[4]

While the Americans made the models for their invasion beaches, Utah and Omaha, the British modellers worked on those for the British and Canadian forces: Gold, Juno and Sword. Each section of the main model was built on a standard wooden base, approximately 4ft by 3ft, which could be fitted firmly together to be viewed as a whole by tightening the clamps underneath. A young model maker was usually detailed to fulfil this task and one day Mary Harrison was busy clamping under the table when an extra-large number of high-ranking visitors arrived and crowded round the table to view the model. Her exit was barred by a forest of legs and she started pushing legs and pulling trousers to escape. Eventually a space cleared and a somewhat dishevelled Mary emerged to find herself in front of the Commander-in-Chief Bomber Command.

> Bomber Harris looked down at me as I emerged and said, 'And what did you do in Civvy Street?'
> I replied, 'I was an art student'.
> To which Bomber replied, 'Oh well, that explains it!'[5]

By a stroke of genius the Section discovered a way to reproduce the individual plaster models, which a limited number of men could be briefed on, into a sturdy, transportable form using a mouldable latex substance. These were unbreakable and small enough to be referred to in the field.

When she heard of the invasion on 6 June, Mary wrote in her diary: 'Invasion of France. I felt cold when I heard the news and wondered if either of the boys [her brothers] were in it.' The following day: 'A twelve hour shift and it seems like the longest day ever.' Three days later: 'Saw some invasion photos today and how they connected up with our work.'

The troops viewing a model of the scene they would encounter as they left their landing craft on the Normandy beaches would memorise the distinctive landmarks, such as a house with dormer windows or the shape of a church tower, in order to orientate themselves quickly. Specially printed maps, known as the 'Bigot' series, at a scale of 1:25,000 and overprinted with complete details of the German defence system and topography of the area, were issued to all units prior to the invasion. In addition, each platoon commander, in charge of approximately thirty men, carried a map of his sector of responsibility with landmarks marked. The Photogrammetric Section worked non-stop on preparing and supplying large-scale maps and plans of individual towns and villages in France, Belgium and Germany in support of the invasion. The speed of map production and delivery was a crucial factor in maintaining the continuity of the Allied forces' advance. The section set up a 24-hour turnaround service from the receipt of a map request at RAF Nuneham Park, to the delivery to the commander in the field somewhere in Europe. This incredibly short period of time included finding and enlarging the relevant photographic cover, possibly of some obscure village the troops were planning to attack the following day, then fine drawing and annotation by hand, followed by quantity machine reproduction. Lastly, transport by truck and aircraft delivered the maps to the field unit that had placed the order. The work for the three Cambridge friends, Sophie, Lucia and Ena, required great concentration and meticulous attention to detail. There was no leave and they did not find any time for off-duty activities: 'We all just wanted to win the war as soon as possible.'[6]

With all the planning and preparations going ahead, the big question remained: where and when would the invasion take place? The 'when' was decided at the Teheran 'Big Three' conference in November 1943, when Stalin pressed for a Western second front to relieve the pressure on Russia. For years Hitler had considered that the Allies would strike in Normandy, while his senior officers were convinced that the attack would be made across the narrowest part of the English Channel to the Pas de Calais. Many inventive Allied deceptions were put into place to support the latter belief, including a bogus British army equipped with rubber tanks in south-east England, designed to provide German reconnaissance aircraft with evidence of a military build-up in that area. In the spring of 1944 Hitler changed his mind and a significant part of the German forces was retained in the Calais area, far from the Normandy beaches where the invasion actually took place.

One of the vital tasks undertaken by air reconnaissance in the preparations for D-Day was to locate all the enemy radar installations, in order to protect the invasion fleet as it crossed the Channel from its bases in southern England. In 1944 the enemy had increased the scope and density of its radar network in northern France by erecting many new stations in anticipation of an invasion. The Wireless and Radar Section at Medmenham undertook this interpretation work and produced very detailed target material of every type for existing radar stations along the Channel coast of France, from the Belgian frontier in the north-east to beyond St Malo in the west and stretching 20 miles inland. In the last two weeks of May 1944 Allied air forces carried out attacks on radar sites all along the Channel coast and destroyed almost all of them – but deliberately left some to function normally. These were to be utilised to ensure that the enemy picked up the signals of a large invasion force heading for the Calais area – except that this was another Allied deception. On 6 June a squadron of bombers flew at a specified speed along the Channel dropping 'window', strips of silver foil, at regular intervals, producing the same readings on the few surviving enemy radar detectors as a flotilla of ships.

Pat Peat recalled the evening of 5 June:

> We stood outside our hut and heard and saw the planes towing gliders going overhead very low. The planes had no doors and they were flying so low that we could hear the men in the gliders talking to one another.[7]

Elspeth Macalister also remembered that time:

> The time leading up to D-Day was exciting and I remember the morning of 6th – wave after wave of gliders going over to France. Two days before, I was cycling up

from Henley to Medmenham and could not cross the main road because of all the Army vehicles, tanks and all sorts trundling past, hour after hour, making their way down to the embarkation ports.[8]

Over 8.5 million photographs were produced for the D-Day preparations alone and similar quantities would be extensively used throughout the Allied advance across north-west Europe. The non-stop processing, the accurate plotting and long hours of patient PI examination of air photography played a substantial part in the success of the Normandy invasion, the advance to Berlin and victory in Europe.

Jeanne Adams wrote about her experience of D-Day:

I had a rare insight into the preparations for the D-Day landings. My unit had been busy examining photographs of the Normandy coast, looking at ports, beaches, harbours and estuaries for suitable landing areas for the invasion. However, despite my work, I was still unprepared for what happened on 6 June 1944.

On the evening of 5th June, I was relaxing with friends at the Compleat Angler Hotel in nearby Marlow. We were having a drink on the lawn. As we stood there, a strange whooshing, rumbling noise began. A huge bomber plane was above us, towing a glider. It was flying very low – so low that we could see the pilot.

There was a strong smell of petrol as the sky began to fill with planes and gliders, all heading for the South Coast and then for Normandy. Security was tight at Medmenham and none of us knew what was going to happen. But on June 5th we knew that D-Day was upon us and that the invasion was about to begin. All those days and nights we had spent poring over the photographs – this is what it had all been for. Every beach, every port and every cliff on the Normandy coast had been plotted and modelled by us and here it was at last!

It was the invasion that I like to think was the beginning of the end of the war. I shall never, ever, forget that evening.[9]

As plans and preparations for D-Day advanced and the bombing offensive continued against enemy industries, a new threat to the Allies emerged. It was a threat so grave that it could have caused the postponement of the Normandy invasion and possibly an evacuation of London. The German V-weapons (*Vergeltungswaffen*, meaning vengeance weapons) were missiles of previously unknown design, fired indiscriminately on the civilian population of southern England, and London in particular. In the early hours of 13 June 1944, just six days after Allied forces successfully invaded Normandy, the first V-weapon fell at Swanscombe in north-west Kent; people living nearby were puzzled that they heard a bomb explode yet did not hear the sound of a plane.

Since 1930 German scientists had developed totally new weapons, including a pilotless jet-propelled aircraft and a long-range ballistic missile. In 1935, an experimental testing base was set up near a small fishing village called Peenemunde, on the Baltic Sea island of Usedom. It was a quiet place with sand dunes and dense forests that concealed the workshops built alongside launch stands for experimental rocket tests, a runway to test fly new aircraft and a factory that produced liquid oxygen to fuel the rockets.

The V-weapons story could have come from the pages of a spy thriller in a race against time, except that these were real events happening to London, whose population became the first in the world to be attacked by weapons of mass destruction. Hitler referred to 'secret weapons' in a speech made in 1939 when war was declared, and a few months later an anonymous package, left at the British Embassy in Oslo, warned of German long-range weapon developments at Peenemunde. Little interest was taken, however, and the whole thing was put down to an enemy hoax and filed away. In May 1942, Peenemunde was photographed from the air for the first time by a PR pilot who, on his way to another target, by chance noticed some heavy construction work on the beach and took a short run of film. These photographs were regarded as 'interesting' at Medmenham, but the poor quality and small scale meant that they did not take priority over more urgent targets and were sent to the library. Unbeknown to the Allies, by the end of 1942 the first successful launches of a V-2 rocket and a V-1 flying bomb had taken place at Peenemunde.

Early in 1943, more hints of rocket weapon research on the Baltic coast came from a Swedish traveller and the Polish underground. Then a recorded conversation between two German generals being held as prisoners of war at a British interrogation centre mentioned rockets; the generals expressed surprise that none had

Air photograph of the experimental ballistic missile site at Peenemunde on the Baltic coast of Germany.

yet fallen on England. This did raise alarm bells in intelligence circles and the Army Section at Medmenham was instructed to look for any rails or scaffolding that might be linked to an enemy long-range projector capable of firing from the French coast. More PR flights were made and the PIs worked on trying to make sense of the large embankments and circular earthworks at Peenemunde seen under their stereoscopes, but nothing resembled a projector. Their report did, however, lead to an investigation into the rocket weapon threat being set up under the leadership of Mr Duncan Sandys from the Ministry of Supply and Winston Churchill's son-in-law.

An intensive photographic search by 'B2', code-named Crossbow, began in April 1943 for potential launching areas on the French coast, with no one really certain what they were looking for. Meanwhile four members of the Industry Section at Medmenham were assigned to search for clues of what the experiments at Peenemunde were producing. Models were ordered that Mary Harrison enjoyed working on as they were a larger scale than those for D-Day. She remembered that the air photographs the modellers worked from were taken from such a low altitude that she could see the faces of the soldiers running from the plane. In June the first rocket lying horizontally on a trailer was photographed there and the following month air photography confirmed the construction of several massive concrete structures inland from Calais and Cherbourg. All indications were that these so-called 'heavy' sites were associated with rockets and linked to Peenemunde. On 17 August 1943 a massive bombing raid was mounted on Peenemunde and against the 'heavy sites' in France. Effective as these attacks were at disabling the launching sites, they only delayed the rocket development work, which the Germans moved to Poland.

It soon became apparent that there was another quite different secret weapon, when the Danish Resistance smuggled to London a sketch of a small pilotless aircraft that had crashed on the Baltic island of Bornholm. The French Resistance then reported on 'catapults able to launch bombs' and 'up to 400 launch sites expected to be operational by November'. Intelligence pointed to flying bombs being the immediate threat rather than rockets, and reports of unidentified constructions at many points in north-east France triggered another intensive programme of air photography. In October 1943, an agent from a French espionage network provided full details of a site at Bois Carre that included a large ramp pointing towards London. This was a standard flying bomb launch site, and as the missile storage buildings looked like a ski lying on its side, they became known as 'ski type'.

However, no flying bomb had yet been seen. Using what knowledge they had, the PIs deduced that they had a wingspan of less than 20ft and that the enemy must be close to launching them from sites in France. The Aircraft Section was instructed to search for a very small aeroplane at Peenemunde and on a re-examination of June photography they spotted something behind a hangar but of very poor definition. On 28 November 1943, a Mosquito took off to photograph Berlin but cloud forced the pilot to cover Peenemunde instead. An examination of these photographs by Constance Babington Smith and her team revealed a launch

The model of the Peenemunde site constructed at RAF Medmenham from information shown on air photography.

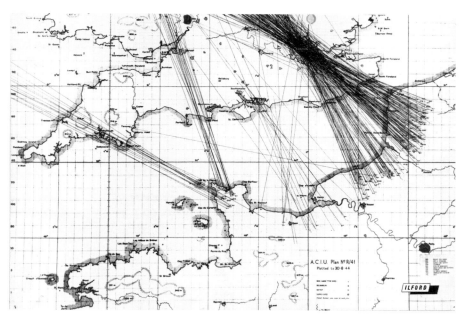

The V-1 firing line plot prepared by RAF Medmenham, showing the concentration of Doodlebugs aimed at London and southern England.

ramp with a tiny cruciform object sitting on it, found to have a wingspan of 19ft. The V-1 flying bomb had been identified, and the launch ramp they found later at the nearby settlement of Zinnowitz was similar to the ones found in France. Here at last was the link between Peenemunde on the northern coast of Germany and the ski sites, hundreds of miles away, in northern France.

Identifying this one small, elusive object in a mass of photography had taken many hours of patient searching and concentration on the part of Constance Babington Smith and her PIs, keeping an enquiring mind even when they might seem to be engaged in a fruitless task. The usual portrayal of randomly picking up a photograph and immediately 'seeing' the relevant object is totally false. The reality was stacks of photo boxes with stereoscopes, magnifying and measuring devices to hand for the PI to pursue a painstaking search. In the V-weapons search PIs were hindered by government scientists who refused to believe that the enemy was capable of producing such weapons, and officials who withheld relevant knowledge from them in the mistaken belief that their search would be more diligent if they had no information on what they were looking for.

Once the flying bomb had been found, it was possible to deduce the fuelling and propulsion of the jet engine, which ran for a pre-set length of time before cutting out and falling to earth to explode. Then the race was on to identify all the ski sites in northern France with which they were linked. It was led by 'B2' sub-section and assisted by any PI who could possibly be spared from other duties – amongst the many WAAFs involved were Mollie Thompson and Kitty Sancto. They found ninety-six sites in all, which by early 1944 were largely rendered inoperable by intensive low-level tactical bombing raids. The V-1 programme was seriously disrupted and the planned firing numbers were not achieved. However, the enemy switched to simpler firing sites, which could be quickly set up, used and moved, and hid them in woods and farm buildings. Although this transitory way of operating made them harder to spot, the PIs found giveaway clues to potential firing sites, which were then targeted.

The V-1s were quickly nicknamed 'Doodlebugs' by people living in the approaches to London, who became all too familiar with the 'putt-putt' sound of their approach, knowing that when the noise stopped they had 5 seconds to seek

WAAF Norah Littlejohn identifies the location of a V-1 launch site on an air photograph.

shelter before the bomb exploded. A three-stage defensive ring was put in place around London with anti-aircraft guns forming the first line of defence against incoming Doodlebugs on the south coast. Behind them, in the skies above southern England, Spitfire and Tempest fighter pilots flew alongside the Doodlebugs with great exactitude and, with the wing of their aircraft, tipped them off course. Lastly, barrage balloons encircled London. The Communications Section at Medmenham provided another solution by detailing the transport routes of V-1s, from their underground factory in the Hartz mountains of Germany to northern France, so the weapons could be destroyed in transit.

Although 4,216 Doodlebugs were destroyed on their journey over south-east England, 2,419 evaded gunners, fighters and balloons to crash on London, and at one point the government considered the complete evacuation of the capital. However, it could have been so much worse without the timely identification and destruction of the projected V-1 launch and storage sites. Instead of the reported 9,251 that did fall, southern England and London could have been facing the planned target of 2,000 V-1 firings every 24 hours.

Pamela Howie, the photographic processor at RAF Benson, saw at first hand what life was like in those parts of London where the Doodlebugs fell regularly:

Fred met me at the NAAFI wagon for a cup of char and a wad, (tea and a bun). I could see he was worried about his mother since the arrival of the doodle bugs (flying bombs) in London. He was arranging to go home for the weekend and asked would I go with him. I put in for a pass and soon we were on our way.

We were not however prepared for what we saw when we came up from the London Underground station at Forest Gate. It was an appalling sight, it was like the devastation I saw constantly on the aerial films we worked on, but at close hand it was unbelievable. I began to think maybe it was not such a good idea to have come here. I could see that it had shaken Fred, naturally, because his mother and sister were among all this. I only prayed that they were still there.

As we turned the corner I heard him sigh with relief as he pointed out his mother's house, on one side of the road. Out of a dozen or so houses two stood intact, of the others, some were completely demolished, others partially so. The rest were rubble, there was a pall of dust hanging in the air and we wasted no more time looking around, it was more than depressing.

Fred's Mum was a frail little lady, but what she lacked in size she certainly made up for in guts to stay among all this, and yet I suppose she had nowhere else to go. She greeted me warmly and made me welcome. Fred busied himself immediately. I could see he was the apple of her eye – he was certainly an attentive son. He explained that as there were only two bedrooms he would be sleeping at his sisters three doors away, which by a miracle was also still standing.

I went to bed and was awakened by an ominous droning sound, one I had not heard before – it was not the noise a plane made. I was aware of Fred's Mum by my bed quietly saying, 'Come on dear, we will go down and I will brew a cup of tea'.

Before the kettle had even boiled the noise abruptly stopped. This we had heard was the time to worry, once the engine cut out and it sounded to be just overhead. I could see the consternation on her face as we both sat perfectly still awaiting the inevitable.

Then there was an almighty explosion and the whole house shook, me included. I enquired in a trembling voice, 'How often do you have to put up with this?' She replied, 'At least once every night dear, and sometimes more.' I took my hat off to her, we didn't know we were born in some parts of the country.

The next day we did our best to cheer her up, or was it the other way around? Personally I was not sorry we were not staying another night.[10]

The area around Medmenham was relatively unaffected, although Mary Harrison recorded on 21 June 1944: 'First taste of a Doodlebug on night shift. Never felt so scared in my life.' A fortnight later: 'Flying bomb in Henley while in cinema.' And two days later: 'Doodlebug dropped near High Wycombe.' On 22 July: 'Terrible evening – a flying bomb dropped on Bovingdon Green (between Marlow and Medmenham) and one or two more too near to be pleasant.'[11]

The last Doodlebug fell on 8 September 1944 and the first V-2 ballistic rocket arrived on the same day. The only launching site needed for a V-2 was a patch of hard standing and there were thus no recognisable sites for PIs to search for. Taking just 5 minutes from launch to impact, the missiles travelled too high and too fast to be tracked down and, as they were silent, civilians had no chance to seek shelter. All the PIs could do was identify the transportation routes for the rockets and their fuel supply, which were then targeted for bombing attacks, while

A V-2 missile firing in 1944.

the invasion forces advanced across the Low Countries and Germany, and eventually overran them. In all 1,190 rockets reached England and more were fired on Liege and Antwerp. The last V-2 rocket fell on Kent on 27 March 1945.

General Eisenhower, supreme commander of the invasion, later commented:

> It seemed likely that, if the enemy had succeeded in perfecting and using these new weapons six months earlier than he did, our invasion of Europe would have proved exceedingly difficult, perhaps impossible. I feel sure that if he had succeeded in using these weapons over a six month period, and particularly if he had made the Portsmouth – Southampton area one of his principal targets, Overlord (the Normandy Landings) might have been written off.[12]

Two years after joining the D-Day planning team in 1942, on another summer's day in London, Ursula Powys-Lybbe had first-hand experience of a Doodlebug:

> I had no sensation of noise, which seemed most peculiar as the flying bomb had driven itself into the roof immediately above us and exploded – all I was aware of was a swaying movement around me, dust rising everywhere, and a feeling of utter desolation and disorientation as many of the dividing walls had collapsed. I turned round to see what had happened to my friends and was horrified to be faced with a pile of rubble blocking the passage between us from floor to ceiling. Five of our personnel had been killed and several injured, as I learnt later. I was too stunned to move, and too stunned to answer the many questions plied to me by a group of air raid wardens and ambulance men who had materialised from a staircase which I never knew existed until the door had been blown off. One of the rescuers handed me an American officer's raincoat, and pushing me towards the staircase, said kindly, 'You're not needed here, love, get on your way home,' and I found myself walking towards Berkeley Square with the rain still pouring down.
>
> Suddenly I was stopped by a young Naval officer, RNVR, brandishing a piece of sodden paper. It had TOP SECRET written all over it and he asked me, 'Does this belong to you by any chance? It came floating down from somewhere.' I replied with something unintelligible and he looked at me closely. 'You look as if you need salvaging, come with me,' and taking my arm led me towards Charles Street. We came to the American Officers' Club of which he was a member, and where I had once disgraced myself by mistaking peanut butter for mustard.
>
> My new friend addressed himself to a very elegant receptionist who was eyeing me with obvious disapproval. 'Is there anywhere for this officer (meaning me) to clean herself up?' he asked. My uniform was concealed under the raincoat filthy with plaster and brickdust, my hair also filthy, with streaks of the stuff all over my face and hands – I was a mess.
>
> The elegant receptionist now stared at me with obvious distaste, and being English, behaved as if she were totally unaware of the mayhem that had been created just down the street. 'Are you a member?' she enquired loftily.[13]

A perspective view of
the entrance to the V-2
launch site at Wizernes,
in north-east France,
drawn in early 1944. It
was prepared by the Wild
Section, entirely from
air photographs, and was
subsequently proved to be
accurate in all respects.

The V-2 site at Wizernes
was built in a quarry.
To obtain this daring
low-level oblique, the PR
pilot flew down into the
quarry, pulling steeply
away once the photograph
had been taken. The site
was extensively bombed
in 1944 and rendered
inoperable.

Damage caused by a V-2
falling in Hornsey, North
London.

On 9 September 1944 the Air Ministry News Service issued a bulletin:

WAAF IN THE FLYING BOMB BATTLE

Thousands of WAAF personnel – Air Ministry Staff officers, photographic interpretation officers, photographers and plotters – the WAAF of Air Defence Great Britain
(ADGB), RAF Bomber Command and Balloon Command, have played an important part in the flying bomb battle since it began eighteen months ago.

One of the 'expert interpreters' mentioned recently by Mr Duncan Sandys MP
was Flight Officer Babington Smith. She was the first to notice unusual features in
the photographs taken at Peenemunde in May 1943, and later was responsible for
drawing the attention of the Intelligence authorities to the speck of a miniature
aircraft which was eventually proved to be a flying bomb. In the ensuing months she
and her section examined many thousands of photographs, not only of Peenemunde
but of all possible localities for flying bomb sites and the factories that might be used
for manufacturing and assembling the new weapon.

In the words of an RAF officer at her photographic interpretation unit: 'These
girls have done a fine job and have played a vital part in warning us of the enemy's
intentions. If it hadn't been for their accurate and thorough work much valuable
information might have been missed.'

Throughout the winter months when the reconnaissance pilots brought back their
pictures of flying bomb bases on the French coast, hundreds of WAAF photographers
who process the films were hard at work night and day developing, drying and printing photographs ready to be rushed to the interpretation experts for scrutiny. They
were not dealing exclusively with flying bomb material but during all these pre-
invasion months handled as many as 50,000 prints a day, including aerial pictures of
the landing beaches, many coastal batteries, railway junctions, troop and freight concentrations. All this time a specially selected handful of WAAF officers were working
at the Air Ministry assisting in planning counter-measures against the new menace.

The post-raid photographs of the V-3 site at Mimoyecques, northern France, on 6 July 1944 showed that, despite extensive bombing, the target had not been destroyed. A further raid would be mounted using heavier bombs.

And when, a few days after D-Day, the long expected flying bombs were launched, WAAF plotters of ADGB tracked on wall and table maps throughout south-east England the height and direction of the new weapon so that accurate information could be relayed to the fighter pilots to guide them to the attack.[14]

Douglas Kendal wrote:

The flying bombs killed 6,184 people in London and seriously injured about 18,000. The number of houses damaged was about 750,000. In addition 2,000 British, American and Canadian airmen lost their lives in the counter offensive. The enemy achieved an average of just under 100 launchings in every 24 hour period, or about one every fifteen minutes, day and night.

In all 1,190 V2 rockets reached England, of which about 500 reached the London area, killing 2,724 people and injuring 6,467, a far higher percentage than the V-1.[15]

The chilling reality was that more secret weapons were on the drawing board to follow the V-1 and the V-2. The V-3 was near to completion and successors were planned to follow.

12

AND THEN IT WAS ALL OVER

As the war entered its final year in 1945 the work at Medmenham continued una-bated. The identification of the transportation routes and storage sites for the V-2 rockets was ongoing, as was the preparation of target material for the bombing raids on Germany's last lines of defence and supply centres. The attacks on synthetic oil factories and underground aircraft assembly plants were of particular relevance to the Allied advance towards Berlin as they minimised the number of aircraft the Luftwaffe could fly. As more male personnel were detached from Medmenham to posts in Europe, where they used their PI for tactical purposes, their places were filled by women. At the end of March 1945 WAAF numbers at Medmenham slightly outnumbered those of the RAF: 684 RAF and 719 WAAF. The overall numbers of personnel for army, navy and air force, including American forces, at Medmenham were 908 men and 794 women. The largest single service group was the WAAF.

In anticipation of the conclusion of the war in Europe, when all resources would be concentrated on defeating the Japanese, increasing numbers of person-nel were posted out to India and Ceylon. Six more WAAF PIs arrived in Delhi from Medmenham, among them Pauline Kraay, Lorna Freke and Diana Kingsley.

Early in the year, Barbara Rugg and her ATS colleagues moved from RAF Benson to the ATS Drawing Office at 1 Air (Survey) Liaison Section, Royal Engineers, in Belgium, to continue their photographic plotting work. This was in support of the Army Photographic Interpretation Section (APIS) of 21st Army Group, providing intelligence to Allied troops advancing towards the River Rhine and across Germany.

In March 1945 four Medmenham WAAF PIs, Margot Collett, Stella Ogle, Betty Holmes and Margaret Price, were posted to Coulommiers, a small town 35 miles east of Paris. They spent their first night in Paris:

In a magnificent French hotel, with red and gold furniture and a private bathroom with masses of hot water! In the evening we went to the Grand Opera and heard 'Boris Godunov'.[1]

WAAF PIs Betty Holmes (foreground) and Margot Collett, with members of 50 PR Squadron, on the steps of the château in Coulommiers, France, 1945.

No. 50 Squadron had moved to Coulommiers to provide photographic cover for the Allied advance, but by the end of March, when they were established, there was little work for them or the PIs to do. An aerial survey of France was carried out to assess the degree of damage caused by Allied bombing. The WAAFs were housed in a villa standing high on a hill outside the town:

> We four women have been cleaning, rearranging the furniture and having the time of our lives – we have no access to any radio and are completely cut off from war news. The locals are tremendously kind and hospitable. My French, which is the world's very worst, is getting me along quite well and I seem to make myself understood far better than I did when holidaying in pre-war days …

Later, Margaret moved to live with the old lady who had owned the château where their unit was based, and as there was so little work to do, she frequently travelled to Paris to meet Joe Hurley, an American model maker based nearby, whom she had known at Medmenham. Stella also enjoyed visiting Paris:

> It was great fun being by myself, because everyone is so friendly – one is continually getting into conversation with friendly natives or lonely Allied servicemen on leave from the front, so in a strange way I feel much more comfortable and at home there, than I do when I am alone in London. Anyone in Allied uniform travels everywhere free, and doesn't pay for museums etc. The shops, of course, are quite prohibitive! I enjoyed looking, but not buying.

Having celebrated VE Day in Paris, the PIs returned to Medmenham, and several weeks later Millicent Laws joined Margot Collett and Betty Holmes at Coulommiers, although there was still very little work for them. Millicent

Servicemen and women preparing for the VE Day parade at RAF Medmenham. The WACs are in the foreground of this squad.

returned to England after VJ Day in August, in style if not comfort: squashed between the navigator and pilot in a 50 Squadron PR Mosquito aircraft.

On 7 May, General Eisenhower, with representatives from Britain, France and Russia, accepted the unconditional surrender of all German forces on all fronts, to be effective from 00.01 on 9 May. In eleven months the Allies had fought their way from Normandy, through France, Belgium and Holland to Germany and on to Berlin.

The Operational Record Book for RAF Station Medmenham for 8 May 1945 (Tuesday) reads:

> News of German Capitulation and celebrated as VE Day. Parade held at 09.00 concluding with a Divine Service and personnel were released (where possible) from duty for the rest of the day. In the afternoon Station Sports were held followed in the evening by an All Ranks Dance and Camp bonfire. A Dance for Officers was held on the night of VE + 1 and for OR on the same evening.
>
> Most of the Sections were operating at peak up to the last few hours of the German surrender since which time personnel have been engaged in bringing Section records up to date.

Personal memories supplement the rather dry official account of VE Day celebrations at Medmenham.

'Panda' Carter and her ATS colleagues had moved at the beginning of the year from Esher to Medmenham to continue their work with the production of maps. They lived in the sergeants' mess hut in the woods and 'Panda' recalled great celebrations around the bonfire on VE Day. They were very fond of 'Rusty', their ATS officer, as she took turns at making the cocoa for them – unlike the WAAF officers, they noticed! They decided that she would go to the fancy dress dance in the officers' mess as Persephone, the goddess of spring. They washed yards of waxed muslin (used as the backing for maps), dyed it yellow and draped 'Rusty' in it before trimming it with flowers.

Pat Donald was in Regent Street in London on VE Day. She had finished working in April two months before her first baby was born. Just before leaving she had offered to take two young Americans, newly arrived at Pinetree, to show them London. They chose to visit the Windmill Theatre, so in a very pregnant state Pat sat through the show of scantily clad dancers and nude tableaux. The Americans thought it was marvellous and didn't want to see anything else in London.

Barbara Rugg remembered VE Day in Brussels:

We went into Brussels by truck and all the rose sellers came up and gave us roses because we were in the services. We went into the AES club to hear Churchill's victory speech and I met lots of people I knew from England, men and women. Then we went to the Monty club which was in one of those tall Brussels buildings – you could get lovely teas there and females could go there for a bath, hairdo, manicure – all sorts of things and all free.

Then we got on a tram and drove all round Brussels. We joined dancing throngs in the streets who would grab us as we went by – they danced all day. We went in lots of clubs – we tried not to get drunk but they kept bringing out champagne that they had kept hidden during the war! In one club we met a group I had been stationed with at Winterbourne Gunner and they invited us to join them later that evening, at the top of the camp, sitting on a truck because it would be a good position to see the lights go back on in Brussels for the first time. Like England there had been blackouts for a long time.[2]

Hazel Furney had visited several Italian cities from San Severo:

In May 1945, 'Coote' and I were planning leave and hoped to get to an island called Vis in the Adriatic, but it was looking like a forlorn hope as the sailing boat that went there would probably be too full. 'Coote' had had a letter from Evelyn Waugh who had been in Yugoslavia, and was an old friend of hers, telling her he'd been told to leave by Tito because he wasn't a communist, so he was sure that she would never get in! When the morning of our departure came, and with it the news that Venice had been liberated, we changed our plans for Vis with an idea of getting to Venice. We got a plane from our airfield to Rome, where we stood outside a hangar, asking every passing pilot if he was going to Venice, and an American said he was and before long we were winging our way there. On landing which, needless to say is on the mainland, we were picked up by someone in a Jeep and, as we were driving along the causeway, our eyes popped out as we passed two car loads of senior German officers, sitting up with grim faces in their own vehicles but with our military police as escorts.

On arrival, we got a gondola and as soon as we reached the Grand Canal, we found ourselves among gondola loads of New Zealanders. They had liberated Venice, but the war was officially over in Italy by then, so it was a peaceful hand-over. They all cheered and waved at us and we at them. One lot had hired a violinist to play bacaroles while they lolled back savouring the occasion.

'Coote' met up with an old friend who'd been liberated from a POW camp and decided to stay, rather than be repatriated. He was one of her upper crust friends and confided to me that until he'd been taken prisoner he'd never had to dress himself. On arriving in Venice his first move was to book a box at the Opera House for the season! He gave us a chit saying we could use it, which we did, taking along two Guards officers we'd met. We saw the 'Masked Ball'. The programme was all written in German and Italian and only 'Coote' had seen it before and had forgotten the story, but it was such lovely music that it didn't matter.

After two or three days the town filled up with service people like us on leave. On VE Day, partisans were shooting rifles all over the place. One of the many people we knew who turned up was an old friend of mine from Belgian days. He said it was much more frightening than crossing the Po.

On VE Day, in the middle of St Mark's Square, the Italians burned all the stuff that had been protecting the statues and danced round it. There were lanterns strung up on the gondolas, several buildings were flood lit, and music resounded everywhere, while we just watched it all. I suppose our soldiers were battle weary and just glad it was over, which we had known would happen any time. This was a memorable evening just the same, and for that reason I've never been back.

We had met forty seven people in Venice that we'd known elsewhere at various times, and I don't think we ever had to pay for a meal!

We hitched back to San Severo to find a mad rush on as we were going to Naples the next day to be shipped home on the Empress of Scotland, in convoy in case not all the 'U' boats knew it was over![3]

Suzie Morrison and her husband had returned to the UK in August 1944 on a troopship in convoy from Naples to Liverpool. It took sixteen days as the convoy circled right out into the Atlantic and U-boat alarms sounded. Suzie returned briefly to Medmenham and was then demobbed to have her first baby. Among others, Pamela Dudding of the 'first Medmenham alliance' and Mary Winmill, whose first married home had been adjacent to 'The Dog and Badger', had also left to start families. By coincidence, two Second-Phase PIs, Diana Byron and Lavender Bruce, by then both married, had their first babies in Penzance Hospital within a few days of each other in October 1944.

Dorothy Colles returned to Medmenham from San Severo in March 1945. After 'demob' she attended St Martin's School of Art but later returned to Medmenham to paint twelve of Garfield Weston's grandchildren; he was the owner of Wittington Hall, next door to Danesfield. She also worked for the Jordanian government, producing records of ancient sites as well as painting portraits of the king's family. She concentrated on portrait painting, of children in particular, working in oils and pastels. She had started painting children in wartime Italy and

Hazel remembered her getting down and playing with them on the floor to get a natural pose. Dorothy had several exhibitions in London, one that featured the paintings produced as a result of her sketches made around San Severo. Many of her PI colleagues from those days attended and were able to buy their favourite landscape to remind them of the days they had spent in Italy.

After the war Dorothy Lygon, 'Coote', worked as a secretary to the British ambassador in Greece, and as a governess in Istanbul, followed by a spell as a farmer and then as archivist for Christie's auction house in London. 'One of her young colleagues there, Simon Dickinson, observed that this fastidious, clever and "very old-fashioned woman" set up a perfect cataloguing system "never bettered" and was adored by the young because of her forthrightness and sense of fun.'[4] Perhaps 'Coote' had learnt something from the cataloguing system at Medmenham, where a sortie of photographs was retrievable in a matter of minutes from the millions held in the print library.

VE Day celebrations in India were more muted. In Delhi Elspeth Macalister wrote:

> Naturally the news of the cessation on hostilities in Europe was received with great joy – no more bombing raids, no more terrible battles and from a more mundane point of view, no more blackout – so we did celebrate mildly. There was floodlighting of monuments such as George V on the Maidan, and there were fireworks. Trader would not even come out for a drink. His was the only light on in the unit – he was preparing reports on the Japanese Navy and the port installations of Malaya in preparation for Operation Zipper, the planned invasion of Malaya. Japan had still to be defeated.[5]

Shortly before the end of the war Flight Officer Mollie Thompson married a Canadian army PI whom she had met at Medmenham. In 2009 Mollie wrote:

> By VE Day, I think most of us, men and women, were a lot more tired – 'burnt-out' – than we realised. For myself, after six years of war (my time in London being quite dangerous), even though much of the work was exciting and important, the idea of married life in a foreign country with children and 'housewifery' seemed to me blissful![6]

Mollie was demobbed in September 1945 and left for Canada with her husband six months later. They lived in Toronto for many years and, although she did 'children and housewifery', she also worked as a volunteer for the YWCA, becoming Canadian national president:

> This I found very interesting as it enabled me to travel throughout Canada – from the Arctic to the Rockies and the Pacific coast through the Prairies; everywhere

except Newfoundland – I tried three times but was prevented each time by either fog, snow and once a typhoon.

Mollie transferred to the World YWCA and spent eight years as a delegate to the United Nations in New York, where she was locked in the UN building with everyone else over the Bay of Pigs episode and when Fidel Castro spoke to the General Assembly. She became vice-president of the World Executive of the YWCA before retiring in 1973.

The American WACs left Medmenham to return to the USA in August 1945. In February 1945 First Lieutenant Lillian Kamphuis had been transferred from Medmenham to the Photographic Intelligence Branch, HQ US Strategic Air Force in Europe, based in St Germaine, near Paris. Her last duty was to travel with an Air Technical Intelligence team into Germany to pick up captured enemy photography.

Another WAC, Captain Alice Davey, was also involved in the end-of-war search for the German photographic library. Alice had been art editor for the *Chicago Sun* when she joined up in 1942. A year later, when the WAC was absorbed into the army, she was commissioned and sent to the PI school at Harrisburg, then worked in the Pentagon. Alice was longing to get overseas, and to Medmenham in particular, and at last her posting notice came through – on VE Day. She went straight to Supreme Headquarters in France and worked with two other PI officers who were intent on finding out as much as possible about German wartime PI. At first they were unsuccessful in questioning prisoners about the subject, although Alice established, when interviewing the head of the German interpretation school, that their PIs were only trained to work on single prints instead of using stereoscopes,

The staff of the Central Photographic Interpretation Command at Hyderabad Palace in Delhi, India, after VJ Day.

and they did not use comparative cover. When they got the news that a barn full of
boxes of photographs taken over Britain had been discovered in Bad Reichenhall,
near Berchtesgarten, they rushed there. The first sortie they inspected was of the
port of Southampton. Although the Germans had excellent cameras and produced
beautiful photographs, they had not exploited their imagery to its full extent as
the Allies had done.[7]

Ursula Powys-Lybbe wrote on the German approach to PI:

> Their training, surprisingly, was much inferior to our own and they were not
> given officer rank, which meant that they held no authority, and if they made any
> errors, they might have found themselves in the equivalent of the 'glass-house' of
> the British Army. According to prisoner-of-war interrogations, Top German Brass
> after receiving an interpretation report would stare at the accompanying aerial
> photographs through antiquated magnifying glasses and pass judgement, thereby
> foolishly throwing away one of the most important weapons essential in win-
> ning wars.[8]

As Alice Davey was waiting to come to Europe from the USA, Pat Peat was waiting to return there after several months in hospital:

> I got out of hospital on VE Day and I had to wait until my sister was ready to go
> so we were together on the ship – I think it was the *Queen Elizabeth*. We waited
> at Studley Priory (near Oxford) until there were enough people to send home to
> Canada and the USA. The ship docked at Halifax, Nova Scotia and we volunteers
> were put on trains going to various parts of Canada and the US. I was heading for
> New York City but they took me off the train in Maine and put me in jail, I don't
> know why. [Possibly because she was not wearing US uniform.] So I said, 'I demand
> a bath and I also want a glass of milk.' The jail people went to a bar and got a glass of
> milk for me and I took a nice shower in the jail and stayed overnight. The next day
> they put me on a train going back to Halifax. I caught up with my sister again there
> and we bought a beautiful white sweater for her husband who was a Polish RAF
> fighter pilot. The Canadians put us with a very prominent person's group, he had
> invented some kind of gun or bullet, something like that, and then we went down to
> New York City.[9]

Pat continued her artwork and in August 2009 held an exhibition of enamels at
the Torpedo Factory in Alexandria, Virginia. These were drawn from watercolour
sketches that Pat had made of the English countryside and villages during her
Second World War service and later converted into enamel paintings.

Peggy Hyne from Second Phase volunteered to go to India in 1945 and was
being interviewed in Air Ministry buildings near Victoria station when an alarm
went off. So used were they to reacting to air-raid warnings that they all went to
lie down in a corridor away from the windows. Instead of going to India, Peggy

was posted to Washington and travelled out with the Australian WAAF Jean Youle and two RAF PIs on the *Queen Elizabeth*, enjoying good food as the ship had been provisioned in the USA. There were thousands of returning servicemen and women on board, mostly Americans and Canadians. Peggy and her colleagues worked in the Pentagon on Second-Phase work and also instructed Americans on PI. She found digs with an Australian couple in Cleveland Avenue, on the side of the Potomac near the cathedral, which had not yet been completed. The most noticeable difference between life in wartime UK and the USA was the abundance of everything, from food to consumer goods, and no blackout – everywhere was well lit. Peggy worked in the Pentagon for three more years before returning to the UK.

In July 1945, twelve more WAAF officers, including Margaret Price and Helga O'Brien, crossed the Atlantic on the SS *Orcades* to Quebec, together with 3,000 Canadian troops returning home after the war. The WAAFs had been posted to the Pentagon to join American PIs working on photography of the Pacific War, but two weeks after they arrived, the atom bomb was dropped and the war against Japan ended. Eight of the WAAFs returned to England but others stayed in the USA and were demobbed there. Margaret married model maker Joe Hurley and they moved to California where he became a Hollywood screen director.

Flight Officer Constance Babington Smith was posted on special assignment to the Pentagon, but the plans for her to give advice on imagery interpretation came to an abrupt end in August. She stayed on in the USA and in the autumn was feted

In February 1946 Constance Babington Smith was presented with the USA Legion of Merit in Washington DC.

by American newspapers as 'The Girl who Saved New York'. This claim was put out initially by the British Information Services in Washington, an agency of the British government. It was based on the six-month delay in V-weapon development that followed the identification of the V-1 and the Peenemunde raid in 1943, together with the belief that the Germans had plans to launch V-1s on America. This publicity rankled with some PIs back at Medmenham, where interpretation was considered essentially a team activity that had been a major contributing factor in the success of Allied wartime interpretation. Constance never made this claim and always played down her section's part in the V-weapon hunt, referring to it as 'a small but fairly important contribution'.[10]

In 1945, Constance was awarded the MBE and on 8 February 1946 in Washington she was presented with the USA Legion of Merit for her services to Allied Air Photographic Interpretation, the only British woman to have received this award. She left the WAAF shortly afterwards and stayed in America to work on *Life* magazine for the next five years as their aviation correspondent. In 1958 Constance published the first book about wartime photographic reconnaissance and interpretation, entitled *Evidence in Camera: The Story of Photographic Intelligence in World War II*, published in the USA as *Air Spy*. Her book told the largely unknown story of the determination of the wartime PR pilots in getting their photographs and of the team of highly individualistic men and women PIs at

Many group photographs of sections were taken at the end of the war. Second Phase, the largest and most international section, posed for a photograph on the terrace and steps of Danesfield House in 1945.

Medmenham who contributed so much to the Allied success. Constance later wrote other books on aviation and several acclaimed biographies.

Thousands of men and women who had joined the armed forces during the war were due to be demobilised; at RAF Medmenham the scheme went into action in May 1945. All married women and those personnel who had civilian posts waiting for them qualified for Class-A release, while subsequent 'demob' dates were arranged by age and length of service.

Anne Whiteman returned to be a tutor in history at Oxford University in 1945 and pursued an academic life, becoming vice-principal of Lady Margaret Hall. Anne Jeffery also took up a post in Oxford and became a leading authority on archaic Greek inscriptions and epigrams. Towards the end of the war, Glyn Daniel had travelled from India to visit Medmenham and encountered his friend Dorothy Garrod. Wing Commander Daniel was smartly saluted by Section Officer (three ranks junior) Garrod:

> 'Remember, Glyn,' she said firmly and kindly, 'that very soon our roles will be reversed and Assistant Lecturer Daniel will be saluting Professor Garrod!'[11]

Dorothy returned to her work in Cambridge and over the years received many honours for her work on prehistoric archaeology. In 1965 the CBE was conferred on her and in April 1968 the Society of Antiquaries presented her with its gold medal, the first ever awarded to a woman. Dorothy's successors to the Disney professorship were Grahame Clark and Glyn Daniel, both of whom had been wartime PIs at Medmenham.

While waiting for her demobilisation at the end of 1945, Sarah Churchill accompanied her father on an election tour of the country and later, when he was voted out of office, went with him to Lake Como for a holiday designed to aid the recovery of his health and morale. In November she was released from the WAAF and on the bus taking her to the demobilisation centre:

> I felt my heart singing like a bird but then I looked across at some of the younger WAAFS, still ACW2s and saw tears in their eyes. Were they thinking of lost loved ones, or was it that they would have to hand in their uniforms, of which they were so justifiably proud, to have them replaced with the rather dull 'civvies'? They would have to return to the more monotonous everyday life of kitchen sinks and bus queues. For some years of wartime everything had been done for them: they had been housed, warmed and fed, they had mingled happily and naturally with new companions from every walk of life and worked alongside them in a great joint effort. My elation dimmed. Perhaps it was not going to be easy for them.[12]

Sarah returned to the world of theatre and films; she was an accomplished artist and published two books of poetry and a tribute to her father in addition to her autobiography.

While awaiting their turn to leave the forces, personnel could choose to attend a range of educational and vocational courses set up at Medmenham and elsewhere, with the objective of getting a job back in 'civvy street'. Some of the younger women filled in time by picking fruit and vegetables for local farmers and PIs at Pinetree worked on the captured German air photography, preparing it for cataloguing and storage. A programme of civic lectures was started, offering a wide variety of topics mostly presented by the resident personnel. Several women remember a particularly prophetic lecture about how the German ballistic rockets, the V-2s, had prepared the way for getting to the moon, which was predicted to happen in about fifteen years' time.

At the demobilisation depot, at RAF Wythall near Birmingham, uniforms were handed in and clothing vouchers were given out to WAAFs; most considered this preferable to the standard 'demob' suit issued to the men. Millicent Laws used her vouchers to get a cerise-coloured tweed suit, made by Hector Powell, which she liked and wore to work for a long time.

With the defeat of Germany and the VE Day celebrations, the preparations for the invasion of Malaya and defeat of the Japanese continued. Six more WAAF officers arrived in Delhi from Medmenham. Elspeth Macalister wrote:

> And then in August, the atomic bomb descended on Hiroshima and Japan crumbled. Trader's reports were used as the Allies took over Malaya and South East Asia, so we did celebrate VJ Day by having dinner at our favourite watering hole, the Imperial Hotel. But for the majority of the Indian population, another objective had to be won, the ending of the rule of the British Raj in India, achieved in 1947. Trader and I married that same year![13]

In Calcutta the three PI WAAFs Eve Holiday, Hester Bell and Margot Munn celebrated VJ Day together and Eve had dinner with Dirk Bogarde at the Saturday Club. With the end of the war there was no work to do in Calcutta or Delhi and all sorts of activities, such as lectures, plays and quizzes, were introduced to keep the staff there occupied. Elspeth spent time at the Museum of Asian Antiquity and worked on cataloguing and drawing many of the exhibits. 'Trader' soon departed for England and 'demob', but Elspeth was to spend several more months in Asia before travelling home. She was posted with a friend to the HQ South-East Asia Command at Kandy, in Ceylon. There was absolutely no work to do so they went sightseeing up into the hills to watch the elephants being bathed: 'and took tea at the Queen's Hotel. One day we even sat beside Peggy Ashcroft and Noel Coward!' Then they were given the job of escorting fifteen WAAF to a naval base to fly to Singapore:

> We took a long train journey right across Ceylon and when we arrived we were given a meal and ferried out to a flying boat. It was a typical romantic scenario – great moon, dark blue velvet sky, coconut palms all bending slightly in the right

direction and white, white sand. We boarded the sea plane and it took off with
enthusiasm. This was short lived however, as one of the engines spluttered and then
gave up. So back we were ferried – consternation – what was to be done with all
these unexpected women? The girls were put up on the floor of the Mess. Rae and I
were allocated a small hut in the jungle – and it really was jungle.

Next morning Rae suddenly said that she had been bitten. I was really worried
about her on the long flight in case I would find her dead beside me. It was a very
long flight and no proper seats. We lay between the struts and as the dawn broke we
looked down on miles of deep emerald green jungle. We re-fuelled at Penang and
eventually touched down at Changi Airport. I had last seen Singapore, my birthplace,
in 1926 from the rail of a P & O liner, which had taken us home to Europe.

Singapore was rather different after three years of Japanese occupation, although
Elspeth saw familiar landmarks. One day she went to the Supreme Court to hear
one of the trials of the notorious prison guards who had inflicted such cruel tor-
tures on their prisoners. She met English people who had been prisoners of the
Japanese in Changi and saw Dutch women and children waiting to be repatriated:

At last my demob number came up, and I embarked at the end of March 1946 on
the Winchester Castle, a liner converted to a troop ship so there were six of us in a
cabin designed for one. One girl had bought three fur coats in Kashmir and these
monopolised our one cupboard – they nearly went overboard!! At Suez mail came
on board, but there was nothing for me. Trader was always a slow letter writer, but I
was a little sad.

The first sight of home … Arriving in a troop ship is always exciting as all ships
are dressed overall, and when we drew alongside the quay there were bands playing.
I looked over the rail, and there at the foot of the gangway was my beloved Trader. I
rushed to the purser's office to get a pass and tore down the gangway. As I fell into his
arms I knew everything was going to be all right.

VJ Day at RAF Medmenham had been a quieter celebration than that for VE Day.
Mary Harrison remembered that a bonfire had been made ready for VJ Day near
their accommodation hut. She was leaving to go on duty when they heard the
news of the end of the Japanese war; the bonfire was lit prematurely while people
danced around it in their pyjamas. The ancient station fire engine, which they had
never seen in use before, had to come to put it out. Later that evening everyone
at Medmenham celebrated the end of the war round a huge bonfire and watched
the fireworks.

By her own account, Jane Cameron took some time to come to terms with
her wartime service, and finally took up a post in an engineering works where
she met and fell in love with a Scottish engineer. They moved to Jamaica, where
Jane recovered her desire to write and completed seven novels, all titled after
friends, keeping them hidden in her linen cupboard. She sent the manuscripts

to a publisher when her husband was very ill, and on his death she returned to Scotland. In 1959 Jane became a publishing sensation when Macmillan Publishers announced that they would be publishing seven of her books; the first one was *My Friends the Miss Boyds* under her nom de plume of Jane Duncan. She wrote many more novels, all based on her life and friends, and an autobiography. Jane's books had a large readership, including many of her former colleagues at Medmenham.

Susan Bendon returned to the world of fashion after her work at Bomber Command in the war. In 1950, she changed direction and opened an antique shop where she founded the company Halcyon Days, which produced decorative enamel boxes, many of which Susan designed herself. She wrote three books on enamels and became a fellow of the Society of Antiquaries. In 2009 she wrote about her wartime experiences:

> Work apart, there was a great deal of fun to be had at the station and we held marvellous parties in the Sergeant's Mess, to which many officers from Intelligence came. I think most people's recollections of being in the forces during the war are the hilarity of so many incidents, and in spite of the tragedies we either were part of or observed, we seemed to have laughed most of the time.[14]

Charlotte Bonham Carter was one of the first to be demobbed. Hazel remembers:

> She came back to see us at Medmenham from a conference in Oxford and not only told us exactly what she had eaten at some banquet, but went around all the sections eating their biscuits, or whatever they had. She was as thin as a rake![15]

Charlotte was a doyenne of the London art world and a generous patron of the arts. In 1946 she inherited her family home, Wyck Place, in Hampshire, where many parties were subsequently held and Charlotte's favourite phrase 'My dear, isn't that marvellous!' was frequently heard. Peter Greenham painted her portrait in 1978 with Charlotte wearing a red gown designed by Fortuny, which she had bought from him in 1922. The portrait hangs in the Tate Gallery in London.

Having completed a course on Far Eastern PI in 1945, Ursula Powys-Lybbe's plans of enjoying a posting at the Pentagon were thwarted, and she left the WAAF to resume her photographic business, taking up portraiture again. She chose to abandon London society, and instead took her 'Touring Camera' to the Australian outback of New South Wales, where for several years she photographed people in their own homes. She returned to England and in 1983 published *The Eye of Intelligence*, a book that relates the technical detail of PI successes at Medmenham and its major contribution to the intelligence gathering processes during the Second World War.

Loyalty Howard from the Night Photography Section went to New Zealand after leaving the WAAF, then travelled to Australia where she became the headmistress of a girls' school. Sophie Wilson, who had worked in the white-tiled cubby hole in the basement of Danesfield House, also took up teaching and in the mid-1950s opened her own school near Tewkesbury which became one of her life's great achievements. In the autumn of 2002 Sophie revisited Danesfield House and, with difficulty, located her old white-tiled office, now sandwiched between the wine cellar and the cleaning materials store, in an area somewhat like the bowels of a large ship.

Sophie's two 'W' Section colleagues pursued surveying careers after the war. Ena Thomas worked for the Foreign Office on Antarctic survey and Lucia Windsor was appointed to the staff of the Directorate of Overseas Surveys computing section, later becoming chief computer. Lucia carried out much technical work on trigonometric adjustments and aerial triangulation concerned with mapping.

After the war PIs Mary Grierson from Second Phase and Ursula Kay from the Aircraft Section worked together as cartographers in a survey company. Ursula left to become a farmer and in 1960 Mary was employed as the official botanical illustrator in the Kew Herbarium at the Royal Botanic Gardens. She had been encouraged by John Nash RA at a series of botanical painting courses held at Flatford Mill, and when he retired Mary took over. The Herbarium archive holds over 1,000 of Mary's paintings and drawings, together with her meticulous record books. No doubt the same observational skills that Mary used throughout the war in examining air photographs were employed in her botanical paintings. She contributed to numerous books and publications, and was awarded five gold medals by the Royal Horticultural Society, an honorary doctorate from Reading University and, in 1999, the Kew Award medal.

In 2011, at the age of 99, Mary was asked which photographs she remembered from her wartime service. She replied:

> The photographs of the Moehne Dam and seeing all the flooding down the valley, sweeping everything away, made a huge impression on me which I shall never forget. I remember too the very brave PR pilots, with no defence or guns, who flew into enemy territory in the days that followed to see what damage had been done.[16]

Fears that women had about loved ones fighting in Europe, and elsewhere, continued to the end of the conflict. In March 1945, just a few weeks before the war ended, Mary Harrison, the model maker, recorded that her brother's ship had been torpedoed off Russia; thankfully he survived. Mary was working on a model of the naval port of Kiel as there were fears that the enemy might retreat into Norway for a 'last stand'. A reconnaissance Spitfire did fly over Kiel on 8 May, VE Day, to see if there were any large ships in the port, but only thick plumes of smoke were seen.

The end of Mary's wartime service is told in her diary entries for October 1945, in a way familiar to many other servicewomen:

1st – Due for demob on October 10th.

9th – Went to Marlow with Nancy Hayes for a last coffee at The Dutch Café. Final pay at Medmenham, 3 shillings. Went to say goodbye to 'V' Section and moved to the transit hut.

10th – Demobbed at Wythall. Left 'Med' for Wythall at 7.45 am. Commenced demob about 2 pm. All happened so quickly one didn't quite know what one was doing.

11th – Can't realise I'm really 'out'.

12th – Went to National Registry Office – got identity card, coupons, ration book etc. In the afternoon Mother and I went shopping and I bought myself a rather nice brown suit. The price broke me for a time – but gosh – to be a civvy!!!

30th – Dyed my RAF cardigan successfully.[17]

The 800 or so women who had worked with air photographs at RAF Medmenham, and all the other women who had served in similar ways on reconnaissance and interpretation units in Britain and overseas, could be proud of the part they had played in one of the Second World War's great achievements. From a few lumbering aircraft and a handful of civilians in 1939, photographic reconnaissance and interpretation had become the major provider of intelligence used in virtually every wartime operation. Unusually for those times, women had carried out the same work as men, were chosen for a particular job solely on their capabilities and had played a decisive part in winning the war. Mary Harrison summed up the effect of war on women:

> It gave women freedom and equality to do jobs that only men did before. It taught us tolerance and how to get on with others.

Many of the Medmenham women had served for nearly six years, some had lost husbands and fiancés, and most knew of a colleague who had not returned from the conflict. They were demobilised into a country scarred and worn from the war and some faced a struggle to find employment and housing. All were affected by more stringent rationing than in wartime and shortages of just about every commodity. A significant number married and took the decision to set up new homes in America and Canada. Many years after the war Mollie Thompson wrote: 'We just wanted to get back to normal.'

As soon as the European war ended, some sections at Medmenham closed and in 1946 the Central Interpretation Unit moved to RAF Nuneham Park and was renamed the Joint Air Reconnaissance Intelligence Centre (JARIC). On 17 July 1946, a number of wartime PIs gathered together and formed the Medmenham Club, with the primary objective of preserving the friendships made during the war.

For nearly thirty years Danesfield House was used as an RAF Signals Unit, before being sold in 1977 to Carnation Foods as their corporate headquarters. It opened as Danesfield House Hotel in 1991, since when the management has

Although we have all gone our different ways and are scattered far apart, our life together during the Second World War left a bond between us for the rest of our lives.

Joan 'Panda' Carter sketched the ATS waving goodbye to their colleagues at the end of the war. The sentiments expressed would be echoed by most women who worked with air photographs in the Second World War.

welcomed the return visits of many of the men and women who worked there in wartime. Golden wedding anniversaries, ninetieth birthdays and other notable occasions have been celebrated in the rooms where stereoscopes, maps and photographs were once used.

In 2010 the BBC used Danesfield House Hotel to film 'wartime scenes' as part of their documentary *Operation Crossbow*, which told the story of the hunt for the V-weapons. A celebratory Medmenham Club tea was held in the Versailles Room, where Second Phase had worked, and afterwards members and guests stepped out on to the terrace to admire the gardens and river, just as the PIs of many nations had during the war. Then, thanks to the BBC, everyone, including men and women who had worked at Medmenham in wartime days, enjoyed a spectacular flying display by a Spitfire, and WAAF PI Suzie Morrison was reminded that:

> Whenever we heard the sound of a returning Spitfire we rushed outside to welcome home our pilot, and hear his news.

ENDNOTES

Chapter 1

1. Wellington, Duke of, Croker Papers (1885), Vol. iii, from *Oxford Dictionary of Quotations.*
2. Ticquet, Cyril, from an article entitled 'Spies of the Skies' in *Chamber's Journal*, January 1946 (Medmenham Collection).
3. Foulkes, Debbie, www.forgottennewsmakers.com.
4. Leggat, Robert, www.rleggat.com/photohistory/history/women.htm.
5. Richards, Peter, *Cam* (the Cambridge Alumni Magazine), June 1998.
6. Obituary, *The Independent,* 28 December 1989.
7. Obituary, *The Independent,* 26 February 1997.
8. Barker, Ralph, *Aviator Extraordinary* (Chatto & Windus, 1969).
9. Chadsey, Mollie (*née* Thompson), correspondence with the author, 2009–10.
10. Plaisted, Arthur, *The Romance of a Chiltern Village* (Village Bookshop, 1958).
11. AOC Wembley Report, *PIU Wembley Organisation and Establishment 18 February 1941* (Medmenham Collection).
12. Cassin-Smith, Jack, *Women at War* (Osprey, 1980).
13. James, Mary, from an article entitled 'The Big Picture' in *Royal Air Force Salute*, 2010.
14. Ticquet, *ibid.*

Chapter 2

1. Muir Warden, Tom, a Canadian wartime PI at Bomber Command, interview with Constance Babington Smith, 1956/7 (Medmenham Collection).
2. Lawton (*née* Laws), Millicent, conversation with the author, 2010.
3. Chadsey (*née* Thompson), Mollie, correspondence.
4. Holiday, Eve, interview with Constance Babington Smith, 1956/7 (Medmenham Collection).

5. Palmer (*née* Ogle), Stella, written memoirs, 1990s.

6. Morgan (*née* Morrison), Suzie, audio recording for the Medmenham Collection in 2002, and correspondence with the author, 2011.

7. Westwood (*née* Bruce), Lavender, conversation with the author, 2010.

8. Scott, Hazel, *Peace and War* (Beacon Books, 2006), pp.47–8. By permission of Hazel Scott. Also in conversation with the author 2010–11.

9. Rice, Joan, *Sand in my Shoes* (HarperCollins, 2006), pp.3–4.

10. IWM 8516 99/44/1 The papers of Section Officer Dorothy Colles, held by the Department of Documents a the Imperial War Museum and printed with their permisison.

11. Benjamin (*née* Bendon), Susan, written memoirs, 2006.

12. Collyer (*née* Murden), Myra, recorded memoirs, also conversation with author 2010–11.

13. Hyne, Peggy, recorded memoirs, 2010.

14. Benjamin (*née* Bendon), Susan, memoirs.

15. Duncan, Jane, *Letter from Reachfar* (Macmillan London Ltd, 1975), pp.18–9. Reprinted by permission of the author's family.

16. IWM 4483 82/33/1 The papers of Sgt Joan 'Panda' Carter, held by the Department of Documents at the Imperial War Museum, and printed by permission of her daughter.

17. Mottershead (*née* Rugg), Barbara, recorded memoirs, 2007.

18. Sowry (*née* Adams), Jeanne, written memoirs held by the RAF Museum, Hendon, and printed with their permission, also conversation with the author, 2009–10.

19. Churchill, Sarah, *Keep on Dancing* (Weidenfeld & Nicholson, 1981), p.58. Reprinted by permission of Lady Mary Soames.

20. IWM 4782 86/25/1 The papers of Air Commodore Felicity Hill, held by the Department of Documents at the Imperial War Museum, by permission of Dame Felicity Hill.

21. Churchill, Sarah, *Keep on Dancing*, pp.58–9.

22. Horne (*née* Macalister), Elspeth, written memoirs, undated, and conversation with her daughter, 2011.

23. Muszynski (*née* Donald), Pat, conversation with author, 2010–11.

Chapter 3

1. Cussons (*née* Byron), Diana, a lecture on the 'Work of the Interpreter' at a seminar on photographic reconnaissance, 10 June 1991, by permission of the RAF Historical Society.

2. Bogarde, Dirk, *Snakes and Ladders* (Chatto & Windus, 1978).

3. Colles, Dorothy, IWM papers.

4. Scott, Hazel, *Peace and War*, p.49.

5. Churchill, Sarah, *Keep on Dancing*, p.62.

6. Powys-Lybbe, Ursula, *The Eye of Intelligence* (William Kimber, 1983). Reprinted by permission of the author's family.

7. Duncan (*née* Cameron), Jane, extract from her wartime diary, quoted in *My Friend Monica* (Millrace, 2011), p.261 Reprinted by permission of the author's family.

8. Scott, Hazel, *Peace and War*, pp.50–1.

9. Komrower (*née* Eadon), Shirley, audio recording for the Medmenham Collection, 2001.

10. Paper on attributes of photographic interpreters, 1945 (Medmenham Collection).

11. Powys-Lybbe, Ursula, *The Eye of Intelligence*, p.14.

12. Sowry (*née* Adams), Jeanne, memoirs.

13. Hick (*née* Johnston-Smith), Elizabeth, audio recording for the Medmenham Collection in 2002 and conversation with the author in 2010–11.

14. Reid, Helena, letter, 2002 (Medmenham Collection).

15. Grierson, Mary 'Bunny', papers on 1 PRU, 1946 (Medmenham Collection).

16. Rendall (*née* McKnight-Kauffer), Ann, interview with Constance Babington Smith, 1956/7 (Medmenham Collection).

17. Holiday, Eve, interview with Constance Babington Smith, 1956/7 (Medmenham Collection).

18. Morgan (*née* Morrison), Suzie, audio recording for the Medmenham Collection in 2002 and conversation with the author, 2010–11.

Chapter 4

1. Starling, Jean, Australian War Memorial REL36872.001.

2. Operational Record Book, Air 28/384, TNA.

3. Cussons (*née* Byron), Diana, RAF Historical Society seminar.

4. Smith, Nigel, *Tirpitz: The Halifax Raids* (Air Research Publications, 1994).

5. Bulmer (*née* Dudding), Pamela, audio recording for the Medmenham Collection.

6. Churchill, Sarah, *Keep on Dancing*, p.60.

7. Grierson, Mary, audio recording for the Medmenham Collection, 2001.

8. McLeod, Norman, 'History of ACIU', unpublished, 1945 onwards, Medmenham Collection.

9. Kamphuis, Lillian, *Pensacola News Journal*, 11 September 2007.

10. Kamphuis, Lillian, Medmenham Club newsletters, spring 1995, autumn 1999, spring 2002.

11. 'Medmenham USA', unpublished account, 18 July 1945 (Medmenham Collection).

12. Grierson, Mary, part of a poem from her personal wartime scrapbook (Medmenham Collection).

13. Skappel (*née* Campbell), Betty, recorded memoirs, 2011.

14. IWM 12598 04/2/1 The papers of Lieutenant Geoffrey Price RNVR, held by the Department of Documents at the Imperial War Museum. The author was unable to locate the copyright holder.

15. Espenhahn (*née* Winmill), Mary, audio recording for the Medmenham Collection, 2001, and in conversation with author, 2005.

16. Churchill, Sarah, *Keep on Dancing*, p.61.

17. Carter, Joan, IWM papers.

18. Mottershead, Barbara, recorded memoirs.

Chapter 5

1. 'Jane', personal memoir (Medmenham Collection).

2. Muszynski (*née* Donald), Pat, conversation and correspondence with the author, 2010.

3. Benjamin (*née* Bendon), Susan, memoirs.

4. Obituary of Charlotte Bonham Carter.

5. 'Jane', personal memoir.

6. Cussons (*née* Byron), Diana, audio recording for the Medmenham Collection, 2002.

7. Sowry (*née* Adams), Jeanne, memoirs.

8. O'Neil (*née* Peat), Pat, audio recording, at her home in Maryland, by Paul and Harriet Richard, 2009–10, and conversation with her daughter, 2010.

9. Chadsey (*née* Thompson), Mollie, correspondence.

10. Colles, Dorothy, IWM papers.

11. Carter, Joan, IWM papers.

12. Cussons (*née* Byron), Diana, audio recording.

13. Sowry (*née* Adams), Jeanne, memoirs.

14. Duncan, Jane, *Letter from Reachfar*, p.20.

15. Carter, Joan, IWM papers.

16. Stone, Geoffrey, letters, 2011 (Medmen ham Collection).

17. Colles, Dorothy, IWM papers.

18. Abrams, Leonard, *Our Secret Little War* (International Geographic Information Foundation, 1991), p.36.

19. Scott, Hazel, *Peace and War*, pp.52–3.

20. 'Jane', memoir.

21. O'Neil (*née* Peat), Pat, memoirs.

22. Hyne, Peggy, memoirs.

23. Collyer (*née* Murden), Myra, correspondence, 2010.

24. Hurley (*née* Price), Margaret, correspondence with the author, 2010.

25. Churchill, Sarah, *Keep on Dancing*, pp.63–4.

26. Palmer (*née* Ogle), Stella, memoirs.

27. O'Neil (*née* Peat), Pat, memoirs.

28. Sowry (*née* Adams), Jeanne, memoirs.
29. Duncan, Jane, *Letter from Reachfar*, p.21.
30. Cator, Group Captain Francis, 'Allied Central Interpretation Unit, Medmenham, September 1943–June 1945' (Medmenham Collection).
31. Daniel, Ruth, letter to *The Independent*, January 1990.

Chapter 6

1. Churchill, Sarah, *Keep on Dancing*, pp.62–3.
2. Scott (*née* Furney), Hazel, interviewed for BBC *Operation Crossbow*, 2011.
3. Daniel, Glyn, *Some Small Harvest* (Thames and Hudson, 1986), p.98.
4. Stone, Geoffrey, letter, 2011 (Medmenham Collection).
5. Scott, Hazel (*née* Furney), conversation with the author, 2010.
6. Babington Smith, Constance, *Evidence in Camera* (Chatto & Windus, 1958). Extracts from *Evidence in Camera* are reprinted by permission of Peters Fraser & Dunlop (www.petersfraserdunlop.com) on behalf of the estate of Constance Babington Smith.
7. Morgan (*née* Morrison), Suzie, interviewed for BBC *Operation Crossbow*, 2011.
8. Collyer (*née* Murden), Myra, interviewed for BBC *Operation Crossbow*, 2011.
9. Carter, Joan, IWM papers.
10. Duncan, Jane, *My Friend Monica*, pp.259–60, 262.
11. Powys-Lybbe, Ursula, *Eye of Intelligence*, p.147.
12. Brachi (*née* Bohey), Joan, in conversation with the author, 2011.
13. Rendall (*née* McKnight-Kauffer), Ann, interview with Constance Babington Smith, 1956/7, (Medmenham Collection).
14. Scott, Hazel, *Peace and War*, p.53.
15. Brachi (*née* Bohey), Joan, conversation.

Chapter 7

1. Saffery, John, Squadron Leader DSO, from a paper, undated but written while he still in PRU (Medmenham Collection).
2. IWM 4009 96/4/1 The papers of Mrs Pamela Brisley-Wilson (*née* Howie), held by the Department of Documents at the Imperial War Museum. The author was unable to locate the copyright holder.
3. Gilbert, Martin, 'Winston S. Churchill, Companion', Volume V, Part 3, *The Coming of War 1936–1939*, Heinemann, 1982.
4. O'Neil (*née* Peat), Pat, recorded interviews.
5. Lawton (*née* Laws), Millicent, conversation.
6. Sowry (*née* Adams), Jeanne, memoirs.
7. Leaf, Edward, *Above All Unseen*, Appendix D (Patrick Stephens Ltd, 1997).
8. Horne (*née* Macallister), Elspeth, memoirs.
9. Hurley (*née* Price), Margaret, correspondence.

10. Komrower (*née* Eadon), Shirley, audio recording made for the Medmenham Collection, 2001/2.
11. Babington Smith, Constance, *Evidence in Camera*, pp. 110–1.
12. Komrower (*née* Eadon), Shirley, document DC 76/46, undated, held by RAF Museum.

Chapter 8

1. Churchill, Sarah, *The Empty Spaces* (Leslie Frewin, 1966), use of 'The Bombers' here by permission of Lady Mary Soames.
2. Jones, Idris, 'Royal Air Force Days 1939–1945', unpublished diary (Medmenham Collection).
3. Palmer (*née* Ogle), Stella, in Ursula Powys-Lybbe, *The Eye of Intelligence*, p. 26–7.
4. Muszynski (*née* Donald), Pat, conversation.
5. Babington Smith, Constance, *Evidence in Camera*, pp. 101, 106.
6. Kendall, Wing Commander Douglas, 'A War of Intelligence', unpublished account of wartime photographic intelligence (Medmenham Collection).
7. Hick (*née* Johnston-Smith), Elizabeth, audio recording.
8. Benjamin (*née* Bendon), Susan, memoirs.
9. Williams, Kathlyn, part of an audio recording of wartime personnel at Hughenden Manor, by permission of the National Trust.
10. Kodak Ltd London, Kodak Datasheet PP-2.
11. Hughenden Manor, information sheet.
12. Brachi (*née* Bohey), Joan, conversation.
13. Williams, Kathlyn, audio recording.
14. Horne (*née* Macalister), Elspeth, memoirs.
15. Benjamin (*née* Bendon), Susan, memoirs.
16. Williams, Kathlyn, audio recording.
17. Duncan, Jane, *Letter from Reachfar*, p. 65.

Chapter 9

1. British Academy, 'Volume 55 Proceedings'.
2. Rendall (*née* McKnight-Kauffer), Ann, correspondence with Constance Babington Smith, 1956/7 (Medmenham Collection).
3. Spear, Major George, correspondence with the author, 2009.
4. Churchill, Sarah, *Keep on Dancing*, pp. 65–6.
5. Abrams, Leonard, *Our Secret Little War*, p. 36.
6. IWM 11602 01/19/1 The papers of Miss Mary Harrison, held by the Department of Documents at the Imperial War Museum, and printed by permission of Miss Harrison.
7. Price, Geoffrey, IWM papers.

8. Harrison, Mary, IWM papers.
9 *More Poems of the Second World War, the Oasis Collection* (Dent, 1989), use of 'My Hands' here by permission of Mary Harrison.
10 Wilson, Sophie, letters and documents (Medmenham Collection).
11 www.britain-at-war-magazine.com/news 'Attack on the Gestapo Headquarters at The Hague'.
12 Wood, Edward, an account of his wartime service at RAF Medmenham, undated (Medmenham Collection).
13 Cator, Group Captain Francis, RAF Medmenham, September 1943–June 1945.
14 Wood, Edward, extract from a letter circulated to all 'V' Section personnel, 1945 (Medmenham Collection).

Chapter 10

1. Colles, Dorothy, IWM papers.
2. Rice, Joan, *Sand in my Shoes*, p.235.
3. Scott, Hazel, *Peace and War*, pp.54–6.
4. Morgan (*née* Morrison), Suzie, recording.
5. Scott, Hazel, *Peace and War*, p.68.
6. Morgan (*née* Morrison), Suzie, correspondence.
7. Byrne, Paula, *Mad World* (Harper Press, 2009).
8. Daniel, Glyn, *Some Small Harvest*, p.175.
9. Horne (*née* Macalister), Elspeth, memoirs.
10. Rendall (*née* McKnight-Kauffer), Ann, correspondence with Constance Babington Smith, 1956/7 (Medmenham Collection).
11. Holiday, Eve, interview.
12. Churchill, Sarah, *A Thread in the Tapestry* (Andre Deutsch, 1967), pp.57, 59, 65.
13. Churchill, Sarah, *Keep on Dancing*, pp.67–76.
14. Reid (*née* Ewen), Helena, script for audio recording for Medmenham Collection, 2001.

Chapter 11

1. Powys-Lybbe, Ursula, *Eye of Intelligence*, p.129.
2. Searle, Adrian, *PLUTO: Pipe Line Under The Ocean* (Shanklin Chine, 2004), p.52.
3. Grierson, Mary 'Bunny', letter about D-Day (Medmenham Collection).
4. The Pegasus Bridge model, with others, may be seen in the Airborne Forces' Museum at the Imperial War Museum, Duxford.
5. An audio recording of Miss Mary Harrison, held by the Department of Documents at the Imperial War Museum, 2001.
6. Windsor, Lucia, conversation with the author, 2003.

7. O'Neil (*née* Peat), Pat, audio recording.
8. Horne (*née* Macalister), Elspeth, memoirs.
9. Sowry (*née* Adams), Jeanne, article in *The Times*, 5 June 2009.
10. Brisley-Wilson (*née* Howie), Pamela, IWM papers.
11. Harrison Mary, IWM papers.
12. From President Eisenhower's book, *Crusade in Europe*, 1948, quoted in Douglas Kendall's unpublished account, 'A War of Intelligence' (Medmenham Collection).
13. Powys-Lybbe, Ursula, *The Eye of Intelligence*, pp.207–8.
14. Air Ministry Bulletin No. 15560 issued on 9 September 1944.
15. Kendall, Douglas, 'A War of Intelligence'.

Chapter 12

1. Palmer (*née* Ogle), Stella, letter, March 1945.
2. Mottershead (*née* Rugg), Barbara, memoirs.
3. Scott, Hazel, *Peace and War*, pp.91–3.
4. Mulvagh, Jane, *The Real Brideshead* (Black Swan, 2009).
5. IWM 13707 Misc 262 (3569) The papers relating to Elspeth Horne (*née* Macalister) that form part of the Kemsing village memoir of 2005, held by the Department of Documents at the Imperial War Museum.
6. Chadsey (*née* Thompson), Mollie, correspondence.
7. Sheldon (*née* Davey), Alice, 1956/7 interview with Constance Babington Smith (Medmenham Collection).
8. Powys-Lybbe, Ursula, *The Eye of Intelligence*, p.14.
9. O'Neil (*née* Peat), Pat, audio recordings and conversations.
10. Introduction to *A History of the Aircraft Section*, May 1945 (Medmenham Collection).
11. Daniel, Glyn, *Some Small Harvest*, p.99.
12. Churchill, Sarah, *Keep on Dancing*, pp.80–1.
13. Horne (*née* Macalister), Elspeth, memoirs.
14. Benjamin (*née* Bendon), Susan, memoirs.
15. Scott, Hazel, *Peace and War*, p.94.
16. Grierson, Mary, conversation with Marilyn Ward, illustrations curator at the Royal Botanic Gardens, Kew, 2011.
17. Harrison, Mary, IWM papers.

Bibliography

Published Works

Abrams, Leonard, *Our Secret Little War* (International Geographic Information Foundation, 1991)

Babington Smith, Constance, *Evidence in Camera* (Chatto & Windus, 1957). A new edition was published by Sutton Publishing, Stroud, in 2004. *Evidence in Camera* was published in the USA as *Air Spy* in 1958

Barker, Ralph, *Aviator Extraordinary: The Sidney Cotton Story* (Chatto & Windus, 1969)

Beck, Pip, *Keeping Watch: A WAAF in Bomber Command* (Goodall, 1989)

Bogarde, Dirk, *Snakes and Ladders* (Chatto & Windus, 1978)

Brayley, Martin, *World War II Allied Women's Services* (Osprey, 2001)

Byrne, Paula, *Mad World: Evelyn Waugh and the Secrets of Brideshead* (Harper Press, 2009)

Cassin-Scott, Jack, *Women at War 1939–45* (Osprey, 1980)

Churchill, Sarah, *A Thread in the Tapestry* (Andre Deutsch, 1967)

———, *Keep on Dancing: an Autobiography* (Weidenfeld & Nicolson, 1981)

———, *The Empty Spaces* (Leslie Frewin, 1966)

Coldstream, John, *Dirk Bogarde: The Authorised Biography* (Weidenfeld & Nicolson, 2004)

Conyers Nesbit, Roy, *Eyes of the RAF: A History of Photo-Reconnaissance* (Sutton Publishing, 1996)

Daniel, Glyn, *Some Small Harvest* (Thames & Hudson, 1986)

Downing, Taylor, *Spies in the Sky: The Secret Battle for Aerial Intelligence during World War II* (Little, Brown, 2011)

Duncan, Jane, *My Friend Monica* (Millrace, 2011)

———, *Letter from Reachfar* (Macmillan London Ltd, 1975)

Leaf, Edward, *Above All Unseen: The Royal Air Force's Photographic Reconnaissance Units 1939–1945* (Patrick Stephens Limited, 1997)

Lee, Celia, & Paul Edward Strong (eds), *Women in War: From Home Front to Front Line* (Pen & Sword Military, 2012)

McKinstrey, Leo, *Lancaster: The Second World War's Greatest Bomber* (John Murray, 2009)

Mead, Peter, *The Eye in the Air: History of Air Observation and Reconnaissance for the Army 1785–1945* (HMSO Books, 1983)

Middlebrook, Martin, & Chris Everitt, *The Bomber Command War Diaries: An Operational Reference Book, 1939–1945* (Viking, 1985)

More Poems of the Second World War: The Oasis Collection (Dent & Sons Ltd, Everyman's Library in association with The Salamander Oasis Trust, 1989)

Mulvagh, Jane, *Madresfield: The Real Brideshead* (Doubleday, 2008)

Nicholson, Mavis, *What Did You do in the War, Mummy?* (Chatto & Windus, 1995)

Ogley, Bob, *Doodlebugs and Rockets: The Battle of the Flying Bombs* (Froglets Publications, 1992)

Olson, Lynne, *Citizens of London* (Random House New York, 2010)

Phillips, Charles, *My Life in Archaeology* (Alan Sutton, 1987)

Plaisted, Arthur, *The Romance of a Chiltern Village* (The Village Bookshop, 1958)

Powys-Lybbe, Ursula, *The Eye of Intelligence* (William Kimber, 1983). Quotations are by kind permission of the copyright holder

Rice, Joan, *Sand in My Shoes. Coming of Age in the Second World War: A WAAF's Diary* (HarperCollins, 2006)

Scott, Hazel, *Peace and War* (Beacon Books, 2006)

Searle, Adrian, *PLUTO Pipe-Line Under The Ocean* (Shanklin Chine, 2004)

Smith, Nigel, *Tirpitz. The Halifax Raids* (Air Research Publications, 1994)

Stanley, Colonel USAF, Roy M., *V-Weapons Hunt: Defeating German Secret Weapons* (Pen & Sword Military, 2010)

Watson, Jeffrey, *The Last Plane Out of Berlin* (Hodder, 2002)

Ziegler, Philip, *London at War 1939–1945* (Sinclair-Stevenson, 1995)

Unpublished works held by the Medmenham Collection.

Babington Smith, Constance: interview notes, papers and letters relating to *Evidence in Camera*, 1956–57

Cator, Francis, 'Allied Central Interpretation Unit, Medmenham, September 1943–June 1945'

Eaton, Hamish, Captain, Intelligence Corps, '60 Years of Army Photographic Interpretation 1914–1974'

Historical reports on the wartime function of each section at RAF Medmenham, written in 1945 immediately after the war ended

Jones, Robert Idris, 'Royal Air Force Days 1939–1945'

Kendall, Wing Commander RAF, Douglas, 'A War of Intelligence', written in 1980s

Operational Record Book for RAF Station Medmenham 1942–1947

ACKNOWLEDGEMENTS

First and foremost, I must thank all the women and men who have written or recorded their experiences of joining the services and working in photographic intelligence throughout the Second World War. Some wrote for publications, and I thank them or the present copyright holders for permission to quote their words. Others wrote, or dictated, their memories as a record for their families, and here I am grateful to the families of Stella Palmer, Susan Benjamin, Barbara Mottershead, Elspeth Horne and Pat O'Neil for bringing them to my attention and allowing me to quote from them. Several writers put their memoirs into national archives, including Joan Zeepraat, Dorothy Colles, Pamela Brisley-Wilson and Mary Harrison, who all deposited their papers at the Imperial War Museum, while the RAF Museum has accounts from Shirley Komrower and Jeanne Sowry.

The Medmenham Collection is the national archive of British photographic interpretation and a major source of much that is contained in the book; this material is reproduced courtesy of the Medmenham Collection, for which I thank the chairman, David Hollin, and the trustees. The archivist and curator, Mike Mockford, his wife Shirley and my husband Chris Halsall, a trustee, have been consistently helpful and encouraging and it is no exaggeration to say that without them I could not have completed the book. I have worked as a volunteer in the collection for ten years, and have compiled biographical notes on many wartime members. When I started the research for the book, the Medmenham Club women members were some of the first to be interviewed. Invariably they gave me informative, and amusing, accounts and provided me with details of other women to contact. I am not forgetting the valuable help that many men have also given me, and I wish to mention in particular Geoffrey Stone, who wrote the foreword with the knowledge of RAF Medmenham and its attitude to women, which could only be expressed by a PI who worked there. I am most grateful to everyone who assisted me in the compilation of all the accounts and memories.

Between 2001 and 2005, Medmenham Club members Sue and David Mander made a number of audio recordings of men and women who worked at RAF Medmenham and overseas during the Second World War. Paul and Harriet Richard, US members of the Medmenham Club, kindly interviewed and recorded Pat O'Neil at her home in Maryland in 2009–10. When the Hughenden Manor staff created a visitor's tour and display explaining its important wartime purpose, Peggy Ewert made audio recordings of the men and women who served there. I am grateful to Peggy and the National Trust for agreeing to the inclusion of some of their words in this book. All these valuable recordings, together with the letters and articles regularly contributed by members to the Medmenham Club newsletter since its inauguration in 1946, provide a unique primary source of information on wartime air photographic exploitation.

Many individuals helped by talking, on my behalf, to women whom, through infirmity or distance, I was unable to visit. Marilyn Ward, of the Royal Botanic Gardens, asked questions of Mary Grierson; Jane Crawford of Peggy Hyne; and Lindy Farrell spoke to her aunt, Betty Skappel. Paul Richard put me in touch with George Spear in Ottawa, who recalled Sarah Churchill's kindness to his wife, while Sheila Middleton in Australia found details of Jean Starling for me. Steve Lloyd, of the Air Historical Branch, helped me find the other Australian WAAF, Jean Youle, with information on her Military Medal. Grant Thompson provided me with the technical information on Kodak Bromide Foil-Card.

Danesfield House Hotel has assisted in keeping the Medmenham Club in touch with its wartime base by welcoming members and guests to partake of splendid teas in the summertime. Sitting in the rooms where photographs were pored over day after day, or strolling in the gardens to the riverbank to contemplate the same view as the wartime staff, provides a remarkable feeling of being where history was made. The BBC documentary *Operation Crossbow* revealed the vital role played by RAF Medmenham in wartime and created a great deal of interest.

Members of staff at the Documents Department of the Imperial War Museum, Lambeth Road, were always helpful, as were those at the RAF Museum at Hendon.

I am grateful to Jo de Vries, Paul Baillie-Lane, Christine McMorris and Kerry Green of The History Press for their support and help.

During the past three years I have asked many questions of many people. Everyone has been unfailingly helpful and generous in their time and diligence in answering. Thank you.

Picture Credits

All the air photographs and the ground photographs of RAF Medmenham, including the personnel at work and off duty, *Evidence in Camera*, the sketches and posters, are held by the Medmenham Collection. All these items are copyright to the Medmenham Collection and reproduced by courtesy of the trustees.

Many women who contributed to the book also provided their own individual and group photographs for inclusion: I am particularly grateful to Millicent Lawton, Jeanne Sowry, Hazel Scott, Pat Muszynski, Elizabeth Hick, Suzie Morgan, Mary Espenhahn, Joan Brachi, Mary Harrison and the families of Diana Cussons, Stella Palmer and Susan Benjamin. The author thanks the copyright holder for permission to use Ursula Powys-Lybbe's photograph, and the National Trust for the photograph of the draughtswomen at Hughenden Manor. The photograph of Jean Youle is reproduced courtesy of the Air Historical Branch (RAF), CH 14552 IWM and that of Sarah Churchill at Teheran, CM 005480 by permission of the Imperial War Museum.

The photograph of Pat O'Neil was taken by Paul Richard, a US member of the Medmenham Club in 2009, while Margaret Hurley and Xavier Atencio were photographed by Tim Dunn, the producer of *Operation Crossbow*, for the BBC in 2010.

Danesfield House Hotel provided the colour photograph of the house on a sunny day in 2011. Other photographs are the author's own.

The WAAF watercolour paintings by Mary Harrison are reproduced with her permission and the daughter of Joan Zeepvat allowed the delightful ATS sketches to be used.

INDEX

Married names for women, where known, are in brackets after the name by which they were known during their wartime service. Ranks at the time, if known, are included, although may have subsequently changed. Colour plates marked CP.